Nîmes

Beaucaire

VIRGILE JOLY
CAVE
PARTICULIÈRE

HÉRAULT

St. Saturnin

Aniane

Clermont l'Hérault

Montpellier

Valmagne
Abbey

Mireval

Marseille

Pézenas

Bouzigue

BASSIN DE THAU

Frontignan

Sète

Marseillan

Agde

Cap d'Agde

Mediterranean
Sea

St. Guilhem - le -
Désert

St. Saturnin

Montpeyroux

Tonquières

Aniane

St. Guiraud

HÉRAULT

Gignac

St. André de Sangonis

Clermont l'Hérault

Nébian

Virgile's Vineyard

A Year in the Languedoc Wine Country

PATRICK MOON

JOHN MURRAY
Albemarle Street, London

A catalogue record for this book is available from the British
Library

ISBN 0-7195-6230 9

Typeset in Adobe Palatino 11/14 pt by
Servis Filmsetting Ltd, Manchester

Printed and bound in Great Britain by
Clays Ltd, St Ives plc

For Andrew

New Year's Eve

MAYBE I JUST need more than twenty-four hours of southern sunlight to melt my northern restraint, but ten o'clock in the morning did seem marginally early for aperitifs.

What do you do though, when the man whose new neighbour you have just become is there on your doorstep, agitatedly shifting his portly frame from one short leg to another, as if all his future wellbeing depended on your acceptance? How can I not say yes? I am, after all, in the land of the *langue d'oc* – the ancient Occitan language, in which everyone said *oc* instead of *oui*. So I meekly cross the wobbly wooden footbridge and follow his eager but elderly steps to the small stone cottage on the opposite side of the stream, bracing myself for a glass of his homemade *rouge*.

1

For Monsieur Gros there appears to be no time to lose. Before he has even puffed his way to the top of his garden path, he has produced a corkscrew from his dirty blue overalls. And before I have fought my way through the curtain of plastic ribbons defending his kitchen doorway, he is already tugging breathlessly at a cork.

'Your uncle Milo always enjoyed his wines,' he chuckles, tapping a conspiratorial finger on a bloodshot nose that bears eloquent witness to more than half a century of equally high enjoyment. 'Until his illness, that is . . .'

He ushers me quickly to a bare wooden table and is urgently scanning the austere, low-ceilinged room for some drinking vessels, when a tall, forbidding figure of similar vintage emerges from the gloom of an alcove.

'*Ah, voici, ma femme,*' he says with a start.

I mumble a hesitant '*Enchanté, madame*' and am rewarded with an almost imperceptible, silent nod.

'Oh yes,' resumes M. Gros, with unnaturally hearty laughter. 'We always knew Milo would leave the house to a wine-lover. *N'est-ce pas, ma chère?*'

The object of this endearment tightens her lips. Madame Gros could hardly look less pleased to see her husband so swiftly replacing my benefactor with a new drinking companion. She produces two glasses of notable smallness and stands with arms firmly folded across her ample bosom, defying us to overfill them.

I begin to suspect a method in my neighbour's madly early invitation. If social drinking is so reluctantly tolerated, solitary consumption must be even more deeply disapproved of. So accomplices have to be rounded up whenever he is thirsty.

Given these onerous social obligations, it amazes me that Uncle Milo ever found time to build the house that is now, unexpectedly, mine. He once told me it took him fifteen years to summon up the energy to drop out. So even for a lapsed architect, his achievement here in the next twenty-five was pretty remarkable. It did, however, leave him no time for the acquisition of wives, children or any heirs more worthy than his nephew – a nephew who hasn't even visited since his student days and therefore feels exceptionally undeserving this morning.

My uncle had only got as far as building two simple rooms when I was last here and younger visitors like me used to sleep in a tiny shepherd's *maset* in the garden. Now the house looks a bit like a miniature Romanesque monastery, with its vast, stone-vaulted dining room and the generously rounded arches of the shady cloister lining all but the south-facing side of its spectacular front courtyard. I can hardly imagine how it kept itself out of the design magazines.

Not that there would be much chance of a photo-call today. The paint on the window shutters has started to peel and a number of the terracotta roof tiles lie broken on the ground. The ancient agricultural terraces stretching up the hill behind the house are crumbling and the once immaculately cultivated vines and olive and fruit trees all look almost impenetrably overgrown with the neglect of my uncle's declining health: uncomfortable reminders of my own less excusable neglect.

'You'll be coming down for the summer holidays, I imagine,' says Mme Gros, anxious to ascertain the limits of the domestic damage that I might do.

As compassionately as possible, I break the news that I've let my English house for the whole of next year. I stumble over the French for sabbatical but I can see from her look of dismay that she has grasped the essential gist.

And this is all before I have braved even my first sip of M. Gros's worryingly thin-looking wine.

'You make a lot of this?' I ask, playing for time.

'Oh very little. Very, very little. Just three thousand litres a year. Just for me and the family,' he says.

Time may, of course, yet reveal the precise extent of this happy group of enthusiasts but I am already trying to calculate how many relatives M. Gros would need before he could divide his annual production into an average daily intake that would be less than life-threatening – especially as the only family member in evidence seems to be so resolutely abstemious. I raise my glass nervously in Mme Gros's direction.

The wine is, as I feared, thin, sharp and characterless. More surprisingly, given the maker's inclination towards intoxication, it also tastes unexpectedly low in alcohol. Which is probably why it is barely eleven o'clock when he proposes that we adjourn to the sitting room for some of his 'secret' home-distilled brandy.

'Don't tell a soul,' he whispers, as he pours me a brimming measure.

Even drinking only one glass to his three, I am beginning to feel the room rotate – a sensation that isn't helped by the walls being covered with the swirliest of brown and orange, carpet-like wallpapers. On closer inspection, so is the ceiling. In fact, the only side of the cube not so decorated is the floor. Perversely, this appears to be hewn directly out of the underlying rock. My glass has been replenished once too often for me to be certain.

As the morning wears on, I become ever more pessimistic that I shall finish my unpacking before the spring. My host meanwhile becomes ever more determined in his health-toasting, back-slapping matiness. By 11.30, Monsieur E. Gros will tolerate no other epithet but Emmanuel; by noon, only the diminutive 'Manu' is ever to cross my lips. Above all, I must, without failure or excuse, accompany him and his lady wife to this evening's Saint Sylvester Night feast.

But Mme Gros is having none of this. With evident satisfaction, she reminds him that the deadline for reservations expired two days ago. (However bad my influence on her

4

spouse in the privacy of her home, I shall not be leading him astray in the Salle des Fêtes.) And speaking of which, isn't it time he was down there setting up the trestle tables?

I am secretly relieved. A preview of the dinner menu, with its opening highlight of 'stuffed neck' (the unfortunate bird or animal undisclosed) inspired little confidence. But with my own simpler New Year's dinner now finished, I feel unable to resist going down to snoop discreetly on the revels.

Uncle Milo's house is well outside the village so I drive as far as the medieval-looking gateway at the bottom of the narrow main street. I have had no opportunity to explore until now and there are very few street lights, but the couples zigzagging unsteadily down the gradient towards me must surely be coming from the direction of the Salle des Fêtes.

My instincts are soon confirmed by the sound of some long-forgotten hits of the seventies drifting tinnily from the far side of the fountain in the little square at the top of the hill. I am not sure whether it is kitchen or disco exertions that have steamed up the windows but I can more or less make out Mme Gros and another equally intimidating matron waging a terrifying war on the washing up. Manu is nowhere to be seen. (Perhaps sent home in disgrace? Perhaps collapsed under one of his trestle tables?) Fractious children are playing football with an empty drink can. A weary young mother dances listlessly round her pushchair on the post-prandial dance-floor. My instinct was right: tonight was not the night for my social debut.

My time was better spent making discoveries and resolutions.

I decided this morning that I ought to drink my solitary toast to the coming year with something fitting. So I asked a local wineshop to recommend one of the best of the local wines. I knew that things had changed since the plastic-stoppered, three-starred litres of my adolescent summers but I had not guessed how radically. I had certainly not been prepared for so much diversity, sparking such contagious enthusiasm from my wine-merchant. Nor imagined that he would persuade me to pay ten times as much for an obscure and rustic-sounding *vin de pays* as I might have given for something with a famous name. Yet, even allowing for a touch of house-moving hysteria, there is no avoiding the conclusion that tonight's so-called 'country wine' was really one of the great experiences of my life.

So, with twelve whole months at my disposal, it seems as good a New Year Resolution as any to try to get to grips with the remarkable wine-making revolution that appears to be going on here. (I can't spend the entire year battling with the brambles.) I shall see if I can understand that subtle something which separates the Domaine de la Grange des Pères from the 'Domaine d'Emmanuel Gros'. And while I am about it, I shall have a go at filling my uncle's cellar with some of the region's finest. It feels like the least that I can do to thank him for letting me come here.

January

I HAVE MADE a big mistake. I have told Manu about my resolutions and, deaf to all protest, he has decided I cannot possibly fulfil them on my own. Imagining a year of joyously uninhibited tastings, far from the censorious supervision of his wife, he has appointed himself my indispensable tutor, protector and guide. Indeed, no sooner was the public holiday over than his battered red van was revving impatiently at the bottom of my drive.

'You're forgetting the size of the Languedoc,' he fretted, as if our only hope of covering the ground in the time available would be 364 unremittingly early starts. 'It spans three *départements*, you know.'

I had not even thought about where I wanted to start but I knew that, if I surrendered the initiative, I might never again recover it. So, with Manu already releasing the handbrake, I frantically tried to remember one of the bottles that impressed me when I was down here to see the *notaire* in the autumn.

'Are we anywhere near Montpeyroux?' I asked, as a possible name came hazily to mind.

'Near enough to take the scenic route,' answered Manu, swinging cheerfully off on to a narrow road winding up into the hills on the other side of the village.

I had thought that few views could match the one from the arcaded courtyard at the front of Uncle Milo's house. Indeed, every front window looks down the hillside, through olives, oaks and cypresses, past vineyards and occasional shepherds' huts, to the river valley far below and then way beyond to the distant, interlocking diagonals of a succession of hills, stretching down towards an invisible coastal plain. But this morning we were climbing higher still – not quite as high as the bleak Larzac moorlands behind us, which I knew from my arrival a couple of days before, but high enough to see as far as the coast, some forty kilometres away, where the January sunshine was gleaming golden on the sea.

Having spotted a sufficiently chilly-looking, windswept crest, Manu swerved to a sudden halt for a cigarette and a geography lesson. 'Montpeyroux', he began, with an ostentatious clearing of his throat, 'is of course a village in the Coteaux du Languedoc . . .'

'The *what* du Languedoc?'

'*Coteaux*,' he repeated, impatient that I had interrupted his oratory. 'Meaning much the same as *Côtes*. As in *du Rhône*. Hillside slopes. Only with the longer word, you get shorter slopes. Anyway, it's a very large wine-making region. Huge, in fact. Stretching all the way from Nîmes to Narbonne, like a . . .' Manu's arms drew frantic circles in the air until at last an appropriate simile hove into view '. . . giant amphitheatre. *Voilà*. And Montpeyroux is, of course . . .'

'Around the middle of the back row?' I suggested.

'One of its best villages,' Manu continued, ignoring my attempt to hi-jack his metaphor. 'And as such, entitled to put its own name on the label as well.'

I was not in fact quite as ignorant about the French wine-naming system as Manu imagined. I knew that the powers that be had comprehensively divided and sub-divided the French vineyards in a codification of positively Napoleonic thorough-ness. It was all supposed to give the customer a sense of what he was entitled to expect from his bottle, by imposing controls on the way in which a wine had to be made, if it wanted to be labelled with the name of a designated area. Hence, the expres-sion *Appellation Contrôlée*.

'All nonsense, of course,' said Manu. 'You get good and bad wines, whatever the name.' But it soon became clear that the real reason why he had so little time for the *appellation* is that it had inconsiderately outlawed his principal grape variety, once the Midi's dominant vine, the Aramon.

'Wonderfully productive,' he enthused, as we drove on. 'Up to four hundred hectolitres per hectare! When the most you get in a Coteaux du Languedoc is a miserable fifty.' I had little understanding of hectolitres and hectares but I got Manu's general drift. 'It's ridiculous, discriminating against Aramon!' he continued. 'I mean, it even does well where it's too flat and fertile for the swanky new varieties . . .' He simply couldn't understand why everyone else had been ripping it up and replanting.

But I could. I'd tasted his wine.

Our third drive up and down Montpeyroux's frustratingly long main street is, however, slightly discrediting Manu's assertion that he knew exactly how to find the Domaine d'Aupilhac. The tall and timeless-looking buildings, squeezed tightly together on either side, all look equally anonymous. I tentatively suggest that an elaborately painted 'A' on the wall beside one of the ancient panelled doors might be a clue. (I have the advantage: I saw the logo on their label in October.) A confident young-looking man, in confidently expensive casual clothes, responds to Manu's rap on his iron knocker with a welcoming, wine-stained hand.

My companion really ought to approve of Sylvain Fadat because he has founded much of his considerable renown on another unfashionable grape: the Carignan – not as deeply disdained as Manu's Aramon but another, it seems, that a lot of people have been accepting European Community subsidies to rip out.

'For a long time, it replaced the Aramon as the dominant local variety,' Sylvain explains, as we follow him through a series of small, low-ceilinged rooms to an office dominated by an enormous modern desk. 'It was a major contributor to the region's bad name, because of its dreadfully high yield.'

'I don't see why that's so dreadful,' grunts Manu, as his plump denimed weight slumps into one of Sylvain's plump leather armchairs.

'It depends whether or not you like bland bulk,' Sylvain answers civilly.

'You decided the Carignan could be rehabilitated?' I ask, remembering my autumn wine, which was anything but bland.

'I didn't have any crusading mission.' He smiles as he pours us a dark, purple-tinged sample of the latest vintage. 'I simply didn't have the money to replant. It was 1989. I'd just finished my oenology studies at Montpellier . . .' (I was right: he is indeed still young, despite his receding hairline.) 'The vines that my father used to cultivate for the co-operative were about fifty years old, and I pruned them hard and harvested late. All of which helped to give me low, concentrated yields.'

Manu drains his glass with an expression of exaggerated concentration, apparently weighing up the wisdom of giving this young upstart the benefit of the doubt.

'But I had far more Carignan than anything else,' Sylvain continues. 'So I had to sell it on its own. Which meant it couldn't be Coteaux du Languedoc.'

'*C'est pas vrai!* You mean, they've criminalized Carignan as well as Aramon?' asks Manu, sensing a fellow-feeling with this young man after all and magnanimously extending a reconciliatory glass for a refill.

'It can't be more than fifty per cent of the blend, *monsieur*. So most of mine ended up as humble *vin de pays*.'

'Even though it's grown on Coteaux du Languedoc land?' I ask.

'Precisely. You see, the bureaucrats didn't think the wine-buying public would get sufficient mental stimulus from just the one complicated system. So they carved up the map a second time, into hundreds of different *vins de pays*. A completely different set of names, running parallel with the first. The same land but different names and different conditions. Less restrictive but less prestigious.'

'Some of them seem to command pretty prestigious prices,' I say, remembering the New Year extravagance that started all this.

'Nowadays, maybe. But in 1990 I could hardly give my Carignan away. Except to passing tourists who were too ignorant about names and grape varieties to be prejudiced.'

I take this as my cue to enquire whether there is any to spare for a passing local today. The telephone has hardly stopped ringing while we have been with him and I am not particularly optimistic but he says he could manage a case. And then we leave him to take a call from yet another hopeful, wanting to reserve an allocation of something he probably once spurned.

*

The village appears to be farther from the house than I thought and I suspect this morning's expedition may well be the first and last time that I walk down in search of breakfast croissants. With most of my belongings at last unpacked and sufficient fallen branches cut into fire-sized pieces to keep me warm for the next few days, I felt it was time for a proper exploration on foot. But I soon realized that what is probably less than a kilometre as the crow flies must be much more than two by the dilapidated tarmac lane that follows the contours round the hill between the vines and the olive trees.

The vines were, of course, completely bare at this time of year – some neatly pruned, others still a ragged tangle – but the delicate, silvery grey foliage of the olive trees gently counter-pointed the starkness of the rugged, fir-clad hills immediately behind me to the north. And somehow, the thought that this must be about the highest altitude that vines and olives can tolerate made these defining features of the Mediterranean seem all the more precious.

Halfway to the village and far from any home, an elderly couple were working in a tiny, terraced olive grove rising steeply beside the lane. Each appeared equally impervious to the cold. The woman's dress was covered only by a thin nylon overall wrapped tightly round her frail-looking figure. The husband was jacketless in a woollen shirt, with braces support-ing well-worn corduroy trousers which hung loosely off his waist, as though they once belonged to some plumper younger brother. They paused as soon as they saw me, apparently grateful for an excuse to massage the stiffness in their backs.

'*Bonjour, monsieur!*' they called out together, as if one voice alone might not have been strong enough to carry on the wind. 'The English nephew, we suppose.'

I was startled to think that my well-worn overcoat and jeans had so quickly betrayed both my Englishness and nephewness but then I remembered that the lane really leads nowhere but to me and the Groses. So it didn't need Chief Inspector Clouseau to crack my identity.

'Did you get a good crop?' they asked in their characteristic, tremulous unison.

'I've no idea,' I confessed. 'I've only just moved in and I can hardly see the olive trees for the brambles and whatever else is climbing over them.'

'Don't leave it much later,' they counselled, as they waved me on my way with a quavery *'bon courage!'*

Rounding the corner, I had the postcard view of the village, perfectly positioned on an oval hillock between two river valleys and surrounded by darker, more dramatic hills climbing up to the sheer white cliffs that support the Larzac plateau high above. As many ancient houses as the ingenuity of successive centuries could contrive clung tenaciously to even the most vertical of the hillock's edges, with a picturesquely fortified château crowning the summit.

The main street was long, narrow, straight and steep. There was no pavement but rather a pair of deep stone ditches filled with fast-running water, making each side narrower still. Most of the houses rose as high as a fourth storey, the ground floor remaining invariably windowless, with a small door for people and a larger one for animals or machinery. Many of them had wrought iron balconies, with enough washing hanging on them to satisfy me that I was genuinely in the South of France but few enough geraniums to reassure me that I was still in one of its less discovered parts. Every twenty metres or so, an even narrower alleyway offered a miniature view of the countryside beyond, often no more than a tiny glimpse beneath one of the curious, arching, stone bridges that the residents seem to favour to link the upper levels of the buildings on either side, facilitating who knows what degrees of neighbourly intimacy.

There was, however, no sign of the master baker whose

trading presence I had so rashly assumed. I did pass one shop professing to butchery but its faded red and white blind looked as if it had not been raised in fifteen years. The only indication of commercial life was a tiny general store up in the Place de la Fontaine, near the Salle des Fêtes. It had three small rooms, strung together in an awkward 'Z' shape and filled, remarkably, with almost everything that the villagers might need, from handmade cheeses to photocopying services. But no croissants. The pretty young woman who appeared to be the owner explained that it operates as a *'dépôt de pain'* but only ten croissants are deposited each day and six of those are reserved for the château. You have to be up early for the leftovers.

I settled for a *baguette* and crossed the square to investigate what appeared to be the village's only café. An outside terrace was shrouded in a zipped-up wall of transparent plastic sheeting. The whole establishment looked closed for the season but encouragingly convivial sounds from within suggested otherwise. I was searching in vain for an alternative entrance when the harassed-looking *patronne* came out to take pity on me and show me the secret panel in the plastic.

About a dozen customers nodded civilly but silently in my direction. They were all male and all perched at the bar on an assortment of stools. The bar itself had started life as a traditional *zinc*, before suffering its more recent mock-wood extension. The centre of the room was completely dominated by a billiard table, swaddled in a protective plastic sheet, which in turn was half-covered by menus, bread-baskets and sauce bottles. Squashed between this and the bare stone walls, a line of small imitation-marble tables, already laid with cruets and cutlery, completed the impression that eating might be the café's secondary sport.

The twelve pairs of muddy boots at the bar testified to several hours already spent in the fields and most of the group were enjoying a mid-morning, restorative, aniseed-flavoured *pastis* or, failing that, a glass of red wine or beer. However, remembering my breakfast *baguette*, I confined myself to a coffee.

The bustling, chain-smoking *patronne* gave no sign that she considered my order effeminate. She simply darted about, as *petite* as most of her *clientèle* were burly, her outfit as curiously matched as her décor. The formal, slightly prim cashmere top contrasted oddly with a loose, almost slovenly skirt, and the neat patent shoes belonged to a different woman altogether from the untidy ponytail. Maybe she was simply trying to be all things to all customers.

Everyone else called her 'Babette'. In fact, everyone else gave her careworn cheeks at least three kisses on arrival or departure and I wondered how long I should have to be here to count as an insider.

'*Et le pauvre Manu?*' she asked, when she brought me the coffee. '*Comment va-t-il?*'

Again I had the eerie impression that someone must have pinned a note of my address to the back of my jacket. Was I really the first stranger that they had seen all winter?

'Manu's my cousin,' Babette explained, as she lit a new cigarette with the stub of the old and left the latter smouldering in my ashtray. 'He said you'd be down before long. By rights, he ought to be my best customer. But guess-who placed the café out of bounds. I'm supposed to inform on him, if he comes here on his own, but I sometimes smuggle him in and out the back way!'

She offered me a well-thumbed copy of the local newspaper and returned to the bar to embrace another wave of thirsty labourers. I had been wondering whether tomorrow's weather forecast might augur well for a first assault on my olive jungle but I didn't think I could face the gothic horrors predicted on the back page. I was just immersing myself in a more comforting report of a local onion-growing competition, when a new female voice intruded from a half-hidden corner behind the billiard table.

'I can see that you've been wondering whether I'm English,' it said.

I was, in fact, wondering nothing of the sort. What I am wondering is how much henna it must have taken to produce the mass of vividly auburn curls bearing down on my table. I suspect, however, that, beneath the expensive cut of an intimidating black trouser suit, she is neither as young nor as slender as she would like to be.

'Krystina,' she booms, above the clank of her costume jewellery. 'With a K and a Y. I live at the château. Bought it with my divorce money. Don't worry, I know who you are,' she assures me, as she draws a chair rather closer to mine than an acquaintance of this brevity would normally justify. 'Steeped in history, of course, the château. Which I love. Used to teach it, you see. History. Before I married my serial philanderer. So it feels like I'm getting back to my roots . . .'

The torrent of self-explanation continues in these conditions of unlooked-for proximity for another minute or two. When I finally have an opportunity to turn the monologue into something closer to conversation, all I can think of to ask is a rather pedestrian 'How much does she know about the history of the Languedoc?' Then I foolishly add that I'm terribly keen to learn all about the region's wine-making history. Not that I'm *uninterested*, of course, but I really should have foreseen how avidly the merest flicker of enthusiasm would be pounced on.

'I don't even know when it started,' I fumble. 'Under the Romans, I've always assumed . . .'

'Wrong!' My history mistress unexpectedly slaps a hand on mine. 'I shall have to take you to Agde to meet my favourite Greek boy. Tuesday would be a good day for me. I'll come up for you at nine. Don't worry, I know where you are. In fact, would you like a lift now? It's raining, I see.'

The rain is actually extremely heavy but I suspect I am in enough trouble already, so I extricate my hand and insist on

16

walking home. However, by the time I arrive it is nearly midday and my soggy *baguette* has lost most of its appeal.

Maybe I should just drive back to the café for lunch.

'Does it ever snow?' I ask Manu. It has been bitterly cold since I arrived and there were icicles on the plants beside the terrace fountain this morning.

'Here?' says Manu, as a shorthand for 'Don't you northerners understand anything?'

We are returning from an expedition to purchase the terrifying quantity of tools that Manu assured me would be indispensable, if I were to have any hope of reclaiming the olive trees. He goes hunting with the manager of the local DIY hypermarket (a great leveller, *la chasse*) and he promised that his networking skills would guarantee me massive discounts. But my credit-card limit has nonetheless suffered a serious assault and somehow Manu's insistence that I buy everything at the top end of the market encourages a sense that many of the more luxurious items in the back of his van are also destined for active service on a neighbouring property.

'Well, maybe it snows once every fifteen years,' he continues. 'Like 1986, for instance. You wouldn't believe it. Completely snowed in, we were. I mean, completely. Up to the windows. For three days it was like living in an igloo. But that must be, what? Fifteen years ago now.'

Making us just about due for another of nature's specials, I calculate, as a car coming towards us from the heights of the Larzac plain passes with snow spilling off its roof. Not quite my vision of life in the balmy south.

'But is there any danger for the vines?' I ask.

'Not in the Languedoc,' says Manu. 'It very rarely goes below minus five down here and you'd need something like minus eighteen to damage a vine.'

'I've heard the Russians bury theirs.'

'Unnatural!' snorts Manu, as if at some scandalous depra-
vity. But then an unfortunate flash of free association reminds
him of some rather special vodka, stashed away in his cellar,
which I really have to sample before lunch.

This morning I made a start on the liberation of the olive trees.
Manu's preferred models of strimmer and chainsaw have been
put into action and I feel unexpectedly exhilarated. All my previous urban gardening efforts in England now seem depressingly mean and pointless: paltry struggles to create tiny
patches of passably abundant life where none would naturally
belong. Here, the opposite adventure of taming twelve acres of
nature's super-abundance seems infinitely more exciting.

Unfortunately, however, it also seems infinitely more
infinite. It is not simply a matter of everything being overgrown. There is, for instance, also the little matter of water. The
house is called 'Les Sources' in honour of the natural springs
that Uncle Milo 'captured' to provide the sole supply of water.
After so many months of abandonment, it is amazing that the
taps are still running – still more so that the water is the best I
have ever tasted. Yet elsewhere nature has started to reassert
itself. The spring that is routed through the courtyard fountain
flows on into a deep freshwater pool farther down the hillside.
Memories of clear, refreshing swimming there on my early
visits have successfully put me off bright blue, chlorinated rec-
tangles for life. However, today it has all the murky greenness
of a forgotten village pond. Another spring that once fed a little
brook running down through the orchard to the river has silted
up, leaving the apple trees paddling in a bog.

There is enough work here for a lifetime, never mind a year.
However, by lunchtime, protesting muscles in every part of my
body were demanding some respite from the morning's unfamiliar impositions. So I generously agreed to treat them to
lunch at a little village restaurant called Le Pressoir, which I

spotted in Saint Saturnin when we were coming back from Montpeyroux. Some homemade chicken liver paté and tender lamb chops grilled on a fire made from gnarled old vine-stocks had revived me just enough to face the afternoon shift. However, hobbling back to the car, I spotted an intriguing, freshly chalked legend above a set of peeling double doors on the other side of the square.

'*Virgile Joly – Cave Particulière – Depuis 2000,*' it said.

And in the second week of January 2001, how could I fail to be impressed? So, for all my good intentions on the olive terraces, I tried a tentative knock.

A cheerful 'Come in, if you can squeeze in!' is the immediate response, because Virgile Joly's *cave* proves to be as minute as it is recent. Though little bigger than a lockup garage it is packed with far more equipment than anyone would have thought possible in such a confined space. Some of it looks conspicuously new, like his dozen or so wooden barrels and the four tall, fibreglass fermentation tanks, or '*cuves*' as he calls them; the rest, including a variety of strange machinery with unidentifiable roles in the wine-making process, looks much more obviously second- or third-hand. Everything, however, is impeccably tidily ordered. Indeed, my arrival has clearly interrupted a fastidious scrubbing of the concrete floor, but Virgile still seems only too happy to lean on his broom for a chat.

'Last year was my first vintage,' he explains enthusiastically, in precise, well-educated French with just an occasional southern twang. (He is well-spoken, well-dressed, well-groomed and, seemingly, well under thirty.) 'Not the first vintage I'd worked on. I'd already been helping other people for nine or ten years. But the first with my own vines. Why don't you come and have a look at them?'

I climb into his elderly but spotless white Mercedes van and we drive a few kilometres outside the village to a spot where rows of vines appear to stretch as far as I can see across the gently sloping plain.

'This is my Carignan,' he explains, pointing to one expanse of vines. 'And here's my Syrah,' he continues, pointing to another apparently identical patch. 'Then over there, I've got some Grenache Noir.'

'Does that mean that you make three different wines?' (I realize I shall simply have to get used to some unfamiliar grapes down here: no sign yet of my old friends, Cabernet and Chardonnay.)

'Not at all. I mix them. In fact, for Coteaux du Languedoc, you're obliged to mix at least two varieties, or *cépages*, as we call them.'

'You mix them after you've made the wines?'

'No, before. Some people make the *assemblage* afterwards but – well, you've seen my cellar – I don't really have room to keep them separate. And, in any case, I think you get a more complex wine, if the grapes ferment together.'

'And these vines – you bought them only last year?'

'They're rented. It'll be a while before I can afford to buy any-thing. But yes, it was only last March that I got hold of them – just in time to give them a hasty prune.' He laughs at the memory. 'The only piece of equipment I had was a pair of seca-teurs. Everything else, including the cellar, came later, as I persuaded the bank manager to lend me a little bit more for the necessities of each new season. The trouble is, I can't get it all in. I'm going to have to move the wine press out to make room for a bottling machine that I'm borrowing.'

'You mean, the wine's ready for bottling already?'

'One of them will be soon, yes. Shall we go and taste it?'

I fail to take in all the technicalities but, back in the *cave*, Virgile explains that he has deliberately made one style of wine for early, relatively easy drinking and another for bottling some time next year, which he hopes will be more complex. He reaches for two of the most serious-looking goblets that I've seen in a long time and, with the aid of a large glass pipette, draws a sample of the first wine from one of the barrels.

'I feel very shy about these tastings,' he confesses, his ruddy cheeks turning a little redder still. 'Especially when they're not yet ready.'

'Does wine-making run in the family?' I ask to distract him.

'My grandfather was a *vigneron* in the Vaucluse. Still is. But I came over here to study oenology at Montpellier. And then I worked for a lot of different people, both here in the Languedoc and in Chile. I could have set myself up anywhere really and I must say I was pretty tempted by Chile. So much less red tape than France. But nowhere else,' he says with evident feeling, 'has this landscape. Or this diversity of wines.'

We move on to wine number two. The first was already deliciously full and spicy but the second, drawn directly from one of the fermentation tanks, promises even more. I make a mental note to ask another day how he achieves the difference. Then suddenly, as I look around the tiny *cave*, it strikes me that here, perhaps, is an operation small enough in scale for me to be able to grasp what on earth it is that a *vigneron* does between one harvest and the next. When I hint as much to Virgile, he declares himself only too willing to instruct me. Indeed, his insistence that I should 'shadow' his operations over the coming year is almost as determined as Manu's resolve to play the chaperon. Not to mention Krystina's apparently obdurate designs on me.

Shall I ever be able to keep them all happy?

'You realize, of course, that what you have here are Lucques?' said Manu last week, when he first came over to inspect my progress in the olive grove. 'The finest olives in the Languedoc. You see that kind of crescent shape? Unmistakable Lucque, that is. Ideal up here, of course, as your uncle realized. They don't mind the cold but they hate the drought. Probably got a bit thirsty, here on their own last summer, though. Otherwise they'd be a lot plumper . . . And of course, you really should have picked them in October. When they were green . . .'

Until a couple of days before this, I had always assumed that there were green olive trees and black olive trees, just as there were green and black grapes. Mercifully, however, a chance conversation overheard in the village shop had brought enlightenment and, thanks to Nathalie the shopkeeper, I now knew that black olives were simply green olives left to ripen longer on the tree.

'You see, Lucques are really green olives,' Manu continued, unaware of how easily I could have made a fool of myself at this critical moment. 'For the table. But I suppose you could always go for oil. Given that you've got black olives. And that you've missed the boat for the table. Although there again, you really should have picked them in December . . .'

I took a small sample branch into Clermont L'Hérault's highly regarded olive oil co-operative – luckily only about twenty minutes' drive away in the direction of the coast – half hoping that the experts would tell me I had missed the boat for oil as well. But unfortunately I was still in time. So I felt I had to ignore the cold and drizzle and make a start but it seemed to take me most of the morning to fill less than half a bucket. My fingers were numb from the chill north wind and I was almost past caring what happened to my crop when Manu arrived with a bundle of blankets under his arm.

'It'll be time for the tree to flower again, if you carry on at that rate,' he laughed, as he spread the blankets on the ground and started shaking the branches with all his might.

The effect was like a hailstorm battering my head, with the coldest and wettest olives finding their way straight down the back of my neck. But it worked. In no time we had enough to fill my bucket many times over and few enough left on the trees to be quietly forgotten.

'Women's work,' announced Mme Gros, appearing from nowhere. 'Always was, olive-picking. Not the young women, though. Never the under-forties. Made the trees infertile.'

Yet for all her conspicuous qualifications on grounds of age and sex, she seemed quite content to confine herself to folklore and set off home, leaving the menfolk to their untraditional labours.

We managed about twenty kilos before the rain forced a retreat and at first that seemed quite gratifying. This morning, however, I feel enormously self-conscious, skulking into the olive oil co-operative with my six bulging carrier bags. The tiny forecourt is besieged by vans and hatchbacks piled to their roofs with crates of shiny, ripe black olives and I am convinced that mine look much more shrivelled than everybody else's. But a brisk young man with a giant set of scales passes them all as perfectly acceptable. And there appears to be no minimum load – as long as you bring six or seven kilos, enough for a litre of oil, you are in. So suddenly, momentously, I find I'm a fully paid-up member of the region's oil-producing community.

Luckily, today is Manu's day for taking Mme Gros to have her distinctively tight perm made tighter still, so I do not have to explain the turquoise open-top BMW that has just roared recklessly up over the potholes of my drive; nor the flamboyant apparition in canary-yellow silk that is waving me into the passenger seat.

'You'll be used to my style of driving by the end of the year.' Krystina narrowly misses the box where the postman leaves my mail at the bottom of the drive, as the morning's lesson begins. 'The date you want to remember is 550 BC. Well, thereabouts anyway. The first Greek colony in the Languedoc. Down on the coast at Agde. Soon be there,' she reassures me, driving heedlessly through a red light. 'Sub-colony of Massilia

– that's Marseille to you, of course – founded fifty years earlier by a bunch of sea-faring adventurers from Phocaea, on the coast of Asia Minor . . .'

Krystina's momentary concentration on the challenges of cornering sharply, with no perceptible reduction in speed, allows me a terrified 'Why did they come to the Languedoc?'

'In those days, nobody sailed *across* the Mediterranean. Journeys were always charted round the edges. They needed lots of safe anchorages and Agde offered one of them.'

This seems clear enough as she says it but harder to under-stand when we actually lurch to a halt in the city centre. Even in the state of shock induced by forty-five minutes as Krystina's passenger, I can see that Agde is not on the coast. The Hérault River is extremely wide at this point but it cannot be confused with the Mediterranean.

'You've noticed the absence of sea?' she asks. 'You'll find it about four kilometres downriver. But this is where the harbour used to be, right at the point where the Hérault met the Med. It's the coastline that's moved. Silted up. There used to be a whole chain of lagoons along the coast – *bassins* I think they call them here – protected by a string of outlying islands. Gave the Greeks wonderfully sheltered sailing, from the Rhône to the Pyrenees. But they silted up as well, turning the islands into much more continuous landmasses, encircling the lagoons . . .'

I seem to have wandered into the geography class by mistake. My head is spinning and I propose a therapeutic coffee in the *centre historique*, having noted that cars – and most especially Krystina's – are excluded. But before we have much chance to explore, a sudden shower steers us into a garish, formica-filled brasserie called the Agathe.

'It's the old Greek name for Agde,' says the beaming, Brylcremed *patron*. 'Means good or beautiful in Greek,' he explains as he casts a proprietorial look at his chipped red tables and cracked black leatherette seating. 'But of course, you won't find any trace of Greek remains in modern Agde,' he adds complacently, as if he were discussing the successful eradication of a contagious disease.

'Nor much justification for the name,' I grumble to Krystina.

'Don't worry, I'll soon be taking you to one of the most beautiful sights in the Languedoc,' she assures me.

'Can't be soon enough,' I think to myself, as I watch the rain trickling down the greasy windowpane. Maybe it's just the effect of the weather and the café but somehow I can't imagine Agde looking much less lugubrious in the sunshine. It must be the ubiquitous dark grey stone. The ochre-painted houses down by the river were pleasant enough but, up here in the oldest part of town, everything from the gloomy-looking market hall to the rather sinister black fortified cathedral shows the same peculiar tendency to emulate some forbidding, soot-stained northern mining town.

'Only to be expected,' says Krystina, as we dash back to the car, 'if you set yourself up beside an extinct volcano and use the recycled lava for your building blocks.'

Her exit from the car park rivals all of the manufacturer's published acceleration statistics. We are apparently now in a hurry because she has booked us a restaurant on the sea front at Cap d'Agde for twelve o'clock.

'*Midi* is so much easier to say than half past,' she laughs gaily, then returns to the Agde colonists to prove that her history is better than her French. 'It was the Phocaeans who introduced the first wine. Brought their own to begin with. About ten million litres a year, to judge by the amphoras shipwrecked off the coast . . .'

Their consumption rates sound even more impressive than Manu's but Krystina hastily explains that it wasn't all for themselves.

'Wine proved a great success with the locals, you see. And very soon the Greeks were planting the Languedoc's first cultivated vines and making the first local wines. Same with the olive trees, because olive oil wasn't just the cornerstone of their cuisine, they also needed it for lighting, medicine, important religious observances, you name it. Absolutely vital. If a Greek wanted to cripple an enemy, he simply cut down his olive trees.'

'It's so hard to imagine the Languedoc landscape without its vines and olive trees,' I manage to interject.

'Not half as difficult as imagining the kind of wine these people drank,' Krystina says, deftly reasserting her monopoly. 'I mean, straightforward fermented grape juice was only a starting point for the most unappetizing selection of cocktails. They added anything from honey, herbs and spices to salt, vinegar, flour, pitch and marble-dust. Even seawater. Anything to disguise the shortcomings of the basic product!'

Cap d'Agde is a 1960s purpose-built resort, a brave attempt to enliven vast tracts of empty lava flow with eight marinas, a hundred thousand beds and countless possibilities for entertainment and refreshment. In summer, that is. In January the floating gin palaces are all deserted, the bedrooms firmly shuttered and every catering outlet serving sustenance fit for consumption apparently closed until the spring – leaving only the one on which we have just for ever turned our backs. I am not sure which was worse: the slimy *terrine de crevettes* or the wilting lettuce that accompanied it; the over-cooked sole or the vinegary sauce in which it was swimming. The only consolation is that the wretchedness of the meal extinguished any possibility of the romantic tête-à-tête that I suspect Krystina had in mind.

'Cheer up!' she says, with a sudden slipping of an arm through mine to make up for lost time. 'You'll soon see why I brought you here.'

The treat that she has been saving for me turns out to be a museum – a deeply unpromising exhibition devoted to the flotsam and jetsam of the river delta. My arm still clamped to Krystina's, I shuffle past an extensive collection of rusty anchors and barnacled amphora fragments, listening to her commentary. Until we turn a corner.

'Still wondering why we came?' she whispers, suddenly hushed.

At the other end of the room, spotlit in its glass case, is one of the most beautiful statues in the whole of France, perhaps the world. It is a figure of a Greek youth, just fractionally under life size – a battered bronze, fished from the Hérault in 1964 – its naked physical perfection somehow movingly heightened by the water's brutal amputation of its hands and feet. We circle it in silence for some time.

'Gorgeous, isn't he?' whispers Krystina, breaking the spell. 'They call him the Ephèbe – from around the third century BC, experts say. A posthumous son of Alexander the Great, perhaps. Call me sentimental,' she laughs as she tightens her grip on my arm, 'but I'll always put him a couple of hundred years earlier. For me, he's the hero who started the history of Languedoc wine.'

'You mean, you went to Agde and you didn't have any Picpoul de Pinet?' said Manu, more scandalized than I've ever seen him. 'When the vineyard's practically next door! The situation must be rectified at once!'

What he really meant was that my exertions in the olive grove had resulted in considerably fewer cellar crawls than he was hoping for. There was still a huge amount of work to be done but I felt my good conduct had earned me at least a day's release.

'Let me guess,' I said, as I joined him in the van, 'Picpoul is the name of some exceptionally obscure grape?'

'Indeed it is – you're learning fast,' said Manu. 'And Pinet's one of just a handful of villages entitled to make the wine. It's the only Coteaux du Languedoc made from a single grape variety and it's pretty special, as you'll see.'

The specialness, Manu insisted, could only be considered in the presence of a substantial platter of *fruits de mer*, for which, he assured me, Picpoul was the only imaginable accompaniment. With this in mind, he had taken the precaution of booking a table for two in my name at his favourite waterside restaurant in Bouzigues, an attractive little port on the Bassin de Thau, renowned for the oysters and mussels that are farmed in the waters of the lagoon.

Our table is the last remaining on a crowded, harbour-front terrace – a crush that, I suspect, owes more to the unexpected warmth of the afternoon sunshine than to any expected excellence in the oysters. I peel off as many layers of clothing as decency allows, while Manu swelters in his habitual blue dungarees. They are the regulation dress of every self-respecting cartoon *ouvrier* but favoured in his case, I suspect, as a purely practical recognition of the fact that he has no perceptible waistline to offer support to more conventional trousering. And little by way of shoulders for braces either.

Manu is, however, less conventional in the choice of headgear covering his sparse grey hair. Blithely ignoring the weight of tradition that should have insisted on a flat black cap or even a beret, he touches instead a slightly faded red baseball cap by way of greeting to our sour-faced waitress.

'No more *tielle*,' she announces with grim satisfaction.

'What's *tielle*?' I ask.

'It's the speciality. But there's none left,' she confirms, as she gestures bleakly towards the rest of her busy terrace. 'It's January. The sun's appeared. Everyone's come to sit in it. No more *tielle*.'

Thankful that we haven't caught her on a day when rain might have dampened her spirits further, we order the *fruits de mer*.

'It'll make a change from the wife's food,' says Manu, pulling a face. 'You thought every French woman could cook, didn't you? Well, it was just my luck to marry the exception.'

Although spared any first hand experience, I do have some sense of Manu's ill fortune, just from the dank aroma of her *potage de légumes* that regularly drifts across from the other side of the stream.

'Don't worry,' says Manu, reading my thoughts as the wine arrives. 'She's not likely to invite you.'

We have ordered some Picpoul, of course, but Manu – a braver man than I and impervious to the waitress's murderous look – rejects the first bottle that is brought to us.

'A good Picpoul', he expounds authoritatively, 'should be crisp and full at the same time. That's how the grape got its name: *"pic"* as in *"picquer"* – to prick – and *"poul"* as in *"poul"*.' (A blank look from me.) 'An old Occitan word meaning soft and rounded,' he elaborates, as if he thought everyone fluent in the medieval language of the troubadour poets. (A more disbelieving look now, as I wonder what dusty volume on the family bookshelves can have been the source of this unexpected, last-minute learning.) But the closet etymologist soon gives way to the more familiar, bibulous incarnation, when a second and then a third bottle measures up to his expectations.

The clean, fresh, pleasantly citric style of the wine is indeed such a perfect accompaniment to our towering mountain of seafood that it is easy to imagine that the grape variety and indeed the whole style of wine-making here must have been deliberately chosen to suit the local produce. But a quick visit to a little harbour-side museum after lunch reveals that, while Picpoul has been grown here for about two thousand years, oyster-farming was not introduced until the mid-1800s. What's more, those early efforts must have been fairly unrewarding, as there was apparently only one oyster fisherman operating in Bouzigues at the end of that century. Today, however, the dark silhouettes of hundreds of wooden frames or 'tables' stretch out in neat rows towards the opposite shore. Each of them supports a thousand ropes and hundreds of shellfish cling to every rope in various states of maturity.

Unfortunately, I see rather more of these oyster tables than I really need to, as Manu struggles to sustain the illusion that he knows precisely where to find the maker of our excellent lunchtime Picpoul. An increasingly flustered exploration of most of the territory within a few kilometres of the lagoon eventually yields a view that faintly resembles the artist's impression of waterside vines, which we remember from the label. And a blast on Manu's horn soon produces a studious-looking young woman in a tracksuit and trainers, who politely confirms that we have indeed located the Domaine Félines Jourdan.

'Is your father not at home?' demands Manu, in the tones of one accustomed to more ceremonious receptions.

'My father?'

'Your boss then. The *monsieur* who makes the wine.'

'But I make the wine,' says our hostess, cheerfully impervious to Manu's incredulity. 'I'm responsible for the cellar and my uncle looks after the vineyard. Would you like to taste?'

Claude Jourdan's offer sends my companion's features into a torment of indecision. Should he seize the opportunity for another glass of the wine that he relished so unreservedly at lunchtime? Or did the heat of the day make him recklessly uncritical of something that ought to have been approached with greater circumspection?

'There's no need,' I tell her to put him out of his misery. 'We got to know your wine extremely well over lunch.'

While Mlle Jourdan sorts out my purchase, she tells us how they made their first Picpoul as recently as 1992 and how a first gold medal followed in 1993. Indeed, to judge from a fat file of press cuttings, few have ever quarrelled with their overnight success. Few, that is, except Manu, who continues to regard this female intruder in the masculine world of wine-making with undisguised suspicion.

Later in the evening, as if to demonstrate more acceptable womanly ways, Mme Gros makes an unprecedented appearance on my doorstep. She is holding a plate with a small round pastry-covered pie, exuding a mildly unappetizing fishy smell.

'We found it down at Hyper U,' she announces. 'My husband says you missed out on these at lunchtime. *Tielle.*'

I am touched by the gesture but, after one bite into the squid-filled cardboard crust, I know I didn't miss out on much. Perhaps because she knows this only too well, Mme Gros stays to watch me finish the last mouthful.

Virgile is worried.

This unseasonably mild weather is no good for his vines. They are supposed to be having a quiet rest after the rigours of carrying last year's crop, patiently sitting out the cold and using the carbohydrates stored in the autumn as a kind of anti-freeze. Instead, the thermometer has been confusing them with spring-like messages and their sap is rising too soon. If it carries on like this, Virgile explains, the buds will burst prematurely and then be damaged by some sudden return to wintry normality.

He is also worried by the sheer quantity of pruning to be coped with in the next two or three months. He has rented some additional parcels of land to increase his production and it is going to be a lot of extra work on his own.

I cautiously follow Virgile's confident four-wheel-drive down a rough grassy track, winding through the endless, anonymous-looking rows of vines on the plain to the south of Saint Saturnin. There are no fences or other badges of ownership and at first I wonder how Virgile can possibly remember which are supposed to be his. But then I notice the subtle changes in pruning styles and maintenance standards every twenty rows or so. When we slow down beside an exceptionally chaotic tangle of last year's growth, where only the metre-wide spacing between the rows seems to have prevented each from intertwining with its neighbour, I feel depressingly certain that we have located his newly rented Syrah.

'Do you see how each of the vinestocks is trained in a sort of T-shape?' asks Virgile, as he pulls aside a jumble of stems to reveal a pair of barely visible horizontal arms, branching off from a central trunk and following a long low wire that stretches down the row. 'It's called "Cordon Royat" – a method of training the vines that's relatively new in the Languedoc but most people use it now for the new varieties. The more traditional method's what you see over there, behind you.'

He nods towards a field already pruned to expose a very different style of vinestock, unsupported by any wires. I recognize this as the way in which most of the vines near Les Sources are pruned. Indeed, it is one of the most striking features of the local landscape, with four or five gnarled and twisted branches curling up from each trunk, as if to grip some enormous bowl or cup.

'Goblet pruning,' Virgile succinctly explains, as he hands me a small pair of secateurs. 'Mainly reserved for Carignan these days.'

The untamed shoots of Virgile's Syrah have been blown in all directions by the wind and the idea is that I go ahead of him, cutting off the worst: a pre-pruning that might have been avoided if the previous grower had exercised a bit more discipline. It's a slow, backbreaking exercise and, to make things worse, one that seems to be perfectly within the capabilities of a rapid-action machine, operating in one of the adjoining fields. But Virgile wouldn't dream of using a mechanical cutter, even for a pre-prune and even if he could afford one.

'Pruning is one of the most important skills,' he emphasizes, keeping a careful eye on my work. 'Apart from just keeping things manageable, it's the main opportunity to impose my policy on the crucial question of *yield*.'

'Is that the "hectolitres per hectare" that people keep talking about?' I ask.

'Exactly,' he says. 'About twenty-five, in my case – half the official Coteaux du Languedoc maximum. But what I'm aiming for, you see, is a low-volume, high-concentration harvest. And by limiting the number of buds, I can start to limit my eventual number of bunches.'

'But what does it all mean in practice? You're talking to someone who doesn't even know what a hectolitre looks like.'

'It looks like a hundred litres,' he laughs. 'And a hectare looks a lot like ten thousand square metres.'

'So your yield of twenty-five . . .' I struggle with the maths.

'Means one litre from every four square metres,' he rescues me. He has done the calculation before. 'But "hectolitres per hectare" doesn't mean very much, unless you also take into account the number of vines per hectare. If you've got low-density plantings, you can achieve the same yield of twenty-five with a lot less work. But the grapes won't be as good because the vines will have had a much easier time. My own densities are quite high – around five thousand per hectare.'

I am once again wrestling with my mental arithmetic but he saves me the trouble.

'My twenty-five hectolitres per hectare means that the four square metres producing that litre are occupied by an average of just two vines.'

'You mean only half a litre per vine? About three good glasses?'

The idea seems immensely depressing as I look back down the row to measure our results so far.

My hands are aching as I struggle to keep ahead of the expert. He takes considerably less time over the more critical, detailed, final pruning than I seem to need for the rough-and-ready preliminaries. His crisply laundered jeans and designer cardigan also remain as pristine as ever, while I end up covered in the mud that the recent sunshine has failed to dry.

With such a meticulous master in command, there's naturally no question of strewing the cuttings wherever they happen to fall. They have to be laid out neatly at right angles between the rows. A mincing machine will then be able to travel down the gaps and turn them into a kind of organic fertilizer.

'I try to make everything as *biologique* as possible,' he stresses. 'That's why I also leave some weeds.'

I always thought this was a sign of a carelessly tended vineyard but Virgile explains that the weeds help to make the vine work harder, pushing their roots down deeper in search of water and picking up tastier minerals as they go.

'A book of Uncle Milo's says pruning starts on the 22nd,' I say as I pause to straighten my aching back. 'St Vincent's Day.'

'Don't believe all you read!' laughs Virgile. 'It can start whenever the leaves have fallen in the first frosts, usually some time in December. The only thing that really matters is that you're finished by the end of March, when the buds start bursting.'

But this is an objective that seems distressingly unattainable as we finish our labours for today, with only two rows, out of I hate to think how many, completed.

Marseillan is another attractive little port, slightly west of Bouzigues on the Bassin de Thau and, according to Krystina, once another sub-colony of Marseille, as its name suggests. But its major claim to modern fame must surely be the production of one of the few alcoholic beverages that have ever – on the rarest of high days and holidays – been known to pass the lips of Mme Gros: the distinctive vermouth, Noilly Prat. So for once, it is she who has urged the expedition upon me.

'Your car, I think,' she announced decisively, when the idea was first mooted. 'My husband will be quite happy in the back. Then we can arrive with a bit of style for once.'

My ancient three-door Renault may not be quite the celebrity limousine of my neighbour's dreams but at least it is not a little red van. Unfortunately, however, the car's designer knew nothing of Mme Gros's taste in millinery. Otherwise, he might have raised the ceiling several centimetres and found a different location for the rear-view mirror. For despite the return of the torrential storms, Mme Gros has graced the occasion with an enormous and unseasonably flowery hat that makes driving extremely hazardous.

In fact, the whole of Mme Gros's outfit is incongruously summery, from the billowing, floral-patterned dress to the unaccustomed pink high heels. The entire effect looks as if she were expecting to open the vermouth factory, instead of merely visiting it. Even Manu has been pressed into a tie. And the fact that he has somehow arranged a private tour in the middle of the normal *fermeture annuelle* (another hunting contact?) accentuates the general air of visiting royalty. Or it would have done, if Manu had succeeded in finding the out-of-season entrance before the silken herbaceous border festooning his spouse's headgear was irretrievably sodden.

She is therefore in no mood to be amused by the rapt attention that he is paying to the vivacious young blonde who has been deputed to act as our guide. After all, who would have expected him to be so fascinated by the fact that a vermouth starts its life as ordinary table wine (in this case, a blend of Picpoul de Pinet and something I have yet to investigate, called Clairette du Languedoc)? Or so enthralled by the addition of fruit-flavoured spirits and a long list of herbs and spices (in a recipe curiously reminiscent of the ancient Greek cocktails that Krystina spoke about but omitting, I trust, the ground-up marble)?

'Pay no attention to my husband,' snaps Mme Gros – a strategy that has clearly commended itself to her over nearly fifty years of marriage. 'A man who manages to forget my umbrella on a day like this.'

The lack of waterproofing is suddenly uppermost in everyone's minds because the blonde has steered us outside again to a rain-drenched courtyard filled with hundreds of ancient-looking barrels.

'Here we observe the special process that makes Joseph Noilly's 1813 invention unique,' says her impeccably memorized script. 'A year's exposure to Marseillan's special combination of blazing sunshine and refreshing sea breezes.'

The irony may be lost on our guide but not on Mme Gros. She glowers first at the heavy black clouds that have so thoroughly soaked her and then at the feckless incompetent whom she holds responsible.

'The heat evaporates six to eight per cent of the wine in every barrel,' the script continues. 'The "angel's share", we call it.'

'Ah, the waste!' sighs Manu, too captivated to notice how dearly he is going to pay for his failure to bring any form of rain-protection.

'But essential, you see, to turn an ordinary bright, fresh wine into the distinctive, rich, amber-coloured liquid that sets Monsieur Noilly's product apart from the opposition.'

'And Monsieur Prat?' asks Mme Gros, with menacingly icy calm.

'Monsieur Noilly's son-in-law, Madame. Our first Marketing Director.'

'No wonder his name's on the label,' says Manu, still blissfully unaware of the impending storm, as he leads the retreat indoors for a tasting. 'Anyone who could get my beloved to buy one of his bottles deserves the *Légion d'honneur*!'

Virgile is worried again.

We are having lunch in the small, sparsely-furnished first-floor flat that he is renting from the Mairie in Saint Saturnin, until the house above his *cave* can be rendered fit for even his own, relatively undemanding, human occupation. The demands of wine-making leave little time or money for home-making but lunch is something that Virgile does believe in.

'Food and sleep,' he says, as he lifts two heavy slices of rare lamb from a frying pan and passes me a large bowl of salad. 'Two things I won't compromise on. Otherwise I can't do anything else.'

But he is still worried. His longer-maturing wine ought to be racked. It is still in its fermentation tank, on top of a bed of sediment known as the lees, and it urgently needs pumping off into a clean tank before the flavour's spoilt.

'Could you taste a hint of rottenness the other day?' he asks, unable to persuade himself that he can't. 'It's the weather that's the problem,' he continues, as he tops up our glasses with the D'Aupilhac Carignan that I brought him. 'We need a nice, crisp, sunny, anti-cyclonic day.'

'But surely racking is an indoor job?'

'We need high atmospheric pressure to push down on the lees. It keeps them settled at the bottom while we're pumping the wine. But look at the miserable wet skies that we've had for the last few days. And that's only part of the problem. In an ideal world, we'd wait for the moon as well.'

'Wait for the moon to do what?'

'To be in the right place,' he says and pulls a much-thumbed booklet out of a drawer. 'Have you not seen one of these before? It's what we call a biodynamic calendar.'

'Bio. . . . ?'

'Dynamic. The bio aspect really just means ordinary organic principles. But the dynamic bit involves doing things when the planets are favourable.'

'Like new moons and full moons, that kind of thing?' I ask disbelievingly.

'Not so much that as the movement of the moon in relation

to the rest of the zodiac. You see, the calendar divides the year into four different categories, each of them earmarked as favouring one of a plant's four key elements: the roots, the leaves, the flowers and the fruits. And if we're doing anything that relates to the wine itself, we try to do it in a fruit period.'

All this sounds a great deal wackier than the weather worries but, before I can betray too much scepticism, Virgile dials a number for a telephonic weather forecast.

'Not good,' he sighs, as he puts the receiver back, looking even more depressed. 'Maybe in a couple of days' time.'

'But won't that be a flower day?'

'Too bad,' he says. 'The wine won't wait. And the weather's more important. I'll call you when the skies are clear.'

February

O N SUNDAY MORNING I was woken by the unrelenting ringing of a telephone.

'*Bonjour, c'est Virgile*,' said the handset, as I fumbled in the dark for the light switch. 'The weather's changed. We need to rack the wine as soon as possible. Can you come straightaway?'

By the time I arrived, he was already busy with a bucket of soda solution, methodically sterilizing everything that he was about to use, from the empty fermentation *cuve* to his ancient, second-hand pump. Then the whole operation was carefully repeated with citric acid. Finally the tap on the tank that needed to be emptied could be turned. The deep purple liquid gushed out into a large plastic tub. The pump swung into juddery action and the frothing wine surged up a pipe to its new resting-place.

'Now this is the really vital bit,' he said, as he dashed over to stir some minutely measured sulphur dioxide into the foaming tub.

'Not very organic,' I ventured.

'But absolutely indispensable,' he explained. 'Even the

Greeks used it as a preservative. It fights bacteria. Prevents oxidation. Without it, you simply couldn't make wine. But the big question is . . .' He bit his lip as he watched the level rising in the receiving *cuve*. 'Have I left it all too late? Has the wine already been tainted by the lees? '

As soon as the transfer was complete, he opened the big circular door in the now empty tank. He put his head inside, lingered a moment and re-emerged, smiling shyly. The wine was not only sound but . . . dare he say it . . . really promising.

Virgile was happy.

The whole of the south-facing end of Les Sources's dining room – from terracotta floor to stone, Romanesque-arched ceiling – is magnificently glazed. An obvious enough idea, perhaps, if you have a view like Uncle Milo's but the masterstroke here was to project the bare stone walls and vaulting of the interior for a foot or so beyond the glass. It makes the window seem to disappear, as inside and outside worlds merge together. More cleverly still, it isolates the room from the extremes of the elements. It will no doubt offer vital shade in summer but, on winter days like these, it is only the rarest and strongest of southerly winds that ever makes the raindrops obscure the glass. It is, of course, impossible to curtain but even dark February nights feel detached and snug, as the warmth of candlelight is reflected back on itself.

On a bright February morning, however, there is no escaping the cruelly panoramic view of all the work that is waiting to be done on the land. Throughout my breakfast, for instance, I tried to ignore the remaining black olives that were obstinately, tauntingly clinging to the tree in front of the window. But in the end, I reluctantly accepted the fact that there is nothing like a glistening, ripe black olive to catch the morning sunlight. And nothing more certain to rob me of inner peace until the survivors were finally picked for the table. Whatever Manu said, if the black Lucque makes such a good oil, I couldn't believe it could be altogether bad for eating.

I took a confident bite to test my theory, gasped with amazement and went straight to the terrace fountain for some water to take away the appallingly acrid taste. Something seemed to be seriously wrong. Perhaps this was what happened when you left them too long on the tree? I needed some advice but I wasn't going to ask Manu and expose myself to another long-suffering 'What did I tell you?' So I nipped down for a quick word with the aged roadside double-act that regular passing pleasantries have revealed to be M. and Mme Vargas.

They were working as usual on the steeply-banked terraces beside the lane leading to the village. They live, so they tell me, just inside the medieval gateway, in one of the main street's tall narrow houses, and normally they bring all their tools out here in a wheelbarrow. Today, however, the *brouette* was full of horse manure, so the tools had travelled in Mme Vargas's two-wheeled shopping trolley.

'You didn't just eat the olives straight off the tree?' they asked in characteristically unified astonishment, as they took a break from fertilizing and hobbled down to shake my hand. 'What you have to do is, you put them in an old pillow-case for a couple of weeks, with plenty of rough salt . . .' Even these more extended utterances were somehow managed in more or less synchronized harmony. 'Give it a good shake every time you pass to drain the bitterness away. Then soak them in some oil – maybe some herbs . . .'

Any remaining stages in the Vargases' recipe (happily, a stiff-jointed gesture of finality suggested that there might in fact have been none) were drowned by the roar of a car being driven far too fast around the corner towards us. The Vargases' body language changed as fast as their infirmity allowed to that of mortal terror but the vehicle swerved to avoid us all with only a handful of the roadside vines destroyed.

'Krystina. With a K and a Y,' the driver introduced herself to the trembling Vargases. 'Oh, don't worry, I know the grower,' she continued breezily, as she turned the BMW on the now flattened corner of the vineyard. 'I'll settle up with him tomorrow. But you seem to have forgotten about our date in Narbonne,' she rounded on me, with an imperious opening of the passenger door.

'Key date for today: 118 BC. Foundation of Narbo,' another quick-fire disquisition began, as the Vargases disappeared in the dust cloud thrown up by our back tyres. 'Important port and capital of the Roman Province of Narbonensis – that's all of modern Languedoc to you, with a good bit of Provence thrown in. Anyway, the surrounding area saw such a rapid explosion of vines and olive trees, people used to think there'd been a climatic upheaval. Planting rights all reserved to the Romans, of course. Mostly veterans of the Legions . . .'

As the fusillade of facts continued, I caught fleeting glimpses of signposts to what Krystina informed me were other places founded by the Romans: Lodève, our nearest local market town, followed by Pézenas and Béziers. Then finally her convertible reached the coastal motorway.

'You don't think we should put the roof up?' I suggested tentatively, as an elegant Gucci sling-back settled into some serious speeding.

'What, and waste all this sunshine?' she laughed, too preoccupied with angling her cheekbones at the sun to notice the illuminated warning about violent winds. Or for that matter, the non-illuminated sign that told us we were following the Roman Via Domitia. But of course, she knew all about the latter.

'Also founded in 118 BC,' she shouted above the wind and the noise of the traffic. 'Vital trade and communication route, running all the way from the Rhône to the Pyrenees, linking Italy to Spain.'

'Taking wine to the Legions?' was all I could manage as I struggled for breath against the constant buffeting.

'Absolutely. But it wasn't just a matter of quenching the military thirst,' she answered, completely unperturbed by the elements, indeed exalting in the sweep of the wind through her improbably red hair. 'Wine was also an important trading commodity, used almost as much like a currency as precious metals. Not that the Romans weren't keen on drinking it. Even slaves were given about five litres a week for strength. Except when they were sick, when their rations were halved. The only Romans who didn't do well on wine were the women. Distinctly frowned on for them, it was . . .'

I was almost tearful with relief when Krystina took the motorway exit for Narbonne East. However, just as we seemed to be slowing down to enter the reassuring haven of a city centre car park, she made a violent last-minute turn to the right and accelerated out of town again.

'I've changed my mind,' she announced, cutting ruthlessly through the petrified pedestrians in the bicycles-only square in front of the town hall. 'Nothing of substance left in Narbonne. I should have taken you to Nîmes for the Maison Carré and the Arena.'

She relented only a fraction to allow me a glimpse of the few square metres of well worn Via Domitia cobbles, uncovered in the middle of the square, then tore out of town towards an open road between vineyards and olive groves.

'At least the Roman landscape survived,' she consoled me as she finally performed an emergency stop in a deserted car park, deep in the countryside.

Ahead of us, impervious to the gale, was a curious, ultramodern construction, built on concrete stilts, with huge, winglike roof structures arching over what looked like an abandoned building site on either side.

'*Amphoralis*,' announced Krystina, with a sweeping gesture

to encapsulate the totality but leaving me none the wiser. 'Amphoras were the most popular vessels for making, storing and transporting both oil and wine until wooden barrels appeared around the first century AD. So the more the Romans planted vines and olive trees, the more they needed local potteries. And this was one of the biggest,' she added.

I looked bemusedly at the uncompromisingly contemporary building that we were about to enter.

'THIS,' she barked and pointed impatiently at the confusion of seemingly half-finished walls and ditches, stretching on either side of us between the tips of those extraordinary roof wings. 'It's an archaeological dig, for heaven's sake,' she sighed despairingly, as she led me into the Amphoralis Museum.

'Amphoras had one great advantage over barrels,' she continued in better humour, once inside. 'They kept on breaking, leaving lots of archaeological evidence wherever you took them – proving, for instance, that the Romans transported Languedoc wines as far afield as Britain and Egypt . . .'

She was just advancing on a map that would illustrate her thesis when the whole museum was engulfed by the world from which her advantageous marriage and subsequent divorce were supposed to have delivered her. A coach had disgorged a swarm of teenage schoolchildren.

'Presumably Rome itself was self-sufficient?' I asked, as we were jostled straight past the map.

'Normally. Except in AD 79,' shouted Krystina above the clamour. 'The Pompeii vineyards were devastated by Vesuvius, so they embarked on a massive emergency planting campaign in the Languedoc, to make up for the shortages. But that then led to a glut, so Emperor Domitian decreed that half the vines had to be ripped out again. You'll see the same thing in later centuries,' she persisted, quite scandalized at the lack of discipline all around us.

'Do the amphoras tell us anything about the wines?' I prompted, in my best placatory manner.

'Not a lot,' she continued, shouting as a wave of adolescent laughter threatened to drown her out completely. 'We know they coated the insides with pitch to make them watertight, which can't have done much for the flavour. But maybe no worse than all their other additives and colourings.'

'Like the Greeks?' I prompted again, with a sense that, for Krystina, there was only one thing worse than unruly schoolchildren and that was unruly French-speaking schoolchildren.

'Like the Greeks,' she bellowed. 'With the same taste for strong, sweet wines, often drying the grapes for extra concentration.'

'Do we know the grape varieties?'

'Not unless you're familiar with the "soot grape".'

A violent turn on a Gucci heel made me wary of the anger that might soon be vented on an innocent accelerator pedal, but as soon as we are back in the relative peace of the car, she acknowledges more moderately that a wine made exclusively from another favourite Roman grape can be sampled on the route back home. So a little north of Pézenas, we double back sharply to our left, in search of Clairette du Languedoc.

The modestly proportioned courtyard of the eighteenth-century Château la Condamine Bertrand is full of windswept activity when we arrive. The owner, Bernard Jany, is manoeuvring a miniature forklift truck, loaded high with somebody's substantial purchase, while his son, Charles-André, cleans up after the day's activities in their crowded *cave*. It therefore falls to the charming young son-in-law, Bruno Andreu, the man in charge of public relations and sales, to deal with Krystina's brusque demand for a tasting.

He starts to tell us how it was his father-in-law's aunt, Marie-Rose Bertrand, who single-handedly secured the Clairette du Languedoc *appellation* in 1948, long before the rest of the

Coteaux in the 1980s, but then he notices the restless drumming of Krystina's heavily ringed fingers on the tasting counter. (She succeeded, under the duress of the car journey, in extracting a full confession about my sorties with Manu and her only reason for coming here was to score the necessary point against a rival. She is therefore impatient to leave as soon as the opposition can be considered bested.) So, sensing a short attention span, Bruno loses no time in pouring a delicious, crisp, fruity white, bearing no resemblance whatever to the oxidized, adulterated Clairette, beloved of Krystina's Romans. He then rapidly follows it with a sweeter, honeyed style, from the same variety.

'You can't make a living these days from Clairette alone,' he says. 'The *domaine*'s been in the family since 1792 but the present generation's made so many steps forward.'

He gestures towards the dozen or so different wines on a display-shelf behind him but we have already hit Krystina's boredom threshold. She extracts a wodge of banknotes, asks him to deliver whatever he thinks best to the château and battles her way back through the continuing tempest to the BMW.

Once on the road, it rapidly becomes clear that Krystina's reluctance to linger sprang partly from the notion that our respective days might each be rendered perfect by an intimate *soirée à deux* at the château. In so far as it is possible both to snuggle and drive down narrow avenues of plane trees at 150 kilometres per hour, Krystina snuggles. As her hand confuses my thigh with the gear stick rather more often than can easily be explained in an automatic car, I try desperately to come up with an alibi. The best I have concocted, as we approach the village, is an urgent domestic inspection for possible storm damage and Krystina is unimpressed.

'I'll say goodnight here then,' she says tartly, as we approach the village gateway, leaving me to cover the last couple of kilometres on foot.

When I finally reach Les Sources, all does at least seem reasonably well, despite the furious winds which have scarcely abated at any point in the day. Around bedtime, however, the merely dramatic turns positively apocalyptic. I have closed all the shutters but they continue rattling alarmingly, as if still unanchored. And the clatter from the rounded terracotta roof tiles sounds as if they are reducing themselves to shards. The bedroom which I selected for its view seems to be bearing the brunt of the storm so, in desperation, I tip my bed on to its side and drag it to another room at the more sheltered end of the house. But sleep is still impossible and I grope my way back across the landing to the telephone.

'*Est-ce normal, Manu?*' I blurt out anxiously, as soon as my neighbour's receiver is lifted. 'Will the house stand up to it?'

'I doubt it,' answers a sepulchral female voice at the other end. 'As a man sows, so shall he reap.'

For hours I drifted fitfully in and out of sleep, wondering paranoically which of my unspecified wrongdoings were judged to blame for the hurricane. Even in the calm and clarity of the morning light, I still felt oddly vulnerable, as if some dark art might indeed have been practised on the other side of the stream. An empty fridge, however, soon obliged me to immerse myself in the bustling normality of a Saturday morning market, where I could at last begin to rationalize those sinister-sounding words. Surely just an eccentric gloss on the effects of global warming, I told myself amidst the reassuring benignity of the foodstalls.

The weekly market in Lodève requires a twelve-kilometre drive from the village but there is no substantial town any nearer, and anyway, I like Lodève. It is a no-nonsense, few-frills town, once extremely prosperous from textile wealth but now just shabby enough at the edges to give it an enjoyably gritty authenticity. The market is blessed with a more than usually souk-like atmosphere, thanks largely to a substantial Algerian population. The majority of this community works in the principal surviving remnant of that former textile glory, the Gobelin tapestry factory. This is a name that I have always associated with France's historic châteaux but apparently the factory still supplies the nation's more modern public buildings.

To reach the foodstalls, I have to jostle my way round the swarming loop of the main street and it is here that I spot Babette buying metre after metre of bright, floral-patterned Provençal cotton.

'I thought I might make some tablecloths for the summer,' she explains, as I push on past mountains of inconceivably inexpensive clothing to find M. Vargas self-consciously trying on a new and better-fitting pair of corduroys behind a makeshift curtain, strung between the trouser stall and a lamp-post.

'We're neither of us getting any plumper,' calls Mme Vargas shakily, from my side of the improvised arras.

I wave to her husband and battle onwards, successfully resisting all the various bargain bed and radiator promotions that are competing loudly for my attention. My goal is the crowded square surrounding an old market hall at the end because it is there that the fresh food is sold.

Food can scarcely *be* fresher than the produce offered this morning and I find it hard not to buy vastly more than I need. The bright-eyed fish on the fishmongers' stalls must surely still have been swimming at dawn, while a poultry-seller's chickens are actually alive and noisily protesting their innocence from overcrowded cages. Where vegetables in England might advertise their country of origin, here I find baskets that cite specific villages, even farms, in their pedigrees. Only the oranges come from as far afield as Spain. My naïve request for basil is simply laughed at. If it isn't seasonal, it isn't here.

My purchases are putting a serious strain on Uncle Milo's

pair of semi-derelict straw shopping bags by the time that I notice the familiar, monumental figure of Mme Gros dominating the herb and spice stall on the opposite side of the street. Surprisingly for one whose cooking is so plain, she appears to be assembling a particularly complicated set of ingredients from a shopping list.

'For one of her spells,' whispers Manu, appearing at my elbow with a wink.

'I think you ought to try some proper pruning,' said Virgile when he telephoned last night.

I was surprised. After all he had told me about the strategic importance of the pruning work, I never thought he would dare to delegate it. Maybe he decided there was only so much horticultural (and therefore economic) damage that I could inflict in a couple of hours. But I still felt apprehensive when I first confronted this morning's Grenache Noir in the windy plain below Saint Saturnin.

'Look, I've bought myself this pair of electric secateurs,' he announced, as he offered me his latest, daunting-looking asset. 'Give it a try. You'll find it much easier.'

I gingerly donned the harness incorporating the battery pack and gently released the safety catch. The lightest touch on the start button sent the twin blades snapping together with a convulsive force that made the whole thing buck violently in my hand, which accidentally activated the start button again . . . and then again . . . until I finally got a grip.

'It takes a bit of practice but once you get the hang of it, it's very quick. I decided it was the only way I'd ever get the pruning finished. But you have to be a bit careful,' he warned me, as the cutters embarked on another of their involuntary spasms. 'Make sure the vines are all you cut!' And here he flourished a heavily bandaged hand, which added nothing to my confidence.

'Remember, we're aiming for high quality, low yield,' Virgile stressed. (So far so good. I'd remembered that much.) 'So we'll be pruning back to a maximum of five or six healthy, well-spaced shoots per vine.' (Seemed clear enough.) 'Where you've got several possible shoots more or less together, always choose the lowest.' (Getting more complicated but I'd manage.) 'Unless the bottom one is unhealthy. Or if it's growing in towards the stock. Or growing too much out at right angles to the row . . .'

By now I was paralysed by agonies of indecision. There were so many conflicting priorities. Any cut that might be justified according to one of Virgile's guiding principles seemed to be automatically proscribed by another. And even when I'd groped my way through this tortuous decision path, I still had to decide precisely *where* to cut.

'Always cut back to the third bud on your shoot,' he emphasized. 'No, that's the fourth. Look, here's the first.' He pointed to a microscopically insignificant protuberance at the base of my selected shoot. 'And always cut directly *across* the bud . . .'

After a few more apparently irreconcilable stipulations in the same vein, Virgile left me to psyche myself up for my first solo snip. He moved rapidly on up the row, while I stood transfixed by the fear that my lethal weapon might be about to decimate his precious vineyard. At least these vines were the ones that had been tended by him last year and were therefore not nearly as wildly out of control as last month's newly rented vines. But even so, they never seemed to stay still for long enough in the wind for me to decide where best to risk a cut. And the smoke from a neighbour's bonfire made it even more difficult to focus. Then just as I was stiffening my resolve for some fearlessly uninhibited, confidently radical action, Virgile threw me straight back into anxious confusion with a casual 'If in doubt, remember it's always safest to prune too little.'

*

'Can't understand all this fuss about pruning,' snorts Manu the next morning.

He knows nothing about Virgile or my labours down in Saint Saturnin but, as a thinly disguised pretext for the liquid hospitality that is threatened in a few minutes, he has invited me over to the terraces directly behind his cottage to admire his own vines. If that is indeed what they are. Manu's terraces may not be quite as spectacularly out of control as mine but the so-called vines look more like giant thornbushes. A few are even growing up the occasional tree.

According to Krystina, Languedoc vines have been pruned since the Romans but not, it seems, those of Manu.

'A lot of it's a waste of energy,' he announces. 'All a vine needs is minimal pruning.' (Leaving plenty of leisure for 'maximum drinking', I reflect.) 'You see these vines?' he continues, getting more dogmatic with every minute that he has to wait for his first glass of the day. 'They may look as if they've got thousands of buds right now, but if you just leave them alone, only a fraction of them are ever going to burst. And when they do, it's only those on the outside, where the fruit can get some sunlight, that will flourish. Those fancy fellows down the hill just don't seem to realize that if they didn't interfere all the time, the vine would simply find its own balance.'

But as we descend towards the bottles awaiting us in Manu's kitchen, I remain strangely unconvinced by this Darwinian 'survival of the fittest'. As I said before, I've tasted the wine.

The original two rooms that I knew when I visited Uncle Milo as an adolescent are now a sort of self-contained studio apartment that will be useful for guests, if I ever find time to invite anyone. The rest of Les Sources, according to Manu, evolved organically but rather haphazardly, as my uncle earned the occasional fee from a local resident for some domestic architectural design project.

'What do you think he built first?' asked Manu when he told me all this. 'After the studio, that is?'

'The kitchen?' I offered prosaically.

'No, the central staircase!' he laughed delightedly. 'And what did he do next? Installed the loo at the top of the stairs. Not the walls. Just the loo! The view was wonderful, he used to say. Shocked the wife though, the first time she saw him sat up there. Oh dear, yes. A very original man, your uncle.'

The house's gradual evolution is partly why it's so clever. For instance, Uncle Milo had time to get used to the angles of the sun and the wind directions before he decided where he wanted his shade and shelter. However, the problem with this kind of organic growth is that every new idea, every fresh injection of cash seems to have brought some additional level of complexity. The water system is bad enough. Every time I clear a new patch of land I uncover yet more plastic pipes taking the spring water to undiscovered parts of the property for unknown purposes. I hardly dare touch any of the half-buried taps that link them all together for fear of the flood that might burst unobserved in some far-flung corner of the land. But even inside the house, things are rarely straightforward.

'You know you've got four different ways of heating your water, don't you,' said Manu helpfully. 'Electricity, obviously. And the oil-fired boiler that powers the radiators. But I bet you didn't know you had a set of solar panels on top of that little conservatory – not much use today, admittedly . . . Then, the *pièce de résistance*, have you noticed the pipes under your log fire in the sitting room? Milo always boasted they'd heat all his water and a couple of radiators into the bargain. You just have to open the right valves,' he explained as I followed him into a dark, windowless room behind the kitchen.

The wall was completely covered with pipes, taps, valves, thermostats, dials and switches, all looking more complicated than the average submarine control room.

'I remember, you have to open one valve and close another, if you're using the open fire,' said Manu. 'And turn off the solar system, before you run the boiler. Various things like that. Your uncle did explain it all to me once. But I forget now which knob is which. Trial and error, I suppose.'

Fortunately, a few of the controls were blessed with faded paper luggage labels giving barely legible clues to their functions and gradually the system and I seem to have sorted out a mutually acceptable *modus vivendi*. I have been scalded almost as often as I have been chilled and the plumbing sometimes gurgles for days at a time, but I think I may finally understand enough to get by.

'You know you're supposed to have truffles on your land, don't you?' says Babette, as she dumps my first course of *terrine aux truffes* unceremoniously on to the plain paper tablecloth in front of me.

There is no sign yet of the colourful Provençal cotton from the market but, looking round, I see numerous fellow lunchers composing shopping lists and other doodles on the current alternative. Nathalie from the shop, for instance, seems to be sketching out some kind of business plan for a man in a suit who looks as if he could be her accountant. So I wonder whether Babette's intended upgrade will ever find favour.

The truffle news, however, could hardly be more welcome, as I scrutinize the microscopically small speck of black set into the middle of my slice of paté and compare it to the size of the supplement that this luxury commanded on the café's lunchtime menu. (Babette and I have graduated to hand-shaking terms by now but sadly the rising warmth of welcome still stops short of greater munificence on the truffle-shaving front.)

'Trouble is,' she explains, as she leans against the billiard table for a cigarette, 'when Manu's brother, Ignace, sold your uncle the land, he promised to tell him where to find the truffles before he died. But then he was up cutting branches off a cherry tree – Ignace, that is – and he made the mistake of cutting the one he was sitting on. Lost his memory in the fall, poor chap.'

'So Uncle Milo never knew?' I ask.

'I've always suspected Manu knows but you'll never get him to admit it.' She returns to the bar, leaving me to speculate about the untold riches that may lie buried beneath my oak trees.

As it happens, I'm already considerably the poorer for knowing the street value of a truffle. I was having some tea at Virgile's after our pruning session when a small, shifty-looking young man called Luc turned up to confirm that he was on the track of a truffle. Apparently Virgile had ordered one for the weekend – proving, not for the first time, the high priority given to gastronomy in his domestic economy – and I heard myself recklessly surrendering to temptation when Luc offered to add me to his client base.

'You know where to find truffles?' I asked rather obviously.

'I know where to find a man who knows where to find them,' Luc answered, with the crafty wink of a middleman who had no intention of being cut out.

'Finding a truffle would be much too much like hard work for Luc,' laughed Virgile.

'We're nearing the end of the season,' the young entrepreneur continued, ignoring Virgile's jibe. 'I can probably get you one for the end of the month but it'll be around two hundred francs, for a reasonable size,' he added, making a tight little circle with his forefinger and thumb to forewarn me of his disappointing notion of reasonableness.

'So, you think I should invest in a truffle pig?' I ask Babette, when she comes to monitor my appreciation of the precious particle adorning my starter. It was meant to be a joke but she draws up a chair to advise me in earnest.

'Pigs are all very well but a dog would be more companionable,' she counsels solemnly. 'Although actually, you could manage perfectly well with a fly. You'll always see them round the foot of a truffle oak. Just as good at sniffing them out and no overheads.'

'If somewhat less easily led on a lead,' I can't help thinking. But the arrival of the village postman with his family of five to occupy the last available table denies me any more practical explanation of the low-cost option. Anyway, where would I *start* in my twelve overgrown acres? I can hardly trail from oak to oak with my tracker insect in a matchbox, waiting for a crescendo of buzzing to home me in on my gourmet target. Unless Manu could be persuaded to spill the beans . . . Perhaps when even less than usually sober? . . . But no, there are some prices that should never be paid, even for truffled self-sufficiency.

'How did those trees get there?' I ask Manu, as the little red van rattles down towards Narbonne. I am certain they were not there yesterday but this afternoon all the dark winter hillsides are suddenly bright with yellow blossom.

'Mimosas,' says Manu, with exaggerated patience. 'In flower.'

'But all since yesterday,' I answer lamely, wondering how a species can achieve such spectacular unanimity of timing.

The ubiquitous splashes of yellow are all the more exhilarating in the clear winter sunlight but most exhilarating of all, when we finally reach the sea, are the colours in the sky. I have only ever seen such blues in the work of the painters who used to flock to this coast for the intensity of its light. The deepest are high above us, the palest nearer the horizon, with every brilliantly reflected variation pulled in different directions across the water by the breezes and currents. It feels as if all my life until this moment has been lived behind sunglasses.

'Sorry, no time to stop,' says Manu, his wife's insistence on the repair of a wind-damaged shutter having already delayed our departure until after lunch.

He has an unusually specific mission to accomplish this afternoon, an important point to prove in the light of researches that he has been conducting in the tiny village library. He is not a regular reader and his first appearance there at this late stage in his life probably caused some surprise. It has, however, enabled him to identify a *vigneron* of incontrovertible distinction who nonetheless makes wine from his much-maligned Aramon.

'You'll see,' he swaggers. 'You should read more yourself. Then you'd know these things.'

He swings off on to a sinuous, snake-like lane leading up the side of a small mountain – the Massif de La Clape, he tells me – separating Narbonne from the sea.

'This used to be an island,' he is able to boast from his researches. 'Until the river and harbour silted up in what, if you studied history, you'd know as the Middle Ages. Look,' he says, pointing back down the hill to the city's distant, half-finished cathedral. 'You can see how the money dried up when the sea trade evaporated.'

Despite the little red van's modest gear ratios, we soon catch up with a battered old lorry, grinding even more slowly up the road ahead of us, laden with dozens of large, wooden, box-like contraptions. They are beehives, Manu tells me, about to be set up for the spring, and it is easy to imagine the pine- and thyme- and rosemary-scented honeys that this landscape will perfume in the summer. Gradually, however, it is vineyards that start appearing amongst the spectacular white limestone rocks.

'Great favourites with your Romans, the wines of La Clape,' continues the fount of village-library knowledge. 'Sent all the way to Rome, they were, leaving the plonk they made over there on the plain for the locals. There's even the remains of a

Roman villa up here, where we're going. Château Pech Redon, it's called, meaning "Round Hill" in Occitan.'

As we reach the highest point of the former island, a round-ish rocky outcrop does indeed loom into view behind a huddle of unpretentious buildings, from which a handsome young man in sweatshirt and jeans emerges to greet us.

I have no idea what story Manu can have spun when making this appointment but Christophe Bousquet is very welcoming. He explains how his father and he moved here in 1988, having first sold all the vines that they used to harvest for a co-operative – the one back in Virgile's village, as it happens. Pech Redon's reputation was already rising. Its forty-two hectares had been extensively replanted by one of the region's pioneers in the 1970s and '80s. But what really attracted Christophe, he says, was the isolation: no neighbours to cope with, like Virgile's in Saint Saturnin, for ever treating their vines in ways that conflicted with his own methods.

'But it's not an area without its difficulties,' he explains, as we pass from the brightness of the sun to the shade of the little forge, which is now his tasting room. 'It's one of the driest parts of France. Less than fifty centimetres of rain a year and virtu-ally all of it in November and March. We get temperatures of fifty-two degrees out there in July. Our well's often dry by September and we have to do a bit of "Jean de Florette", just to have water for the house. Not that it's always warm like today. Well, you know the Mediterranean weather – up and down, like the mood of the people. But anyway . . .' He takes a bottle of white wine from the fridge. 'This is a mixture of Grenache Blanc . . .'

'Grenache *Blanc*?' I check, remembering Virgile's black variety.

'Exactly . . . and Bourboulenc.'

'Bourbou . . .?' I query. (This surely beats all previous obscurities.)

'. . . lenc,' he confirms. 'Grown here since Roman times. The ultimate Mediterranean grape, I always think, thriving only if it's right by the sea. Often called Malvoisie, in other regions. You know, I only really feel at home in the Mediterranean, so even my holidays are always in places like Corsica and Malta – which gives me plenty of opportunities to see what others get up to with their Malvoisie!'

Fanciful as it sounds, the scent of the wine is unmistakably reminiscent of the Mediterranean herbs that lure those bee-keepers to the surrounding scrubland. Indeed, the same impression is confirmed in the mouth, I decide, as the fridge yields a couple of *rosés* – in contrasting styles, so Christophe explains, for summer and winter drinking. But Manu is quite uncharacteristically distracted, continually craning over the tasting counter to check the labels on the cluster of reds await-ing their turn and, even as each is poured for us, curiously impatient to move on.

'Ah, saved the best till last, you see,' Manu nudges me smugly, when Christophe pours the final wine.

'The Alicante?' asks our host in surprise.

'The Aramon, surely,' says Manu, casting an eye around for a possible extra bottle.

'Oh, now I know which book you found me in,' laughs Christophe. 'The authors made a mistake. I don't grow Aramon. I mean, I may be eccentric but there are limits.'

Manu listens crestfallen, as we hear how the Alicante is a crossbreed created in Montpellier. In the 1820s, it seems, a certain Louis Bouschet de Bernard crossed the notoriously high-yielding but colourless Aramon with the intensely deep-coloured Cher to create what he called the Petit Bouschet. Sixty years later, his son crossed the Petit Bouschet with the Grenache Noir and called it Alicante.

'So it's the only truly Languedoc *cépage*,' says Christophe, holding one of the darkest, inkiest reds I have ever seen up to the light. 'Yet it's one of the few that's actually outlawed – even for a *vin de pays!*' (The label, I see, reads simply *vin de table*.) 'I'd like to see a small percentage permitted for La Clape,' he continues animatedly, 'giving a bit of extra complexity. But even with my father being President of the Coteaux du Languedoc, I can't see much hope. So I make it on its own, using very low yields. It's my little amusement . . . My chance to show that there are no bad grape varieties – only bad wine-makers.'

I do not think I have ever seen Manu look so downcast. I have certainly never seen him show so little interest in a glass of wine. Suddenly, all he can think about is how long it will take us to drive home, as if every moment spent away from Mme Gros were torture.

It is already dark by the time we round the last of the bends to see the welcoming sight of our respective post boxes, perched on their poles at the bottom of the shared drive. It is not, however, too dark to notice an unfamiliar dark-coloured Deux Chevaux parked in the shadows beside them, or the glow of a cigarette from the driver's seat. It is a couple of days since I checked inside my box and I really ought to do so now but Manu is strangely unwilling to stop the van. He hurries twice as fast as usual, up over the pits and bumps of the rough ascent, as far as Uncle Milo's parking area. He would normally drop me at the point where my part of the drive forks away from his, but tonight he seems to want to usher me all the way to my door and see it safely closed behind me. However, he underestimates my stubborn desire to audit my mail. Having counted to a number high enough to allow the van to speed back down to the fork and up to Manu's ramshackle garage, I steal outside again.

The moon is fuller and brighter than I realized when we were returning in the van. From the corner of high land overlooking the stream that divides our properties, I am rewarded with the intriguing sight of Manu tiptoeing delicately down his garden path, with many a nervous glance in the direction of my house. Instinctively I conceal myself in the shadow of the big Mediterranean pine near the *maset*, as my neighbour scuttles furtively out of his gate and down the main drive towards the post boxes and the mystery car. Every so often he stops and listens and casts a secretive look over his shoulder but he fails to see me following him.

March

'IN OTHER WORDS, you've been had,' laughed Babette on the evening following Manu's mysterious meeting.

She had seen that I was in a bad mood as soon as I arrived. After all, I didn't usually complain about the awkwardness of the billiard table filling the centre of the room or the fact that the *plat du jour* was always *coq aux olives* whenever I called in for a meal. But with the café nearly empty tonight, she had time enough to spare to puff her way through half a packet of Gitanes at my table and uncover the underlying cause of my grumpiness.

'But now I want the whole story,' she insisted, so I started reluctantly with the unexplained car.

I told her how it had still been down there in the shadows beside the post boxes and how its driver had emerged as soon as Manu came close enough to be identified. I was too far away, I explained, to hear much of their exchange, except when the driver unwrapped the tiny parcel that Manu extracted from the pocket of his overalls.

'*Et alors?*' pressed Babette, serving me one of her less ambitious desserts in the shape of a banana. '*Qu'est-ce qu'il a dit?*'

' "A beauty!" was his exact response,' I told her bitterly and she laughed some more. Then I related how the driver had started counting notes into Manu's outstretched hand.

'*Et combien?*' she urged.

'I couldn't see. But it wasn't as much as Manu seemed to expect, so the driver reluctantly added another and that seemed to satisfy him. Then they said a quick goodnight and I just had time to beat a retreat before Manu started panting up the gradient behind me. He made a last check that no one was watching and vanished inside his own front door. Then almost immediately there were car lights bumping up the drive. A dark grey Deux Chevaux was paying me a visit and it was driven by Virgile's friend – Luc, the truffle-man.'

'*Oh, j'adore!*' giggled Babette.

'He said he'd "just made it". The end of the month, that is. Like he'd promised. And no extra charge for delivery to the door.'

I winced at the memory, as I told Babette how Luc had produced a little loosely screwed-up ball of newspaper and immediately started justifying his pricing policy. The small black lump nestling inside was much bigger, he emphasized, and therefore (he knew I'd understand) much more expensive than his estimate – at this end of the season, an absolute bargain for 400 francs.

'Exactly twice the sum I'd budgeted,' I lamented.

'But twice as good for being home-grown,' chuckled Babette.

'I'll say one good thing for the Church,' said Manu, as the single village bell swung into a faltering summons to the faithful. 'They did at least keep the vineyards going after the Romans gave up on us.'

A fairer man in his situation might have conceded a second

good thing because, unfortunately for me and my liver, the call to Sunday morning Mass had given Manu an effective dispensation to pour us each an unprecedentedly large tumblerful of the dreaded house red. It's only on rare occasions that the diocese rustles up a priest for a parish as small as ours but, whenever it does, Mme Gros can be relied upon to add her formidable contralto to the shaky descants of the sparse and predominantly aged congregation. Moreover she makes a point of walking all the way there and back, whatever the weather, like some medieval penitent, which gives her less religiously-minded husband nearly two hours of unsupervised drinking time.

The morning was supposed to be dedicated to the mending of Manu's roof, which suffered even worse than mine in last month's winds. I could scarcely afford the time with so much work needed on my own house, but the quantity of terracotta that he talked me into buying for my own repairs turned out to be substantially more than I needed.

'*Je suis désolé!*' he apologized, in his most convincingly desolated manner. 'I must have miscounted. But if it helps at all, I think the extra tiles might just be enough to plug some gaps over at my place. That is, unless you had other plans for them.'

We had, however, hardly replaced the first of Manu's breakages when the tolling of the church bell occasioned the most abrupt reordering of priorities. No sooner had Mme Gros's Sunday headscarf disappeared around the bend towards the village than Manu was down the ladder with the speed of an athlete half his weight and a quarter of his age.

As he pours me a second glass, my survival instincts tell me my only hope is to keep him focused on ecclesiastical history. The only trouble is, I suspect I know even less about the subject than he does.

'You mean, the Church took the lead in wine-making when the Roman Empire declined?' I offer feebly, to keep the conversation on track.

'Had to, didn't they?' says Manu, emptying the last of the bottle. 'Needed it for the Mass . . . Blood of Christ and all that. But not as much as you might think, because for centuries the priests used to drink the wine on behalf of everyone else . . .'

For a few moments, it seems that Manu might have been successfully sidetracked but the pulling of a second cork soon disabuses me.

'It was the monks who really saved the day,' he resumes with glass recharged. 'Part of their daily rations, you see. Only a bottle a head, it's true. But they gave you more if you were sick . . .'

A charming vision of a tonsured Manu, permanently laid up in the monastic sickbay, is interrupted by the baleful crunch of Mme Gros's sensible lace-ups coming back up the gravel drive. I have just enough time to make both my excuses and my escape but, as I tiptoe away by the back door, the late morning air is already ringing with the wrath of the returning righteous.

'Manu's quite right,' concedes Krystina, from behind her enormous sunglasses. 'Every monastery had its vineyard. And I don't mean just a few little vines in the back yard. We're talking whole wine districts here. Like most of the Coteaux du Languedoc belonging to this place,' she explains with a toss of her copious curls (surely even redder than the last time I saw her) towards the pair of abbatial doors behind us.

As the day had dawned unexpectedly sunnily, I was summoned to lunch in Saint Guilhem-le-Désert, a brazenly picturesque little village, huddled round a diminutive Romanesque monastery in a narrow, rocky river gorge. 'Too popular to visit after Easter,' Krystina announced when she telephoned. 'But we'll be all right today. The only thing is, do you mind if we meet there? I have to stop at my manicurist's.'

For once I arrived with my nerves intact. Krystina was already sunning herself in front of the eleventh-century abbey church, her fingernails newly filed to unnerving glossy red points.

The medieval-looking square was filled with brightly colour-coded tables, in four separate groups belonging to four different cafés, but like everyone else, we ordered in 'yellow' because that was the only way we could sit in the sun. However, by the time the food arrived, the shadows had moved, so Krystina insisted on eating her first course in 'blue' and her main course in 'red'. Initial reluctance to accommodate our peripatetic meal soon warmed into a series of enthusiastic welcomes as portions of Krystina's divorce settlement were discreetly disgorged from her handbag.

'Benedictine,' she says, resuming her monastic theme, as we shuffle across the flagstones to 'green' for coffee. 'Founded in 804 by Guilhem – that's Occitan for William – Count of Toulouse, friend of Emperor Charlemagne and star of umpteen troubadour epics. Spent most of his life driving Arabs back into Spain.'

'The Arabs had invaded the Languedoc?'

'Absolutely. Captured Agde, Narbonne and most of the major coastal towns. Totally opposed to alcohol, of course. Biggest threat to wine-making the region ever knew. No wonder everyone considered William such a hero. Such a saint indeed, when he took to the cloister . . . Anyway, dozens of abbeys were springing up all over the place, thanks largely to a childhood friend of William, the great Benedictine reformer, Saint Benedict of Aniane – so-called to cause maximum confusion with Saint Benedict of Nursia, the founder of the Order, a couple of centuries earlier. *Our* Benedict didn't really approve of wine but he more or less bowed to the inevitable because, quite apart from any alcoholic expectations on the part of the monks, their abbeys were important resting places for travellers, especially those on the Compostela pilgrimage route to Spain. Talking of which, it's time we walked off our lunch on a bit of the pilgrim path.'

She thrusts more cash than lunch can possibly have cost under her saucer to avoid the tedium of waiting for a bill and strides purposefully off up a narrow lane.

It is definitely time to be leaving the village square. All the colours-of-the-rainbow tables are now in the shade and the sunlit rocks above us look much more inviting – or they did, until I saw what a punishing pace Krystina's designer sandals were going to set. I think she must have doubled as a gym teacher. She is certainly a lot fitter than I am, and the steep, almost blinding white path up the hillside does nothing to stem the information flow.

'Pure self-flagellation,' she calls, as I scurry to catch her up, 'pilgrims choosing this route to Spain, when they could have taken the Via Domitia by the coast. But a gift of a chunk of the True Cross from Charlemagne had turned this into a three-star stopover.'

We are climbing high above the irregular red roofs of the village, past a ruined keep where everyone would have sheltered, if the abbey was under attack, to a rough, arid landscape, dotted with fragrant tufts of thyme, straggly flowering rosemary bushes, stark wind-warped pines and stunted, scrubby evergreen holm oaks.

'They call this the *garrigue*,' continues Krystina, with never a hint of breathlessness, '*garric* meaning holm oak in Occitan, apparently. It gives you an idea of what the monks were up against when they wanted to plant a vineyard.'

'I know just how they felt,' I wheeze, remembering my own terrace-clearing, scheduled for the late afternoon. However, Krystina insists that we can squeeze in a second monastic case study, if we are even less than usually scrupulous about the prevailing speed limits.

'Cistercian, this one,' she announces in the Abbaye de Valmagne car park, before I have a moment to marvel at any of our luckier escapes *en route*. 'Founded in 1155 – a time when wine was becoming an important source of wealth and power. It was also a time when monasteries were doing remarkably well from the Crusades. Knights departing for the Holy Land made endless gifts of vineyards to ensure that prayers were said for their souls. The Cistercians probably did best of all. They were more rigorous than the Benedictines generally and they were more serious about wine-making – part of their commitment to perfection in all things. You name it, they researched it: pruning, training, grafting, soil types . . .'

Her list tails off. She has noticed that it is almost six o'clock. By the time we have sprinted to the ticket desk, the entry deadline has passed, but happily there is a significant shortfall in the abbey's restoration budget and Krystina has remembered her chequebook, so we are favoured after all with an unhurried private view.

'Much better than trudging round with a French-speaking guide,' she says, as she snaps her handbag closed. 'But I wanted you to see the Languedoc's only monastic building which still functions as a wine estate.'

'But not as a monastery?' I ask, as we enter the abbey church.

She gives me one of her more withering looks.

'There was this little thing they called the Revolution.' She points to some enormous oak barrels squeezed between the arches of the nave. 'Most of the abbeys were simply treated as stone quarries but the relative cool and darkness here made it excellent for wine storage.'

'Are the barrels still in use?' I ask and receive a second withering look.

The modern wines, it seems, are made in rather more modern conditions and Krystina's benefaction proves also to have been sufficient to secure us a leisurely private tasting in one of the adjoining château-like wings of the abbey. We start with a curiosity made from Morrastel – allegedly a medieval grape variety, much beloved of the monks – and we work our way quietly through a dozen or so wines to the finest of their reds, named after the Counts of Turenne, the owners of the property since 1838.

Even allowing for the 'anything Manu can do, she can do better' factor, I am amazed at Krystina's unaccustomed patience this evening. I can only imagine it is the challenge of establishing her own stately-home-owning credentials within limited French vocabulary which lengthens her normally short fuse. Unfortunately, however, this gives the clouds that were gathering and blackening as we arrived ample time to fulfil their promise.

We emerge to find my rain-soaked Renault refuses to start. This is not at all how Krystina had planned the climax of our day – another attempt at a cosy, candlelit supper at the château was more what she had in mind. She is accordingly all for abandoning my modest motor, as if there were simply 'plenty more where the likes of that came from'. Indeed, I think she would willingly have bought me another, rather than waste a wet evening drying spark plugs. But impecunious pride prevails.

It was barely light but I could see that the rain had stopped. And yet there was an alarming roar coming from the direction of the stream. I had heard it from my bedroom as soon as I woke up. I dressed quickly and hurried down through the long grass of the still dripping orchard to find a noisy, racing torrent in the place of the normally gentle brook.

'Your first Mediterranean storm!' shouted Manu cheerfully from the opposite bank where he had been enjoying a furtive cigarette, while Mme Gros prepared some of her famous breakfast coffee. (I could hardly believe it, the first time I saw her throwing random quantities of 'instant' into water drawn straight from the hot tap.)

'I must have slept through something pretty spectacular!' I called back above the din.

'*Incroyable!*' he yelled, as we watched some dead branches tumbling rapidly over a little waterfall. 'Another few centimetres and it would have taken the bridge! Wonderful exercise for the fish though!'

'Fish?' I hollered hoarsely.

'Trout,' shouted Manu. '*Délicieuses!* Especially upstream a bit, in that pool in your wood. You ought to try them. When things are calmer.'

My drive to meet Virgile for another round of pruning told much the same story after the storm. The rivers had turned a dark muddy brown and the track leading down to the village road was half washed away.

'*Quelle nuit!*' called M. Vargas, from the foot of his dramatically eroded terraces. He looked as if he had aged four or five years in the last few hours but I was surprised to see him alone. 'Of course, it would be the morning that Agnès goes down with flu,' he lamented, more despondent than I had known him. '*C'est une catastrophe!*'

I felt that I should have offered to help but I was already late and I knew that Virgile liked punctuality.

As I drew into Saint Saturnin, I found him opposite his *cave*, killing time with the owners of Le Pressoir. Neither of them had been in evidence when I had eaten there in January, so Virgile introduced me.

'Marie-Anne . . .'

'*Enchanté.*'

'Pius . . .'

'*Enchanté.*'

'My English "apprentice" . . .'

'*Ah, c'est vous, donc.* It's you who's brought us this English weather!'

Marie-Anne pointed accusingly at the blackboard from which the long night of rain had washed every trace of yesterday's '*suggestions du jour*'. She looked tired before the working day had even begun – a condition no doubt explained by the two toddler daughters who came running out of the restaurant to tug at the calf-length hem of her chic linen skirt.

'*Enchanté, quand-même,*' said Pius warmly.

He looked equally stylish in well-cut trousers and narrow-striped shirt but noticeably less ruffled by the vicissitudes inherent in attempting to run both a restaurant and a family on the same morning. He insisted that we had to go inside to see the new exhibition of abstract paintings that he had just been hanging.

'This isn't really a restaurant,' laughed Virgile. 'More of a picture gallery with food.'

'Nonsense, it's a jazz club with food *and* pictures.'

Pius is clearly passionate about all three and it is some time before he has finished detailing the coming season's concerts.

'I hope you brought your boots,' says Virgile, when we finally set off. 'It'll be wet.'

The Carignan that we are going to work on is another of his newly rented *parcelles* but the fact that he has already carried out the kind of pre-pruning that was left to me in January should have made our task easy. Our boots, however, are soon so caked with mud that we are lumbering down our respective rows like a pair of lead-weighted astronauts, ponderously tending some boggy lunar vineyard.

Yet somehow Virgile remains immaculate. For a moment, I thought a small smudge of mud had besmirched his forehead but then I realized it was only the distinctive little birthmark above his left eyebrow. His denim creases are, of course, impeccable and his dark, neatly trimmed hair as unruffled as if it had just left the barber's shop. He could pass for a city professional on a 'dress down' day, were it not for one small detail. As he stoops to show me the first sign of life in the vineyard – the rising sap 'weeping' gently from one of my cuts – I catch sight of a single, narrow, tightly knotted plait of hair, starting just at the nape of his neck and disappearing subversively down the back of his collar. A discreet but significant glimpse of a less conformist spirit.

'Will you still be bottling your early wine this month?' I ask, as I ponder how best to make sense of a particularly lop-sided old vine.

'I can't. You see, I still can't decide between paper labels and something printed directly on to the glass,' he calls from a distance, making much faster progress down his own row than I am managing on mine. '*Sérigraphie*, the process is called.'

'Are labels more expensive?' I ask, having only ever seen the alternative on a mass-market supermarket wine.

'No, it's the serigraphic method that costs most. But labels mean an extra process, sticking them on. An extra machine to organize. It all depends whether I can achieve something smart enough. But bottling and labelling are the least of my problems right now. I'm much more concerned about the bank.'

'Why, what's happened?'

'They've rejected my business plan. Refused to finance it. Everyone else that I've shown it to thought it was fine. But this is politics.'

'I don't follow . . .'

'I'm the only private grower in Saint Saturnin. At least, I'm the only *particulier* who sells his wine in bottles. There's the Poujols family, round the corner – two geriatric brothers who have always made their own wine – but they sell it all in bulk to a *négociant*, a middleman. So they don't really count. Everyone else in the village takes his grapes to the co-operative. So there are those who'd rather I didn't succeed.'

'You're joking . . .' I bought some wines there only last week and although the premises on the edge of the village were utterly factory-like and charm-free, I have certainly been enjoying the best of their bottles.

'No, believe me. It's the same with some extra Grenache I

71

was hoping to rent. The owner's been leant on. He's says he'll either let the land to some youngsters in the village who work with the co-operative or he'll take an EC subsidy to rip out the vines – even though they're perfectly healthy. In other words, anything except rent it to me.'

'But that's outrageous! I'm amazed you seem so relaxed about it.'

'Well, what's the worst they can they do to me?'

All sorts of possibilities for agricultural sabotage spring to mind but I keep them to myself.

'Don't look so anxious,' he laughs. 'I can manage without the Grenache. And I'll find another bank – I've got a meeting this afternoon and another next week. I'll be all right. But I ought to be on my way. As soon as I've smartened myself up a bit.'

I wish him luck and head back home, wondering what I can find in the fridge for a late lunch. But no sooner have I opened the door to consider my limited options than Manu is there on my doorstep with a glistening fresh trout in a plastic bag.

'A little treat for you – from your wood,' he explains. 'I think you'll be impressed. The two we had for lunch were excellent. *Formidable!* Even the wife's cooking couldn't spoil them . . . No really, there's no need to thank me,' he adds. 'What else are neighbours for?'

Before I have time to ponder this nicety of etiquette, a furious female voice thunders from the other side of the stream.

'MANU! Come back here! I want to know how I'm supposed to put my shopping in the deep freeze when you've filled it up with fish!'

'You didn't tell me you were off to Saint Chinian,' said Krystina, as soon as I answered the telephone. 'Escorted by your neighbour, I gather.'

'Well, you see, it's more of a wine day,' I faltered, as I realized that I must have mentioned the excursion to Babette who must have felt it her duty to give the event some wider publicity.

'I'm not your keeper, of course,' she bristled. 'But I can't send you off in a state of historical ignorance. I'll pop up at once.'

'I was just locking up,' I explained, as Manu's horn reminded me that we were already late.

'Then we'd better do the crammer's course right now,' she decided, as I performed an elaborate mime in the doorway entitled 'person reluctantly taking telephone call', in the hope that Manu would go easy on the horn. 'You remember our friends Saint Guilhem and Saint Benedict of Aniane?' (Loud horn blast.) 'Well, the Languedoc in those days was a very small world. They had this other friend called – confusingly enough – Saint Anian.' (Louder, more insistent horn blast.) 'And it was Anian who left Aniane and founded Saint Chinian in 782. Hence the name.'

'You're losing me.'

'Saint was pronounced "Santch" in those days,' she explained, in the special, exaggerated tones perfected long ago for her slow learners. 'Santch Anian . . . Saint Chinian.' (Even louder, syncopated rhythmic horn blast.)

'Krystina, I've really got to go . . .'

I had no time to feel guilty. I was too busy feeling car-sick, as Manu did everything within the little red van's power to make up for lost time. The village of Saint Chinian lies only about fifty kilometres to the south-west but it is separated by winding river valleys and tortuous mountain passes that double that distance. And for much of the cliff-edge mountainous stretch, the hairpin bends were made hairier still by a programme of roadworks which had recklessly removed every last metre of safety wall before starting to renew even the most vital parts of it. Not that such trifles inhibited Manu from using both hands to point out distant beauty spots at the bottom of precipitous drops; or from accelerating down the middle of the only straight descent to make sure that none of the high-performance vehicles trapped behind us could overtake. Indeed, as we arrived in Saint Chinian, I was half wondering whether Krystina's driving might have been more soothing.

Manu has already briefed me on Saint Chinian's key facts as he sees them: 'Twenty villages . . . Separate *appellation* since '82 . . . Mostly red, bit of *rosé* . . . What more did I want to know?' He is therefore straining at the leash to sniff out a grower or two before lunch, but I somehow feel that I owe it to Krystina to track down the abbey first. There is nothing obvious on the skyline, so we ask at the elegant seventeenth-century Mairie, where every member of staff pulls the blankest of faces until one of their number remembers Mme Guibert.

'You're standing in it,' says this small, serious-looking lady, having sped to our rescue on her bicycle. 'What's left of it anyway. It used to be the abbot's lodgings, before the Revolution. Just as our Salle des Fêtes was part of the church's gothic nave. There was also a second, smaller abbey on the other side of the river but they flattened all that was left of that to build the rugby stadium in about 1900. No, there's really more monastic legacy in our wines than in our buildings nowadays.'

Manu's thirst-riven features could hardly spell 'I told you so' more clearly. Returning to the village square, he would happily knock at the door of any *vigneron* possessed of a bottle and a corkscrew, but Virgile has advised me to look out for the Moulinier family.

'We'll have to ask,' says Manu, hurrying into an impressively comprehensive-looking wine emporium, where he accosts the energetic young man restocking the shelves. 'Moulinier,' he barks. 'Can't find the blighters anywhere. Just like all the rest – too damn full of themselves to put up a sign! Been looking for hours!'

'Then look no further, *monsieur*.' The young man politely

offers a business card. 'Pascal Moulinier. Welcome to our shop.'

Manu's discomfiture is only momentary: if a tasting is to be organized before lunchtime, there is no time for apologies. But to his dismay, the youngest of the Moulinier line proposes a preliminary visit to his vineyards.

'Everyone thought my father was crazy,' he chuckles, as we head for the countryside. 'Giving up a solid job with the Customs to try his luck at wine-making. No experience. No money. No vines. Just some long-abandoned hectares of *garrigue*, picked up cheaply because no one else would touch them. In the early eighties, this was. Then a couple of years, just clearing and planting.'

'Like the medieval monasteries,' I suggest, with the fellow feeling of a man who really ought to be strimming his own wilderness.

'Exactly. And just like them, we spent a good few years experimenting to find out what worked where. Did you know the monks would often wait a whole generation to see if land was good enough for wine, before committing themselves to building? Well, here's our own belated gesture of commitment.' We are now in the middle of a very muddy building site. 'By this year's harvest, we'll finally have somewhere big enough to house both the family *and* the wines – and right at the heart of our vineyards.'

His excited confidence is surely belied by the surrounding half-built chaos. Manu taps an impatient foot in the builders' rubble; he has correctly deduced that there can be little prospect of a tasting here amongst the scaffolding and concrete mixers. But Pascal has mysteries to unfold for us first.

'How's your geology?' he asks unexpectedly.

'Non-existent,' I admit.

'It's very important in Saint Chinian,' he enthuses. 'Well, we think so, anyway. We've got perfect examples of the area's three soils on these slopes here.' A sweeping gesture encompasses the carefully tended patches of vines alternating with substantial tracts of untamed *garrigue* all around us.

'Oh, please don't make him tell us about them!' reads the thought bubble above Manu's head but his prayer is unanswered.

'Those steep, grey, gravelly slopes behind us are called *schiste*. Slate, I think you say in English. Marvellous, heat-retaining soil, giving vivid, high-definition wines. Over here, a mixture of clay and limestone. More pebbly, producing fuller, softer wines. Wonderful soil again, except when you're breaking it up for planting. Then finally down here, we've got sandstone. Quite rare in St Chinian but fantastic for Grenache . . .'

Manu cannot believe that so many vital 'tasting minutes' are being sacrificed to this pointless classification of the earth's crust. 'Is your old *cave* anywhere near?' is the closest he gets to subtlety.

'Just a bit far before lunch,' comes Pascal's hammerblow, as Manu's face crumples so fast, I fear I may be about to see a grown Frenchman cry. 'That's really why we started our shop. But I tell you what, join me for lunch in the village and we'll see how our "Terrasses Grillées" '96 is getting on.'

Manu's face brightens as rapidly as it fell. He even turns politely conversational in the back seat of Pascal's car, asking who does what in the family business.

'I concentrate on the *cave* and shop and my father and brother look after the vines,' Pascal explains. 'They're the important guys. It's the work in the vineyard that makes the difference. Much more than anything I might do in the cellar.' He stops outside the shop and dashes in for the wine. 'I thought maybe two bottles,' he says as he returns, having clearly got my companion's measure.

Pascal's exaggerated pantomime of wiping the mud from his shoes at the door succeeds in extracting laughter from the theatrically pursed lips of what must surely be the region's most formidable-looking restaurant proprietress – her broad, powerful shoulders undoubtedly the envy of the village rugby team.

'My father had no training at all,' Pascal continues, as soon as the prop-forward has taken our order and offered to decant the wine. 'But travelling round the country for the Customs gave him an open mind, especially for grape varieties. I mean, everyone thought he was completely mad – planting Grenache, Mourvèdre and Syrah and refusing to touch Carignan. I suppose two years of study in Burgundy had much the same effect on me. Took the famous regions off their pedestals.'

The first course arrives, and with it the decanter, but Pascal makes no move to pour. Manu is so transfixed by the sight of it that he can hardly focus on his salad but it is clearly unthinkable to sample the top Moulinier *cuvée* before it has breathed a little. Pascal offers water but Manu signals with a shudder that this would be one mortification of the flesh too far.

'For a couple of years, we took our grapes to the co-operative,' continues Pascal. 'But all they seemed to care about was weight. There was no real incentive for low yields or high quality. So although we were signed up for twenty-five years, we broke away. We're still getting the writs but we just couldn't work that way. We wanted yields as low as fifteen for the wine we're drinking now.'

The use of the present tense is almost too much for Manu. He half chokes on his lettuce and mops a fevered brow. However, finally, with the arrival of our steaks, the glasses are filled. And in Manu's case, rapidly emptied again. As Pascal worries that his pride and joy is still not showing its best, Manu can restrain himself no longer and helps himself to a second generous pouring.

'People ask how long this should be kept,' says Pascal. 'But it's the one question I can't answer. We've nothing older than '94. It's too early to say. We'll just have to wait and see.'

One of our number, of course, has no intention of waiting another moment. He is already wondering whatever can have happened to the second bottle.

Virgile's remotest vineyard, down at Nébian, must surely be his most beautiful. It lies high on a hillside to the south of Clermont l'Hérault, overlooking picturesquely patchworked vines and fruit trees. Its sheltered situation has encouraged a few of the buds to burst already, washing just the palest hint of green across the vines, while the edges of the field are exuberantly carpeted in deep purple and pale lemon by hundreds of heavy-headed, stumpy-stalked irises.

There is, however, nothing very picturesque about the afternoon's activity. As always, Virgile the fastidious pruner has made neat piles of his cuttings but these, he has decided, will have to be gathered up and burnt. Too many of the vines were diseased to mince them up as fertilizer.

'Only a tiny vineyard,' he assured me on the drive from Saint Saturnin, but it feels quite big enough to me as I trudge up and down the gradient, gathering armfuls of severed vine shoots to stoke the fire that he has lit at the bottom.

'A new variety for you,' says Virgile, as we work. 'Cinsault – mostly planted as a table grape, which is why I could rent the land so cheaply. You don't need slopes like this for table grapes. And if you don't need them, why make the extra effort? On the other hand, it's outside the Coteaux du Languedoc boundaries, so wine-makers weren't exactly falling over themselves either. Indeed, the fact that I'm using these grapes for wine obliges me to declassify a proportion as *vin de pays*. But then, I'd have to do that anyway, simply because I've got a higher percentage of Carignan than the fifty permitted for a Coteaux du Languedoc.'

All this reminds me that I wanted to pick his brains. I need to know whether April will be too late for planting vines on my own land. 'Only for the table,' I hasten to emphasize. 'I'm not setting up in competition.'

'But I thought you said your uncle had some vines.'

'He did until he diversified into sheep. He decided it was the easiest way of keeping the grass under control. But from what I've cleared so far, it looks as if his four-legged lawnmowers did a lot of damage to the vines while they were at it.'

'You never know,' he says. 'Vines are tough old creatures.'

'Well, come for lunch next Sunday,' I suggest as we watch the last of the cuttings burning. 'Then you can tell me the worst.'

My first breakfast in the sunshine.

I've decided to stick to the alternative bedroom in which I sought refuge from last month's storm. It opens on to a little balcony terrace and I found I loved being able to wander straight out there from my bed to enjoy the flowers on the fruit trees in the morning light. The almonds were the first, followed quickly by the apricots and plums and now the dazzling creamy white of two magnificent old cherry trees.

'All right for some,' grumbled Mme Gros last week. A rash expression of delight from my side of the stream had undammed a bitter tide of self-reproach from hers. 'Here we are with about a tenth of the land that you've got and I was foolish enough to let Manu cover it with vines.'

'But everything's flowering too soon,' warned Mme Vargas yesterday, when I found her struggling with her weeding on her own, having passed the flu to her absent Albert. 'There'll be no fruit in the whole *département* if things carry on like this.'

But early or late, who would not have been glad of the blossom this morning? The balcony is always the first part of the house to be warmed by the sun as it pushes over the wooded hills behind and this morning I installed a little break-fast table at the sunniest end.

Sitting there contentedly, asking myself why I would ever want to be anywhere else, I suddenly remembered that I was supposed to be down in Clermont l'Hérault, collecting my hard-earned olive oil from the co-operative. I quickly hung out some washing to take advantage of the weather and set off excitedly, my thoughts full of mouth-watering, dark green *extra vierge*. To everyone else, of course, my three precious litres would be indistinguishable from all the thousands of bottles and plastic jerrycans filled from exactly the same vat. But not to me.

The sense of anticipation survived the long-winded bureau-cracy of the collection process. It even survived the prosaic realization that, by the time I'd paid the co-operative's hand-ling charges, my long hours of picking in the freezing January rain would have saved me little more than fifteen pounds on the ordinary purchase price. It has, however, been slightly undermined by the discovery that the oil to which my docu-mentation entitles me is not the highly prized, single-variety product to which my cherished Lucques will have contributed but the co-operative's rather humbler *diverses variétés*.

'It does include some Lucques,' the co-operative's director, Mme Pagès, tries to reassure me. 'And it is the genuine local article. Not the cheaper one we make from bought-in Spanish olives. You see, there simply aren't enough in the Hérault to satisfy demand,' she continues, as she senses my surprise. 'Not since 1956.'

'What happened?' I ask, sufficiently intrigued to forget my disappointment.

'February temperatures were exceptionally high,' she elab-orates. 'The sap was rising exceptionally early. Then suddenly the thermometer plunged from plus twenty to minus twenty in just twenty-four hours, wiping out nearly every olive tree in the *département*. Most had to be cut back down to ground level. They sprouted again but it was five or six years before the new shoots bore fruit. We were the only mill that managed to stay open. Recovery was very slow, especially as so many decided to replant with vines, which were paying much better. Small wonder, I suppose, when doctors were telling people that oil was unhealthy. It was only in the early eighties that they decided it discouraged heart disease and the pendulum swung back.'

Mme Pagès speeds ahead down a spiral staircase to show me the surprisingly modest processing-room, with its mills and presses, centrifuges and conveyor belts, below the shop. Most of her 3,500 members operate on a rather different scale from mine, she is quick to emphasize, and when she tells me she has handled seven hundred tonnes this season, it's hard to imagine how the tightly packed chain of machines surrounding us ever manages to cope.

She tells me she is married to the grandson of the man who founded the co-operative in 1920, but hers is clearly no nepotistic appointment. She is passionately committed to her product, particularly the range of single-variety oils that she makes from Lucques and other exotic-sounding olives that I've never heard of.

'I'm specially keen to develop the Ménudal,' she enthuses. 'It would do very well up where you are and, of course, with a government grant for planting . . .'

'Oh, no,' I shake my head and back away defensively towards the car, cradling my priceless oil in my arms. 'I've got enough problems already.'

These turn out to include a dramatic change in the weather. My car is barely visible on the other side of the road, obscured by the kind of rain that I've only ever seen in films. Then, of course, you know perfectly well that some supercharged fireman's hose has been invoked to drench the few square metres in front of the camera, but here it is universal and sensationally real. The road is many centimetres deep in water and I have to drive away at something slower than walking speed. Yet within a quarter of an hour, the deluge has given way to brilliant sunshine and a perfect double rainbow.

Ignoring the washing, which must now be wetter than it was when I hung it out, I unlock the front door and the first thing I hear is the electric water pump. The principal spring is pretty vigorous but it still needs some help to push the water round the house for showers and so on. Yet the pump is only activated when water is actually running in some part of the house. So why can I hear it now?

I scurry round the house to check whether I left a tap on this morning, but everything is as it should be. Except for the continuous rasping of the pump. Manu has already told me that it was never this noisy in Uncle Milo's day and I suspect it is on its last legs but that does not explain why it is in constant action right now. I go to the submarine control room and look helplessly at my baffling collection of pipes and valves, wondering whether there might be some new permutation that I could usefully try. There must be a logical answer. I just need to think it through quietly. So for want of any better inspiration, I decide to fill a kettle for some coffee. And now I learn the terrible truth: there is no water.

Impossible surely, after the morning's downpour, but yes, another tap confirms the same alarming reality. No water. Which is why the pump is struggling away – straining to replenish something somewhere in the system from a supply that appears to have dried up. The nightmare possibility that I have been pushing to the back of my mind since the day I arrived is suddenly upon me.

Ridiculously, the first thought that occurs to me is what a nuisance it will be if I can't continue to call the house Les Sources. All those change of address cards. And the carved wooden sign at the entrance . . . Then I remember that I won't even be able to live here without water. I'll have to go back to England. But I won't be able to throw my tenants out. So where am I to spend the rest of my sabbatical?

April

Hᴏᴡ ᴄᴏᴜʟᴅ ᴍᴀɴᴜ have been out last night? He never goes out. It's not approved of. But yes, Mme Gros assured me, when I telephoned (and surely I only imagined the ring of delight in her regrets) her husband was going to be out until very late. '*Désolée*,' of course, but nothing to be done until the morning. And then as soon as I dared call this morning, after an essentially sleepless – not to mention waterless – night, I found he had gone out again. Doubly '*désolée*' by this stage, naturally, but it had somehow slipped her mind to give Manu my message.

'Too busy sandbagging the source of my spring, no doubt,' I muttered bitterly to myself, as I slumped despondently at the table in the courtyard with the yellow pages, wishing that I could just call the water board like everyone else. I felt sure I needed an expert but I had no idea what kind. It didn't seem like a job for a plumber. Maybe someone down at the café would know who to ask. At the very least I could have some breakfast coffee. And get away from that irritating fountain – normally such a soothing sound, splashing down to the pool, but this morning the constant babble was simply stopping me thinking straight . . .

And then the penny dropped. The fountain! How could I have been so stupid? If the fountain was still flowing freely the spring could not possibly be dry. So where in Uncle Milo's labyrinth of inside and outside piping did he decide to separate the fountain supply from the one for the house?

I am still asking myself this question a couple of hours later, having conducted every empirical test with valves and taps that I could think of. Every pipe that looked as if it might be heading in a domestic direction has turned out to activate some maddeningly irrelevant sprinkler in a remote part of the garden. So, parched and caffeine-starved, I am just trying to fill the kettle from the fountain when Manu appears with an open bottle of the red peril.

'A little liquid refreshment,' he says tactlessly, 'while we crack the problem.' But as soon as glasses are charged, he addresses himself to the matter in hand. 'You've looked in the little reservoir where the supply divides, I assume?'

'Little reservoir?'

'On the ramp beside the garage. Underneath the pile of stones.'

'I always thought that was a pile of stones . . .'

'How long have you lived here?' he laughs, uncovering a crude trapdoor beneath my uncle's curious cairn. 'The stones are just to weight the wood down but, under here, you've got a reserve tank. Helped Milo put it in, I did,' he boasts, as he surveys the primitive structure with pride. 'Without it, the fountain used to stop whenever you turned on a tap. But it's here that the water divides. And just as I thought, you've got a jammed ballcock.'

It *was* a problem for a plumber after all, if only he could have known where to look. The ballcock wedged against the rough concrete sides of Manu's rudimentary reservoir had duped the system into thinking that the house and the tank were awash with water. So it was stubbornly redirecting the entire supply to the fountain, impervious to the clamour of a desperate pump that had long since sucked the tank dry.

Or something like that. I am still not sure how the fountain could be taking priority when I thought Manu said the tank was there to compensate for the house having first call. But as he prods the ballcock into action with the bottom of his almost empty wine bottle, I am too relieved at the sudden, satisfying surge of water towards the house to bother with technicalities. All I want now is my coffee; but any such hopes are dashed by the observation that our triumph calls for 'a little celebration'.

'My vines are shooting after all,' were my first excited words when Virgile arrived for Sunday lunch.

'But only from the roots,' was his dispiriting verdict when he saw the extent of the damage done by Uncle Milo's sheep. 'They're alive but you'll never get any grapes. You could have a go at grafting some new vines on to the old rootstocks but it's almost as cheap and certainly easier to replant.'

'And it's not too late?' I ask from the depths of my disappointment.

'Not if you're very quick. But the trouble is, you need to get rid of the rootstocks first. Otherwise they'll infect the new vines. Much better to clear the land in the autumn and plant next spring.'

As we settle in the courtyard for a drink and the last of my precious home-grown olives, this feels like the last straw. I thought I already had cleared this part of the land when

I finished hacking back the weeds and brambles. I hadn't bargained for anything more radical.

'Maybe I can give you a hand,' offers Virgile. 'After all, I've got a tractor now.'

'Does that mean you've sorted out a bank?'

'Since Friday, yes. Everything's signed and settled. And just as well too. I managed to muddle through on a shoestring last year, with just my one and a half hectares. But now with seven and a half – and all on my own – it's a slightly different proposition.'

'I don't know how you do it,' I call from the kitchen, where lunch is now ready.

'Most of the time, I don't know myself,' he laughs.

'And here's me worried about a few dozen vine plants,' I say, as I carry out a dish of the local asparagus, which has just appeared in the market.

'You're tired of the wild *asperges*, then?' asks Virgile, helping himself.

'I don't follow.'

'Over there,' he points. 'Under the olive tree in front of your dining room window. I can see you've been picking pretty hard.'

I can't see anything much myself, apart from a bank of white irises. Well, nothing except some tall spindly weeds that I don't recognize. Although, now that I look more closely at their wispy little side-shoots, branching out at right angles, I suppose, yes, their tips could be considered asparagus-like. It's difficult to be certain when so many of them have been broken off . . . And then illumination dawns: it was here, only yesterday, at the very spot where this unacknowledged delicacy was reaching a perfection of ripeness, that Mme Gros surprised me with an offer to help me with my 'weeding'.

'Imagine getting a barrel of wine up this hill,' says Krystina, as we start the steep ascent to the ruined ramparts of the Château de Quéribus. 'You think I'm joking, don't you? But it wasn't just the monks who liked to see some wine in their daily rations. It was considered absolutely indispensable for medieval soldiers. Even for the Brits in the Hundred Years War, when presumably they'd have stuck to beer in normal circumstances.'

'Dutch courage?' I ask, already a little breathless.

'Partly that and partly the fact that it was much safer to drink than water,' answers Krystina, as indefatigable as ever on the rugged uphill slog. 'Especially during sieges. Even used it as a disinfectant.'

Halfway up the track, I feign an urgent interest in the view to get my breath back. A long line of jagged peaks stretches down the skyline, but high above us, on the most jagged of them all, the imposing stone defences of Quéribus seem to soar directly out of the cliff face. It is as if the solid, stocky polygon of the keep had been chiselled like some half-finished sculpture from the gargantuan block of stone that we are climbing.

'We're right on the edge of the Languedoc, here,' explains Krystina, as a new surge of energy signals an early end to our rest. 'This ridge makes a natural frontier. Go down the other side and you're into Roussillon. A different world in many ways. Still part of Spain in the seventeenth century, so it's not surprising really that Quéribus was once a border fortress for the Kings of Aragon.'

'I thought it was a Cathar castle,' I interject, having read as much on the signpost below.

'They're the ones who put it on the map,' she continues, ignoring my uncharacteristic display of knowledge. 'The sieges may have been bloodier at some of their other castles – hundreds of Cathars burnt alive, that kind of thing – but this was the last stronghold to fall in 1255 . . .' Then, belatedly, surprise begins to register. 'How much do you know about the Cathars?' she asks suspiciously.

'They had a lot of castles,' I flounder unconvincingly. 'And a lot of sieges . . .'

Krystina snorts dismissively. She has seen too much bluffing in the classroom to be taken in by my feeble performance this morning.

'*Kathari* means "pure ones" in Greek,' she continues, as we approach the castle gatehouse. 'They didn't believe this imperfect material world could be God's creation. It had to be the work of the Devil. So men's spirits – trapped here, they believed, by a Satanic ruse – could only be freed and restored to a spiritual world of purity, beauty and light through poverty, chastity and humility. All of which compared unfavourably with the laxity of a lot of the Catholic clergy. So in 1209, the Papacy launched a crusade – the Albigensian Crusade, it's always called because the heresy was particularly prevalent over in Albi. But as you can see,' she says, as we penetrate the last of the castle's complicated triple fortifications, 'the crusade met some pretty solid defences.'

'But were they Christians?' I congratulate myself on a few further syllables.

'They sought to emulate Christ but denied his divinity. So, yes, it was doctrine as well as lifestyle that upset the established Church. But the conflict soon got complicated by politics. Cathar supporters like the Count of Toulouse and the Viscount of Béziers were much more interested in political control of the Languedoc so . . . *Merde!*'

The rare display of French marks the fact that, after negotiating the ascent in the most unsuitable high heels, Krystina has suddenly fractured one of them on the totally unchallenging flatness of the battlements at the top of the castle.

'Who won?' I ask, as she flings both the good shoe and the bad into the abyss below.

'In a sense, the French Crown,' she answers, tiptoeing shoeless down again. 'The Languedoc was annexed to the royal domains in 1229. The beginning of the end for the *langue d'oc*,' she adds between winces and curses. 'In 1539 the Occitan language was formally outlawed in official documents. Boring Parisian French extinguished the romantic, courtly tongue of the troubadours.'

She languishes theatrically against a battlement: clearly the romantic, courtly thing expected of *me* is to sweep her off her stockinged feet and carry her down to something nearer sea level; but mindful of the forces which such gallantry might unleash, I remain unchivalrously empty-armed.

'She dragged you all the way to Quéribus?' marvelled Manu. 'Practically to the Pyrenées and you didn't taste a single Corbières?' He was absolutely scandalized: I had driven from one end of the Languedoc's largest *appellation* to the other without so much as a trickle of its delectable product passing my lips. 'This must be rectified at once!'

Undeterred by the morning's wind and rain, he scribbled a hasty note to Mme Gros with one hand and rummaged for his keys with the other. 'If you'd come to me in the first place, you'd have tasted wines that were actually *made* in one of your Cathar castles. Two for the price of one, and half the journey time,' he assured me as we sped south.

Unfortunately, like so many of Manu's promises, this one was to be only half fulfilled. The Château de Lastours was certainly more accessible than Quéribus, being only a little farther down the coastal motorway from Narbonne. Indeed, as Manu probably intended, we arrived in time for me to buy him lunch in the château restaurant. But the Cathar connection proved to be wishful thinking.

'Hundred per cent orthodox, I'm afraid,' says Jean-Marie Lignères, the château director. He is a thin but commanding presence behind his desk, distinguished-looking despite his jeans and pullover and somewhere, I imagine, in his fifties, with a sharp intelligence that will not take him long to see through to my companion's baser interests.

'Maybe it was fortified *against* the Cathars?' suggests Manu to save what face he can.

'Maybe,' concedes the director tactfully. 'But this was primarily a resting place for merchants on the trade route into Spain. The château wines supplied the travellers' drinking requirements.'

'As your family's excellent production supplied ours at lunchtime.' Manu's compliment only thinly obscures his appetite for further samples.

'Oh, but this isn't a family estate. I thought, from the way you introduced yourself to my secretary . . .' He barely suppresses a smile. 'Well, anyway, no, it was bought in 1970 by one of the big Marseille banks, or rather its *Comité d'Entreprise*.' He sees me looking blank. 'A kind of works council. Every large business in France has to have one. But this one was unusually altruistic. It bought the estate to provide employment for sixty mentally handicapped people, to help them lead as full a life as possible through their work.'

'In the vineyards?' I ask.

'And in the *cave*. And more recently in the restaurant.'

Now I understand the strange intensity with which our lunchtime waiters concentrated on every tiniest detail. The service was perfect and yet there was something disconcertingly obsessive in the perfectionism, each piece of cutlery laid precisely parallel with the next, each row of glasses a mathematically exact diagonal. But now that I know, I find the achievement quite remarkable.

'Everyone starts with the vines,' emphasizes M. Lignères. 'Sorting out a relationship with nature before they try their hand at people.'

'And they help with everything – the pruning, for example?' I ask, remembering how challenging I found my own introduction to that complicated art.

'Most things, yes. With "normal" – for want of a better word

– workers alongside. We try to make their work as varied as possible. They could, of course, perform the same mechanical action day after day but that wouldn't do much to help them reintegrate – which is our overriding aim.' He explains in parenthesis how he came to this as his first and only job, after finishing his wine studies, but has since completed a doctorate in psychology to cope with the parallel challenge. 'You have to accept a different pace for the handicapped. But we're lucky – we've got enormous altitude variations here. The vineyards at three hundred metres ripen up to a month behind those at thirty, which gives us extra time – even with a hundred and sixty hectares.'

'What sort of condition was the estate in when you started?' I ask.

'Appalling. I mean, totally abandoned. We more or less rebuilt the château. And practically every hectare of vineyard needed replanting – except for a little ancient Carignan and Grenache that we still use for our top wine, the Château de Lastours itself.'

'We only tasted your regular red at lunchtime,' says Manu, plumbing new depths of unsubtlety.

M. Lignères, however, simply nods approvingly and tells us how it was another of their *cuvées* – named after Simone Descamps, the handicapped project's original driving force – which has perhaps done most to publicize the *domaine*. In a recent blind tasting it was ranked alongside some of the world's most exalted and expensive properties. But when I voice the prosaic thought that most of us would consider winemaking at this level quite ambitious enough, without the added 'complication' of a substantially handicapped workforce, his answer betrays a fascinating ordering of priorities.

'We *have* to make something exceptional,' he explains with passion. 'The reintegration of the handicapped depends on it. The feeling that they're contributing to something great helps them recover a sense of their worth.'

Before Manu can formulate any less oblique reminder that my niggardliness with the restaurant wine list has left him unacquainted with these finer efforts, we are joined by a figure as well-padded as M. Lignères is lean but of similar age and, to judge from the spring in his plimsolls, imbued with the same energetic commitment.

'André Puyal,' says M. Lignères. 'My number two.'

'Maybe this is the man with the corkscrew,' says Manu's brightening expression. But André Puyal turns out to be the man with the four-wheel drive – for, despite the continuing rain, M. Lignères thinks we should see a bit of the estate.

When Manu first bluffed our way in here, M. Lignères was quick to explain his difficulty in more than half rising to greet us. 'A bad crash in one of those.' He gestured ruefully towards a giant photograph of a racing car behind him. He used to be a driver – when not otherwise engaged as master wine-maker and psychologist – and the accident left him partially para-lysed and wheelchair-bound for many years. However, a com-bination of physiotherapy and the iron will that he clearly brings to all things has recently enabled him to walk again – not without difficulty but with only occasional support from a stick. He can also drive but M. Puyal is more the man for what's in store.

I am not entirely sorry that Manu insists on sitting in the front of the Land Rover. M. Lignères's 'enormous altitude vari-ations' are linked by such steep ascents and precipitous descents that I am soon regretting the richer elements of my lunch. Indeed, M. Puyal explains that many of these inhospit-ably stony tracks are used for testing racing cars.

'All the top names come here with their new designs,' he says, as we skid downhill through the rain-soaked golden gorse. 'You see those guys on the ridge over there? That's the Mitsubishi team. They'll stay with us for as long as it takes to break the car. Then, when they've seen where it's broken, they'll take it away to decide how to make it stronger. But we also hire out four-wheel drives for ordinary drivers to use the circuit. It helps attract people from other regions, who then discover our wines. It's also why we developed the hotel side of our operation,' he continues, as I begin to wonder whether this multi-faceted enterprise has any limits.

'You can't just stand still,' he says, as if reading my thoughts. 'We live in what Jean-Marie calls a "Kleenex Society". Everything is disposable. New ideas are needed all the time to keep the public's interest. But all the fringe activities, like the concerts and the art exhibitions – did Jean-Marie mention those? – they also help to "socialize" our disabled employees.'

There is little sign of the disabled this afternoon, except for some shadowy silhouettes huddled in a distant, steamed-up minibus. There has also been little sign of Manu's hoped-for tasting but, just as we are taking a more promising turn towards the *cave*, we stop to greet an approaching tractor.

M. Puyal introduces us to Georges, the serious, slightly anxious-looking driver. His report on his afternoon's activities proves him a man who knows his Grenache from his Syrah and his 'goblet' pruning from his *cordon royat* but he is rather surprisingly one of the handicapped.

'Needed a lot of shelter and support at first,' says M. Puyal, as Georges drives on. 'But then he teamed up with one of the handicapped girls and we gave them a little flat on the estate. Now they're well enough to live together in the village. Someone pops in to help them sort out their bills but they're well on their way to integration.'

As we speed back to the *cave*, he declares Georges to be 'one of their best successes' and he is right: when you have met Georges, the notion that the wine which you may be about to sample has rivalled the legendary Château Pétrus somehow seems less important.

*

'*Tu veux aller ébourgeonner?*' asked Virgile, when I picked up the telephone.

I had no idea what 'ébourgeonning' might involve but I said I could be with him in half an hour. He told me I'd be working for the first time *dans le vert*. I had no idea what working 'in the green' meant either but it sounded more fun than pruning dead wood from olive trees in a howling gale.

I had in fact been pruning quite worrying quantities of dead wood. I needed to ask the Vargases' advice – or rather that of Madame Vargas, since Monsieur was still not back on his feet – but that would have to wait.

Just as I found a parking space in front of Le Pressoir, some rain hit the windscreen. Nothing so remarkable about that, except that this afternoon the sky was brilliantly, cloudlessly blue – so blue that it made you wonder how the rainclouds could ever return – and yet there it was: rain on the windscreen.

'It's the wind,' said Marie-Anne, coming out from the restaurant with her two little daughters to greet me. The children laughed at a couple of elderly villagers who were struggling to remain vertical for a windswept game of *boules* at the bottom end of the square. Then a sudden gust threw rain in all our faces and the children's laughter turned to tears. But still the sun shone on. 'It must be raining up on the Larzac and blowing all the way down on the wind,' Marie-Anne explained, as she took her protesting offspring back inside. 'No wonder we get these rainbows!'

It was every bit as blustery when Virgile and I reached our target patch of vines near Montpeyroux.

'Grenache Blanc,' he announced, 'Don't ask me what I'm going to do with it. It was part of a job lot that I'm renting but I haven't any other white grapes.'

'For a blend, you mean?'

'You have to mix at least two *cépages* for a white Coteaux du

Languedoc – the same as for a red. I suppose I could make a single-variety *vin de pays* but I can't say I'm very convinced by the idea of pure Grenache Blanc. So it was rather a crazy acquisition.'

But of course, it would take much more than a few doubts about the usefulness of a vine to make Virgile relax his usual exacting standards, as rapidly becomes clear when he starts explaining the business of the day. The *bourgeons* prove to be the buds, which have burst in a windswept profusion of delicate, fluffy new leaves and fresh, pale green shoots (hence our working *dans le vert*). However, they are mostly *too* profuse for Virgile's liking. I had fondly imagined the winter pruning to be more than rigorous enough to achieve his intended low yields, but no. If we are to have any hope of reaching that target half-litre per vine, we must examine every one of the five or six points of growth and strip off all but two of the shoots sprouting from each.

'Not just any old two,' he emphasizes, as if I could have been naïve enough to imagine anything so simple. 'Always keep the strongest. But favour the shoots that are most in line with the row. And of course, lower rather than higher, where possible. We're thinking ahead to the next round of pruning here, deciding where we want next year's shoots.'

Virgile leaves me grappling with the conflicting priorities – every bit as indecisive as I was at the pruning stage and thinking surely three-dimensional chess would have been less stressful.

A couple of weeks ago Babette put up a new sign. 'Between 19.30 and 21.30 meals only,' it said.

'You mean, we can't call in for just a drink any more?' I asked, surprised that her dinner trade at this time of year could be brisk enough to exclude the casual imbiber.

'Oh, *you* can,' she said. 'All the regulars can.'

'Is this your new summer régime or something?'

'Hardly,' she laughed, as the wind howled outside. 'It's just that I've been getting a lot of rough types coming up from Lodève, looking for trouble. But now I can point to the sign.'

This seemed to make sense until I made my first ever Saturday evening visit last weekend. When I arrived at about eight o'clock I could hardly open the door, there were so many villagers drinking at the bar.

'So how will you explain this lot to your undesirables?' I asked.

'Easy – I'll say they're waiting for tables.'

Babette was cheerfully oblivious to the fact that there was only one table laid, let alone occupied. The recently widowed octogenarian Monsieur Privat was, as usual, tucking into one of his twice-a-day, every day meals at his regular table near the kitchen. (No one knew how he survived on her *jour de ferme-ture*.) Otherwise there didn't seem to be the slightest interest in food; but before I could put this to Babette, another wave of 'regulars' forced its way inside and she was overwhelmed with drinks orders.

Babette's new dining rules may have nothing to do with summer but there are many indications that warmer times are finally on their way. She herself has taken down the café terrace's wall of plastic weatherproofing and poked some artificial roses in amongst the neglected-looking greenery in her concrete planters. Down in Saint Saturnin, Pius is busy constructing a big wooden platform in front of Le Pressoir to quadruple his outdoor capacity. And back here in the village shop, Nathalie has put up a notice that, as from next month, she will be offering fresh milk as well as the disgusting 'long-life' that we have endured all winter. ('The visitors prefer it,' she told me.)

Even closer to home, a trio of the noisiest frogs imaginable has arrived to keep me awake throughout the summer, croaking loudly beside the pool in three-part counterpoint every night. They are also the greenest frogs imaginable – a thoroughly implausible, children's story-book green. Tree frogs, according to my uncle's dog-eared but vividly illustrated Mediterranean nature book. I spotted one of them jumping into the water and could hardly believe that such a tiny, three-centimetre body could generate such reverberating, sleep-banishing volume.

Meanwhile, all around the garden, there are dozens of once anonymous, indistinguishable shrubs bursting into vibrantly varied life. Geraniums for the breakfast balcony have found their way into my shopping basket and the first – but certainly not the last – of the new season's insects have delivered their bites.

But surely the most striking indication that the seasons are changing is the number of friends who are starting to telephone – ostensibly to check on my welfare but rapidly progressing to explore my receptiveness to visitors.

There are two bedrooms in the main house but the separate studio has always seemed the ideal lodging for all but the closest of guests. However, some vital work is needed to make it safe, especially a few repairs to the wrought-iron staircase leading up to the galleried sleeping area. So yesterday Monsieur Parrouty, a convincingly burly-looking blacksmith, came up from Lodève to take a long, thoughtful look.

'What do you think?' I asked, as I shook his blackened, vice-like hand and introduced him to Uncle Milo's rickety spiral.

'Bawf,' said M. Parrouty.

In fact that proved to be mainly what he said. He was a man of few words. He was more preoccupied with stroking his opulent moustaches. Indeed, metalwork, I decided, could represent only a minor sideline for a man whose principal activity was clearly the winning of the local whisker-growing competition. A pair of luxuriant S-shaped curls looped nearly down to his chin, before twisting magnificently back again to reach almost as high as his ears. In fact, they obscured so much of his face that it was quite impossible to interpret the stream of ruminative noises, as he sized up the assignment.

'Baaaawfff,' he said in tones that could as easily be read as an expression of admiration for Uncle Milo's staircase design as one of dismay at its state of repair. But before I could elicit any more articulate estimate of the problem, my powers of speech were cut short by a blood-curdling scream from the roof.

In retrospect, I suppose, it was not so much a scream as a screech. Certainly not a squeal. The sheer volume, let alone the violence of the noise put it far beyond the frontiers of squealing. A shriek perhaps, something halfway between fear and anger – but whatever the *mot juste*, there was evidently something up there that was not best pleased to be disturbed. And something substantial too.

The shriek was rapidly followed by a tumultuous frenzy of movement. As far as I could tell, and improbable as it seemed, the furious scrabbling seemed to be coming from an almost negligible gap between the steeply sloping ceiling boards and the roof tiles immediately above them. I tried to console myself with the thought that the sound of a pigeon on a slate roof in England could reverberate below as if an eagle had chosen to perch there but, deep down, I knew that something formidable had taken up residence beneath the terracotta.

'Bawaawaawaawff,' said M. Parrouty, still cogitating regardless.

His moustaches twitched ever more animatedly with every new aspect of the staircase project that he considered but with never a flicker of interest in the violent agitation above us. Either he enjoyed the society of similar visitors in his own rafters or some highly developed sense of *politesse* precluded him from passing comment. It was inconceivable that he could have failed to hear it.

However, as soon as M. Parrouty had uttered his last farewell 'bawf', I rushed to the main house for the nature book. Heaven knows why I thought this was going to help when I had nothing visual to go on, but I turned to the page that covered a local selection of comfortingly harmless-seeming mice, only to encounter, at the bottom of the page, a painstakingly detailed drawing of a dark, glistening turd. It looked worryingly familiar.

I hurried back out to the courtyard and, sure enough, there in the corner near the studio were three perfect forty-millimetre specimens. I hadn't taken much notice when I had seen them in the morning but now I felt absolutely certain that the beast with which they had not long since parted company was a *'fouine'*. And yet I had no idea what a *fouine* might be.

Every other living thing in the entire book had been favoured with a graphically lifelike, full-frontal pose. So why not the *fouine*? Was the creature's physical reality so terrible that the sight of anything more than its excrement would have potential purchasers fainting throughout the bookshops of Southern France?

May

SEVERAL DAYS AND several freshly delivered, telltale traces later (at least there are none *inside* the studio) I am still hearing the same alarming scuffle in the roof whenever I enter the studio. And worse than that, this morning I heard the high-pitched squeaking of what I can only imagine are babies. But I am little the wiser about my adversary, except that my diction-ary offers an Anglo-Saxon alias: 'stone martin'. Otherwise, all that the nature book adds is that my *fouine* is (a) a notorious leaver of turds (which is hardly news) and (b) carnivorous (which is hardly reassuring).

Meanwhile, the need to prepare the studio for my friends' arrival grows ever more pressing, so I decide to assert a few pro-prietorial rights – nothing over-sophisticated, just a few judi-cious whacks of a heavy broom-handle on the wooden ceiling, at the epicentre of the commotion. This quickly teaches me something that the nature book could have mentioned: the female *fouine* has no qualms about abandoning her young within seconds of the going getting rough. Her exit from the roof is, however, so rapid that I have no time to catch sight of her.

I do, nonetheless, get several more chances, as the second thing I learn about the *fouine* is that it is exceptionally persistent about returning as soon as things quieten down again. At first, I get a glimpse of something brown and furry disappearing into the bushes. Then, in the afternoon, a sighting of a bushy-tailed rear view – much larger than a squirrel, I'd say, but a little smaller, I think (and hope), than a cat. And finally, towards evening, a flash of white on a fast-moving chest.

As usual I need advice, but Manu is away for the weekend, dragooned into visiting a sister-in-law whose fulminations against the demon drink apparently make his life with Mme Gros feel like a Bacchanalian orgy. And the Vargases, I know, are now both out of action. Madame sprained her wrists in a fall from a ladder while engaged in some over-ambitious olive-spraying, and Monsieur has taken her for a rest-cure at a cousin's on the coast. So I am forced to resort to the collective wisdom of the village café.

I join the crush at the bar and initiate a 'supposing a friend of mine had this animal in his roof' kind of conversation, expecting the usual hotly-debated range of views. But tonight the zoological consensus is both immediate and unanimous.

'*Vous avez une fouine!*' they chorus.

Unfortunately, however, opinions as to how the animal's unhappy host should best proceed in these circumstances are less united.

'*Elles sont protégées,*' calls M. Privat from the corner table where he is enjoying another of his twice-daily meals *chez* Babette. (The man's appetite for *coq aux olives* must be inexhaustible.) The *fouine*'s protection, he insists, precludes even the civilest of invitations to consider alternative accommodation. '*Mais pourquoi les chasser, alors? . . . Je les aime, moi,*' he adds affectionately.

'*Elles sont vicieuses,*' counters Monsieur Puylairol, the bee-keeper.

For a man of his profession he is surprisingly timid-looking but he speaks on this occasion with unaccustomed vehemence. Presumably, the life of an *apiculteur* exposes him to quite enough aggression without confronting a *fouine*.

'Only my opinion, of course,' he continues, more character-istically diffident. 'But I wouldn't go nearer than twenty metres, if I were you.'

'Not without a full suit of body armour,' Babette supports him more emphatically, and I set off home wondering whether the studio will ever again be fit for human habitation.

I am too depressed to return to the battlefield until the morning; but when I do, the crack of the broom against the ceiling boards is greeted with unaccustomed silence. The *fouine* is clearly learning not to panic at the first hint of hostilities. Another more savage prod produces the same mute response. Perhaps it has gone in search of breakfast. But a few more bat-terings at intervals throughout the morning and still there is no hint of protest.

Cautiously, I face the improbable truth: I seem to have won. The *fouine* appears to have decided that there must be easier places to raise a family.

The vines are surely now at their most beautiful – vibrantly limey green, profusely, flutteringly leafy yet still distinctly independent shapes, set off by newly ploughed soil, in neat rows, all across the region. Even Virgile has ploughed the weeds into his soils, though perversely, he is now wondering whether he might even sow some replacement grasses in the spaces between his rows for better organic balance.

Everywhere the tiny round buds are starting to form, looking so much like miniature grapes that I thought I must have somehow missed the flowering. But the surprising thing is the sheer quantity of these buds. After all that winter pruning and April shoot-removal, Virgile's vines are still remarkably heavily laden.

'Will we have to thin them yet again?' I ask faint-heartedly, remembering Virgile's masochistically modest three glasses per vine.

'Nature will probably find a way of doing that bit for us,' he assures me. 'Disease or hail or something usually helps us out.'

The vines that seem to be growing fastest are his Syrah, and the assignment for the day is to reorganize their *palissage* – the system of wires on which this variety in particular needs to be trained, before its exceptionally high-reaching shoots get snapped off by the wind. The wires are already there, a relic of the previous owner, stretching all along the length of each row. However, they are still where the last vintage left them and now need repositioning to support the delicate young growth. At roughly eight-metre intervals down the rows, there are metal posts with supporting hooks at different heights, and the object of the exercise is to lower the wires from one of these pegs to another without damaging the new shoots.

'Hey, careful,' says Virgile, as I tug with excessive enthusiasm at a wire already tangled by tendrils. 'I know I don't want a lot of grapes but I do want some!'

As we work down the vineyard together, on opposite sides of the row, I ask about progress on his much-deferred bottling. I know that he opted in the end for 'serigraphic' labelling, printed directly on to the bottles, but the last time I enquired the initial designs had failed to please.

'Next month,' he says. 'Definitely. I must get some wine on the market to appease the bank. But goodness knows how. I mean, I know Pius will take some for Le Pressoir but as for the rest . . . There just aren't enough hours in the day.'

'You'll have to get yourself a wife,' I suggest. 'Someone with nothing better to do than hang around the *cave* all day, giving tastings . . .'

'You're right,' he laughs. 'When she isn't answering the telephone and paying the bills and doing the paperwork for the

Customs . . . I knew there was something missing in my business plan!'

'You must be mad,' said Babette, when I told her yesterday that her hearty *confit de canard* was going to have to fortify me for an afternoon of tree planting.

I didn't need her to tell me that it was far too late in the year but, back in March, when I ordered the trees from another of Manu's shooting cronies, I was naïve enough to assume that it might need fewer than twenty reminders to secure the promised 'same day delivery'.

'Madder still,' she said when I telephoned a couple of hours later to ask whether she knew of anyone with some dynamite.

Uncle Milo had left the level, paddock-like area immediately behind the house unplanted – simply fencing it off in his unavailing effort to separate sheep from vines. Having cleared away the canopy of brambles, I was now determined to plant this area but, as Babette was quick to point out, land is often left unplanted for a reason. In this case, the soil's unyielding resistance to my pick-axe suggested no one had disturbed it since whatever seismic convulsion shaped these hillsides in the first place.

'I thought you had more trees than you could cope with already,' she observed with ample justification.

'Not peach trees,' I explained defensively. 'And Manu says I ought to replace a couple of dead Mirabelles. And the paddock looks so empty,' I continued, knowing privately that, more than anything, I was simply impatient to make a creative mark on my landscape after so many months of cutting and clearing and burning.

Our famously resourceful café proprietress was disappointingly unhelpful in the dynamite department but she did know someone with a giant, tractor-mounted drill, which she thought should solve the problem. As long as the job didn't need too much discussion.

The importance of Babette's proviso became clear as soon as Monsieur Mas applied himself to this morning's doorstep preliminaries. A big broad smile beamed down at me from a big round head on big broad shoulders. But the smile was entirely toothless. If I had not already seen a mechanical drilling device, with accompanying tractor, lurching up the lane, M. Mas's sibilant speech of self-introduction would have given me no hint as to his identity. He, on the other hand, was too busy fiddling with a whistling hearing aid to guess that my own first words might merely be ones of greeting.

'*BON. . . . JOUR,*' I tried again more slowly.

'*M'ssssshhhuhhMassshhh,*' he announced once more.

I was already hoarse with fruitlessly repeated salutations before I could even begin to address the subtler message that the stakes so mysteriously dotted round the paddock coincided with the spots where his drill was to dig the required holes.

But now that the holes are dug and the fruit trees duly planted, another thought has struck me. The field where I have chosen to plant my trees is effectively the only part of Uncle Milo's estate where there is no convenient water supply. Almost everywhere else, there appears to be some sort of outpost of his still untested watering system. But not in the paddock, I realize belatedly.

'You'll need to do that every day, when it gets warmer,' calls Mme Gros contentedly from the other side of the stream, as she watches me hobble out of the bathroom with a watering can for the tenth time.

'I wish I didn't have to do this,' says Virgile gloomily, as Laurent, his friend with the filtering machine, presses the start button.

Laurent looks silently on, as the pump starts noisily sucking the wine from the peace and quiet of its fibreglass tank and forcing it down the pipe to the point where it pushes its way through the multi-layered, card-like filter before returning again to the calm of another newly sterilized *cuve* on the other side. Laurent's wordless solemnity suggests that he considers it a great shame too but maybe he is just taciturn by nature. It is Virgile who voices the concern.

'You never know how much intensity you're losing,' he frets. 'I didn't intend to filter it at all but I had a problem with the wine in one of my barrels. I thought it was developing too much volatility – too much acetic acid. So I was afraid to bottle without filtering first.'

'But I thought it was the wine that you're keeping to bottle next year, which was now in the barrels,' I respond, confused.

'Oh, didn't I tell you? I decided to mix them after all. I thought the weightier wine for next year needed balancing with some of the freshness of this year's. And vice versa. But the net result is, everything now needs filtering.'

He takes a sample of the newly clarified wine in a glass. He sniffs it, tastes it and passes it to Laurent. 'What do you think?' he asks tensely.

'It certainly looks more brilliant,' says Laurent, avoiding the issue.

'Great pus-filled swellings in the armpits and groin,' said Krystina, as Babette thrust two generous *salades niçoises* on to our sun-dappled table.

It was the first day that extra tables and chairs had spilled out beyond her café terrace to fill as much of the Place de la Fontaine as the chaotic parking of cars and vineyard machinery permitted. Scores of lunchers were celebrating this first confirmation of summer. Monsieur Privat seemed only too pleased to be sharing his shady table under an ancient plane tree with a trio of Scandinavian girls, while the Vargases, back from the coast, continued Madame's convalescence on the sunnier side of the square. Babette had still not found time for tablecloth-making but nobody cared. They were much more interested in their carafes of well-chilled *rosé* and the colourful salads that were giving the *coq aux olives* a well-earned rest.

So who but Krystina could have chosen such a moment to regale me with a grisly account of the Black Death?

'Disastrous for wine production,' she persisted between mouthfuls.

'Lack of workers?' I asked, having lost most of my own appetite.

'Lack of customers as well,' she explained. 'Wiped out a third of the population by 1400. You'd never think Montpellier was Europe's most important medicine school. But the professors seemed to be much more interested in doctoring wine. You see, the medieval stuff was still very short-lived. Anything left by summertime was likely to be sour and the spicing of wine to disguise the deterioration became one of the Medicine Faculty's specialities. You'll get a better idea when we're down there.'

Krystina's threat, however, reckoned without my secret knowledge that Wednesday was 'Aromatherapy Day'. So this morning, in a gesture of rare defiance, I have taken advantage of this prior claim on her liberty to find my own independent way to the university city.

Arnaldus de Villanova is the man I am looking for. Not the man himself – he died in 1311 – but his bestseller, the *Liber de Vinis*, the first book ever to be printed on the subject of wine and endlessly reprinted, it appears, until at least the sixteenth century. But no one seems to have thought fit to give him a statue in the Faculty's imposing classical entrance hall of fame. Only the librarian upstairs seems to show proper respect, as she ushers me to a research desk with surprising lack of interest in either my motives or my credentials.

'You can choose from about twenty editions,' she explains,

without even consulting the catalogue. 'In Latin, that is. Unfortunately, there's no French translation worth reading. There's one coming out in Catalan next year but maybe you don't want to wait.'

Stupidly, I came all this way without a moment's thought for the subtle linguistic warning in Villanova's title. But I know it would take me months to understand the Latin, and the Catalan I wouldn't even recognize. So I brave her scorn and ask for the vilified *version française*.

I am not sure what I expected. Some kind of technical vini-cultural treatise, I suppose. Or a first compendious encyclo-paedia of local wines. But what I get is a bizarre, fifty-two-page mixture of astrology and alchemy, much of it devoted to some very dubious-sounding 'recipes' for a series of wine-based Wonder Drugs. My favourite infuses straightforward wine with a mixture of garlic, cinnamon, liquorice, resin and 'mastic' to produce an elixir allegedly capable of warming the kidneys, purifying the blood, banishing melancholy, relieving haemor-rhoids and stopping your hair going grey, all in the same miraculous dose.

But at last Mme Gros's love of Noilly Prat is explained: she must see a similar promise of eternal life in its own only slightly less extraordinary list of ingredients.

A sobering thought indeed.

The first of my visitors has come and gone. And waving her off, I hardly knew which had done me more good – the un-accustomed separation from my strimmer and chainsaw or Sarah's unfeigned enthusiasm for the house and the land, the village and the countryside, the food and the wine. Her amaze-ment made me listen with new ears to the morning birdsong, evening frogsong and night-time cicadas and her bright-eyed curiosity took us into corners of Uncle Milo's land that I had never found time to explore.

One day for instance, at the far extremity of the wood, we found a curious, circular, stone-built, stone-roofed shelter, half-hidden by creepers.

'Another shepherd's hut?' speculated Sarah, as we ventured inside to admire the unexpected intricacy of its dome-like ceiling.

'A *capitelle*,' corrected Mme Gros, appearing from nowhere in the doorway. Her primary objective was to check that Sarah represented only a temporary addition to the community but, having come this far, she was willing to share another of her nuggets of folklore. 'You'll find lots of *capitelles* round here,' she explained. 'They were used by women field-workers for giving birth.'

She looked meaningfully at Sarah, as if to say 'let that be a warning'.

'I won't be a tick, I feel a baby coming on,' Sarah giggled, unaware of my neighbour's underdeveloped sense of humour.

'*Pas de respect, ces jeunes gens,*' snorted Mme Gros, as she tutted her way back through the wood.

On another day, Virgile joined us for lunch and we sat together in the shade of the courtyard arches, sampling something new to me, as well as to Sarah – a local speciality, which he had forgotten to tell me he made. 'Cartagène,' he called it, as he poured us each a glassful from the plastic bottle in which the continuing delays in his *mise en bouteille* had forced it to travel. 'I can't think why we didn't taste it back in January. It's one of my passions.'

The curiosity in our hands looked exactly like an ordinary pale pink *rosé* but the taste was quite different: intensely grapey, yet somehow noticeably higher in alcohol than wine.

'It's a blend of pure unfermented grapejuice, with pure unflavoured alcohol,' he explained. 'The addition of the alcohol – the *mutage* as it's called – stops the juice fermenting and preserves its natural freshness and sweetness: an invention, as it happens, of your mate Arnaldus, down at Montpellier.'

'But how do you make it pink?' asked Sarah. 'Mixing red juice and white juice?'

'Not at the best addresses,' replied Virgile, more tolerantly I suspect than if I had asked the same question. 'You use red grapes – in this case a blend of Syrah and Grenache Noir. But you allow the juice only a brief contact with the skins, especially if you want a delicate colour like this.'

'Well, it's one of my passions too,' declared Sarah. 'I'd like a dozen when it's bottled.'

Virgile had also brought us a couple of the wines that he made in 1997 on his grandfather's land in the Côtes du Ventoux and we dutifully set about comparing them over our *charcuterie* and salad. Both bottles were simply and stylishly signed 'Virgile' in gold marker pen – a prototype, he told me, for the rather more sophisticated serigraphic design now commissioned for his Languedoc wines. But intriguingly, each of the bottles also bore a different barrel number: 32 and 46.

'How many barrels did you make?' asked Sarah, imagining a long and tunnel-like *cave*, lined with casks.

'Two,' answered Virgile with a grin that showed he understood as much about marketing as he did about wine-making.

'Well, I think they're the best two reds that I've tasted in years,' announced Sarah, as she placed another substantial order for his Coteaux du Languedoc.

Both the Ventoux and the Cartagène were undeniably delicious but I couldn't help wondering whether Sarah's purchases might have owed less to the charms of the wines than the charms of the wine-maker. She has, after all, always claimed to be allergic to anything red and indifferent to anything sweet. And she did tell me it was particularly tactless to return to the courtyard with the cheeses, just as Virgile was enquiring about her marital status.

So, while I can hardly see Sarah abandoning her high-powered city career for dutiful days behind his tasting counter, I think she may well be back before the summer is much advanced to see more of his 'black gypsy eyes'.

'Marvellous man, your uncle,' said Manu, surveying my ripening cherries at the beginning of the month. 'Always very generous with his produce.'

'Marvellous quality,' he said, when he appeared on my doorstep before breakfast this morning with a basketful of the glossy, black-red fruits. 'But you mustn't be disappointed with the quantity. It's the same across the region. Too much temperature variation from day to night in the early spring,' he insisted as he mopped the juice stains trickling down his chin.

However, my later discovery that Mme Gros had bought up the village shop's entire supply of preserving sugar left little doubt that I had unwittingly emulated Uncle Milo's generosity.

Not that Manu has stripped my trees entirely bare. He has left me plenty that could still be reached if I had a taller ladder and others that could perhaps be used for jam, if I had the patience to cut away the little blemishes where the insects have sampled them first. (If only they would gorge themselves on one cherry at a time, instead of these roving comparative tastings, there would be plenty for everyone.) But after an hour or so of unrewarding exertions, punctuated by vicious attacks from an insect population jealously defending its prerogatives, I decide to make do with Manu's little hamper.

Virgile's mighty empire now extends to a rented garage in one of the winding and exceptionally narrow streets behind the church. This is where he keeps his new (but not, of course, brand new) tractor. It is also where a small but formidable-looking herd of many-armed mechanical spraying monsters is kept in captivity – each, he explains, designed to tackle a different phase of the vine's development or a different kind of treatment.

There are two main enemies, apparently: a downy mildew and a completely different powdery mildew, otherwise known as oïdium. Each is matched by two main weapons: the first, a pale blue mixture of lime, copper sulphate and water, popularly known as Bordeaux Mixture because Bordeaux is where it was invented, and the other, a white powdered form of sulphur. It seems that the current hot, dry weather will reduce the risk of the downy mildew but, unfortunately, somehow favour the spread of the powdery kind. The only consolation is that the same climatic conditions will also be good for the distribution of the remedial sulphur dust.

'It's all I seem to do at the moment,' Virgile yawned, as we inspected the new garage annexe one stifling hot afternoon. 'Very early every morning too, before the sun's too high, and then late in the evening when it's cool again. It'll go on like that for weeks. The worst is the land down at Nébian. It's too far away to tow the big machines behind the tractor, so I have to go in the van with a spray that I can carry on my back. And carrying thirty-five kilos of liquid and motor in these temperatures is no joke!'

'Is it normally as hot as this in May?' I asked, as we returned to the airless heat of the alley. Some village women who had been gossiping in the shade of an adjoining doorstep when we arrived, were now clinging to the changing shadows on the other side.

'This is pretty exceptional,' he assured me, as we settled under Le Pressoir's awning for two of the coldest beers that Marie-Anne could muster. 'More like the end of June or July.'

Twenty minutes with a beer proved long enough for us to have essentially the same heat-struck conversation with half a dozen passing wine-growers. (If there is one social group that spends more time talking about the weather than the English it must surely be the wine-growing community, and no one was in much of a hurry to relinquish the shade of our awning that afternoon.) The other burning issue in each of these exchanges was the great *palissage* debate: to raise or not to raise it. Everyone agreed that the vines were growing at the rate of about four centimetres a day and badly needed support. Opinions, however, differed on the risk that hoisting up the wires might shake away the latest application of sulphur dust. Decisive as always, Virgile concluded that there was only one solution in such temperatures: a second beer.

'Rather bad luck for you,' he commiserated, as he handed me my refill. 'With all those late-planted trees.'

As if I needed reminding about my twice-daily watering struggles! So, to shift the focus back to someone else's problems, I asked why his spraying goes on so long.

'It has to be repeated every ten days or so,' he sighed. 'Much easier, if you're non-organic. Systemic fungicides last the whole year but the organic treatments are only good for about a week and a half – even less, if there's any significant rainfall.'

'If only,' I think to myself, as I set off home to the evening watering cans.

'Sparkling wine was invented in Limoux in 1531,' said Manu, determined to prove that Krystina didn't have a monopoly on dates. 'Well, here in the Abbey of Saint Hilaire to be more exact,' he added as he fanned himself with his baseball cap.

We were resting in the welcome shade of the abbey cloister, enjoying a picnic lunch, after driving as far as the yellow broom-filled hills and lush green valleys to the south of Carcassonne. The picnic had been assembled by me, having learned from experience that it was well worth getting up half an hour earlier to avoid Mme Gros's packed rations. I think she regards a sandwich filling as an opportunity to clear her fridge.

'It was all thanks to an early spring,' Manu elaborated. 'The monastery wines started fizzing of their own accord, in their stoppered jugs.'

As he helped himself to thirds of salami and another foaming glass of the oddly named Blanquette de Limoux that we had purchased on the way, I began to suspect further hours in the village library.

'So how come everyone outside the Languedoc gives the credit to a different monk – Dom Pérignon, in Champagne, in the following century?' I challenged him.

'Ah,' said Manu, as we hit the buffers of his historical knowledge. 'Good question.'

'Ah,' echoes Jean-Pierre Cathala at the Caves des Sieurs d'Arques, on the outskirts of Limoux, an hour later. 'Good question.'

The PR man for this huge and highly sophisticated co-operative has just done an Internet search for an answer. The best that he has come up with is a claim that the same (necessarily long-lived) Dom Pérignon invented the process here in 1531 and then took the recipe up to Champagne a hundred and thirty years later. Monsieur Cathala seems quite satisfied with this, being far too busy promoting the story of 1531 to worry overmuch about its verification (as indeed might we be, if we had marketing responsibility for a thousand growers and five thousand hectares).

'Or maybe,' he suggests, as an afterthought, 'it was our monks who did the inventing, while others perfected the technology when corks and bottles arrived in the following century.'

This sounds potentially more plausible but I am still not sure that I entirely follow the point.

'You do understand how the "Champagne Method" works?' M. Cathala asks Manu who has been nodding sagely.

'Oh, indeed . . . One of the great methods,' he stumbles. 'But perhaps, for the benefit of my English friend . . .'

'All fermentations produce carbon dioxide,' M. Cathala obliges, as Manu assumes an attitude of bored all-knowingness. 'In a *Méthode Champenoise*, however, there's a secondary fermentation inside the corked bottle. The closed environment dissolves the carbon dioxide in the wine – from which it can only escape, in the form of bubbles, when the bottle's opened.' (Manu tries a 'couldn't have put it better myself' kind of expression.) 'Unfortunately, the secondary fermentation produces a sediment and it was certainly in Champagne that they found the technical solution to this.'

'It's called "riddling",' he adds, after an expectant pause. (Manu experiments with more of a 'tip of my tongue' sort of look.) 'In the 1810s, the Widow Cliquot discovered that, if you gradually twist and turn the bottle upside down, the sediment ends up in the neck. Then if you open it, the built-up pressure spits the sediment out and you can quickly top it up and recork.'

'All there is to it,' endorses Manu, with an improvised, two-handed gesture, which he hopes approximates to the requisite twisting and turning action.

'Of course, we no longer do it by hand,' says M. Cathala, deciphering Manu's semaphore. 'We've got mechanical riddlers, like mechanical most things. But come – I'll show you.'

It takes some time for us to tour the co-operative's impressively high-tech production line, from batteries of computer-controlled pneumatic grape-presses, through forests of temperature-regulated, stainless-steel fermentation vats, to a dazzling white laboratory full of gadgetry for every conceivable sophisticated analysis.

It takes almost as long for M. Cathala to outline the stringent quality controls that they impose on their members. At harvest time, for instance, they issue tickets authorizing the picking of particular *parcelles* on particular days. Anything brought in late is rejected, just as anything arriving in trailers loaded above a certain marked level (risking damage to the grapes and even premature fermentation) is automatically down-graded for *vin de pays*.

By the time we reach a line of curious, metal cage-like cubes – each about a metre and a half across, suspended at odd angles from metal stands and filled with scores of bottles of Blanquette – I have almost forgotten about Mme Cliquot and her clever idea.

'Riddling machines,' M. Cathala reminds me, as one of them gently rattles its way through a precisely timed and carefully measured partial rotation.

'But why *Blanquette*?' I ask, as we pass the impressive conveyor belt where the bottles will be automatically disgorged, replenished and recorked.

'Cos it's white, of course,' chimes in Manu, suddenly over-confident.

'Not exactly,' comes the mildest of put-downs. 'It's a local name for the principal grape variety – the Mauzac. Probably so called because of the fine white down on its leaves. Not that it's much known by any name outside Limoux,' he admits, with a smile.

He explains that the 1938 Blanquette *appellation* – almost the oldest in the Languedoc – allows the Mauzac to be blended with up to ten per cent of Chardonnay or Chenin, while a newer 1990 classification known as Crémant de Limoux permits up to twenty per cent of each of those *cépages*. In fact, he says, Chardonnay does exceptionally well here, as recognized by an even newer designation, called simply Limoux, introduced in 1993 – apparently the only *appellation* for pure Chardonnay in the whole of the Languedoc.

'We mature the Chardonnays in oak,' he tells us, as we enter what is apparently almost a kilometre of underground barrel-lined galleries. 'But these are the cream,' he announces proudly, as we reach a perceptibly smarter tunnel, 'the Tocques et Clochers.'

He was expecting even us to have heard of the co-operative's most ambitious marketing idea but he quickly resigns himself to further explanations.

'First we choose the best grower, or just occasionally two of them – with the best *parcelles* – from each of our villages. We supervise the production of a couple of exceptional barrels from each. Look, this one's from Saint Hilaire, for instance. It's the first time this chap's been selected. His predecessor no longer wanted to work within our extra-rigorous quality controls for these special wines. Anyway, we auction the results on the Sunday before Easter every year. Wine merchants and restaurateurs come from all over the world. But not just for the Chardonnays. There's also a gala dinner cooked by a celebrity chef – that's the *Tocque* bit, the chef's traditional tall white hat. The auction proceeds go to a different Limoux wine village each year – to be used for the restoration of its bell-tower . . .'

'The *Clocher*,' says Manu, catching on faster than usual.

'*Voilà*,' endorses M. Cathala. 'But there's a small catch for the village that's about to benefit. On the day preceding the auction, it has to host the biggest street-party-cum-wine-tasting you've ever seen. More than twenty thousand visitors descending on a village of maybe seven hundred and fifty inhabitants.'

'Ah well, all in a good cause,' says Manu, as he tries to remember whether Easter will be early next year.

I do not linger over my goodnights.

Manu may not be the Languedoc's greatest mental arithmetician but, when Jean-Pierre Cathala excused himself to meet a Canadian television crew, he could swiftly calculate the eighty minutes remaining before the co-operative's tasting counter closed. And his insistence on putting them to productive use made the little red van's return not just long and hot but also terrifying.

I stagger exhaustedly indoors for some water and am halfway to the kitchen tap when I am hit by a sense that something has changed. Something outside is not quite as I left it.

I return to the courtyard, wondering what it was that I dimly noticed in my haste. The fountain is still bubbling away. The outdoor dining table and chairs are still in their places, the arcade as shady as ever, the garden the same half-tidied semi-chaos . . . And then I see it.

On the hillside to the south-east of the house, there is an entirely new building. I am certain it wasn't there when I was having my breakfast on the balcony terrace. But it's there now – a huge, metal, barn-like structure, the walls painted sandy brown and the roof sandy pink in perfunctory imitation of the traditional local stones and terracottas. Now that I think about it, I have been vaguely aware of some tree-felling and earth-moving activity up there over the last few days. I just innocently assumed that someone was preparing the terrain for some new vineyard or olive grove, never dreaming that a pre-fabricated eyesore of indeterminate function was about to shatter forever the fragility of paradise.

June

I WAS TOO TIRED to investigate the monstrous new blot on my landscape last night. I went straight to bed before it was even fully dark but immediately my imagination raced into frenzied overdrive. All sorts of alarmingly plausible explanations chased one another through my semi-conscious dreams, lurching luridly from the noisy to the noisome. I woke, convinced that any hopes of future peace or beauty had been shattered, and went outside for a better look from one of the higher terraces behind the house. And there I found Manu up even earlier, inspecting the ripeness of my apricots.

'Goats,' he said, pointing to the barn. 'Owned by a complete rogue, as well,' he added, more cheerfully than I felt the situation warranted.

Just my luck, I thought. Both noisy and noisome.

'Didn't he need planning permission?' I asked, as if the situation might still be reversed.

'Even rogues can book tables in the Mayor's favourite res-

taurants,' he answered. 'But listen, I've an idea to cheer you up
– the Feria down at Nîmes. I was supposed to be taking the
wife this evening but her back's playing her up. No good at all
on those benches.'

'Benches?'

'You'll see.'

'She won't mind my going with you?'

'I wasn't going to tell her,' he whispered conspiratorially. 'But
then I thought, if you sent her some flowers for her sickbed?
Your roses being so much more plentiful than mine . . .'

I left Manu stripping my rosebeds and went down to the
château to see whether Krystina knew anything more about
the goat farm. She didn't but, predictably, she did know a lot
about Nîmes and, as soon as she knew I was heading that way,
she insisted on a little 'preparation' over coffee and croissants.
The founding by the Romans I knew about but not the Wars of
Religion.

'Nîmes was a major Protestant stronghold,' she explained,
piling Sèvres porcelain carelessly on to a tray, 'and consequently, the scene of a major massacre of Catholics in 1567.'

'I always thought of Protestantism as more of a northern,
cool-climate religion,' I remarked, as Krystina squeezed herself
on to the tiny gilt-legged sofa where I was already sitting.

'Well, they certainly flourished in the heat of the
Languedoc,' she resumed, moving closer still to accommodate
her coffee cup on a minute expanse of cream-coloured damask
behind her. 'Three-quarters of the population of Nîmes went
over to Calvinism. Or Huguenotism, as the French variety
called itself. And when they'd done enough damage in Nîmes,
they quickly found other places for a scrap. They even attacked
our own dear Lodève in 1572.' Krystina's coffee cup wobbled
dangerously as the drama heightened. 'The Bishop and most
of the local nobility were forced to seek refuge in – would you
believe it? – this very château!'

Carried away by the excitement of the village's hour of fame, her hand descended on my thigh in a gesture of emphasis that suddenly turned the delicate damask coffee-coloured.

'Never mind, I was getting tired of it,' she muttered non-chalantly.

Manu was right. Driving into Nîmes in full Feria fettle, the miseries of life in goatland do seem very far away. As do the austerities of Calvinism.

Manu's choice of festive attire had set the tone before we left. It would, of course, take more than the Feria for him to dispense with his trademark blue dungarees and red baseball cap. However, today the overalls are disguised beneath a multi-coloured Hawaiian beach shirt and brightly spotted necker-chief – the striking *ensemble* only slightly marred by the fact that he must have purchased the shirt when he was several sizes slimmer.

I have rarely seen so many people so single-mindedly intent on enjoying themselves. As the little red van searches for a parking space in the heart of the city, it seems that almost every centimetre of the city's broad pavements has been filled by temporary terrace restaurants – surely more than even these hungry hordes can collectively hope to patronize. And every-where there is music, sometimes piped and sometimes live but always competitively loud to drown the efforts of neighbour-ing revels.

It is only as we start our third and slowest crawl around the city centre (we should never have ignored the invitation to 'park and ride' from the outskirts but Manu knew best) that I notice the unmistakable Spanish air of the festival banners stretching between the plane trees. Huge, shallow cooking pans of bright yellow paella outside the pavement restaurants reinforce the Spanish flavour, as we proceed on foot (Manu having barged his way into a space to which a timid tourist had a better claim). The same could even be said for much of the music, in so far as anything much can be distinguished in the general cacophony.

It is all very surprising, so far from the Pyrenees. But then comes the biggest surprise of all. The highlight of our day – Manu can keep his secret no longer – turns out to be a bullfight. And that, of course, is why the banners looked so Spanish. Half of them were covered with images of bulls and matadors.

Bullfighting is something over which I always assumed the Spanish had a monopoly but *La Corrida* turns out to be very big in Nîmes. Indeed, it is difficult to believe that the streets are still so populated when we see the crowd that has already flocked in its smartest festival best to the well-preserved Roman arena, which serves as the city's bullring.

Manu's tickets indicate that we are destined for a section of the arena unpromisingly billed as the *Vomitoire*. Knowing how reluctantly he and his money are parted, I have visions of somewhere vertiginous at the top of the steeply tiered banks of seating. However, his absent consort must have insisted on the best because the minute section of hard wooden bench reserved for us is remarkably close to the action.

'Got the tickets from a chap called Luc,' says Manu. 'Oh, but you know him, I think. Didn't he sell you a truffle? Thought so, yes, amazing fellow, Luc. Nothing the blighter can't track down, if the price is right. But then, you see, he's owed me a favour or two, since the winter . . .'

Our seats may be close to the action but they are a long way from the nearest entrance staircase, so we have to squeeze past a tightly packed selection of Nîmes' plumper citizens before we can reach them.

'*Les coups de pied sont gratuits chez vous?*' protests one of the plumpest, when Manu trips and kicks her in the back.

Apparently, the distinctive combination of dungarees and beach shirt have set him apart as an outsider – or maybe it's just the company he keeps. In any event, Manu's grudging apologies are drowned by the opening fanfare.

In the rush to get here, there was very little time to consider how I felt about my first bullfight. I didn't even know whether it was part of the Nîmes tradition to kill the bulls; but some twenty minutes into the proceedings, the answer becomes bloodily clear.

Manu is appalled – not by the killing but by the unpardonable ineptitude of the first matador's performance.

'Mere embroidery,' he snorts at the Spaniard's clumsy business with sword and cape. 'The woman on the meat counter at Hyper U could do better.'

Not only a vociferously opinionated commentator, he is also uncompromisingly biased.

'You'll soon see how things ought to be done,' he nudges me as a strikingly handsome young matador takes his turn in the arena. 'Sébastien Castella,' he explains excitedly. 'He's only nineteen and he's from our *département*. Well, all right, he lives near Seville now but he was born in Béziers.'

Manu rises wheezily to his feet to applaud his undisputed *'héro de l'Hérault'*. However, to my puzzlement, Castella has hardly started engaging his first bull before Manu starts jeering with all the volume that his smoker's lungs permit.

'*Honteux!* . . . *Scandaleux!* . . . *Execrable!* . . .'

The strident derision continues unabated while the slender youth faces five hundred and fifty kilos of opponent with what, to my untutored eye, seem entirely admirable bravery and skill. Only belatedly, as the beast slumps lifeless to the sand, do I realize that it was the bull, not the boy, that was the object of this scorn – the two of them regarded by the crowd in general as equally important and equally judgeable competitors, albeit with subtly unequal life expectancies. But now, as suddenly as the hero's sword pierced the animal's heart, Manu's limited lungpower joins the cheers of an ecstatic crowd. A red baseball cap soars skywards, while jubilant white handkerchiefs are waved all round the arena, and for this signal of universal approbation, Castella is awarded one of the little-lamented bull's ears to decorate some remote Sevillian mantelpiece.

What Manu needs, of course, is more informed opposition than I can hope to offer, with which to argue the merits of the matadors and the aptitude of the animals long after the event has ended. And so it is that a succession of innocent strangers, who might have had other plans for their evening, find themselves embroiled in a series of fierce-fought controversies in the streets and bars surrounding the arena, before Manu will at last contemplate dinner. He then insists on one of the bargain pavement paellas and a giant jug of Sangria, at a table as close as possible to the brass band so that we can be as close as possible to its accompanying trio of tight-T-shirted gogo girls. I can therefore scarcely hear his 'Never think this used to be a Huguenot city, would you?'

'Too puritanical for wine, I suppose, the Protestants?' I shout back hoarsely.

'They needed it for communion,' I can just about lip-read. 'And not just for the priests, for everyone.'

'But social drinking?' I yell back at him.

'Mr Killjoy, Calvin,' is I think what Manu replies. 'Told his followers it was a sin to buy a round of drinks!'

A man after your own heart, I reflect, as the bill lands on my side of the table and Manu leads me off to discover the Feria nightlife in earnest.

I wake with a profound sense that I have discovered enough nightlife in a single night to last me the remainder of the year.

Having persuaded me that there could be no question of driving home when the festivities finally calmed down around four in the morning, Manu had booked us a hotel, which was

firmly at the wrong end of the budget category. (I think it was
the derelict awning flapping outside my window that woke me
but it might equally have been someone cursing the discomfort
of the beds on the other side of the paper-thin walls.) However,
at least Manu decided that sharing a room would be one
economy too far and I thus remain innocent of all that lies
beneath the blue dungarees.

When I cross the corridor to check on his welfare, I find him
unable to face daylight, let alone breakfast, until I have been
out to buy him a pair of the biggest and darkest sunglasses
known to Nîmes. He groans wretchedly when I remind him
that we have only half an hour to get to our rendezvous in the
Costières de Nîmes, outside the city. He winces painfully at the
crunch of the gravel when we turn into the picturesque courtyard of the Château Mourgues du Grès. He then squints in
bemusement at the motto on a sundial, set high on a sun-
drenched wall: 'SINE SOLE NIHIL'.

'Nothing without sun,' says Anne Collard, the slim, smartly
dressed young woman who comes out to greet us, with hardly
a hint of disbelief at the outsized sunglasses and the paella-
stained Hawaiian shirt which are steadying themselves
against a balustrade. 'It's been there since the Revolution but
we took it as our logo. It so much expresses our philosophy, our
aim of capturing all the intensity of the purest, sun-ripened
fruit . . . But is your friend all right?' she hesitates.

The buzzing of the cicadas in the late morning heat isn't
helping Manu's headache.

'Perhaps he'd prefer the *salon* to the tasting room?' she offers
as, with saintly generosity, she ushers the grubby overalls on
to a comfortable white sofa. '*Mourgues* was a Provençal name
for Ursuline nuns,' she resumes, assembling six or seven different Costières de Nîmes on a coffee table. 'The farm belonged
to a convent over near Beaucaire.'

'And *Grès*? That's a kind of sandstone, isn't it?' I ask, more to drown the muffled moaning from the sofa than to prove how much I remember from my Saint Chinian geology course.

'Exactly. But you must have seen the most distinctive feature of these vineyards, driving in – the *galets*, the lovely rounded pebbles? Did you notice the colours? From golden yellow, through pink to red? Well, it's after them that we've named our first three wines – the freshest, fruitiest white, *rosé* and red – "Les Galets Dorés", "Les Galets Roses" and "Les Galets Rouges".'

Her pouring of the first of these is eyed by Manu with unprecedented wariness. For a moment I think he is about to decline but, heroically, he stiffens his resolve and visibly wills himself to lift the glass.

'The *galets* make wonderful storage heaters,' she enthuses, as she lines up some *rosé* beside the white. 'Absorbing sunshine by day and reflecting it back on to the grapes at night. They're unique to the Costières de Nîmes, washed all the way down here from the Alps by the Rhône.'

'You're only a couple of miles from the Rhône, aren't you?' I ask, the burden of small talk falling to me, as Manu conserves his limited powers of speech for a whispered '*Juste un petit peu*' at the approach of the Galets Rouges.

'Yes, in many ways we feel more a part of Provence and the Côtes du Rhône than the Languedoc. You'd even see the Mont Ventoux from the top of our slopes, if it weren't for the heat haze.'

'So are your slopes quite high?' I ask prosaically, finding it difficult to scintillate with Manu muttering prayers for deliverance to the elegant, vaulted ceiling.

'A *costière*'s a pretty gentle sort of slope,' she replies. 'Although our own are steeper than most. Thirty hectares in all, with the different *cépages* spread around as much as possible for maximum complexity. But the wines from this *parcelle* are the richest, the most concentrated,' she says, as she pours a second white labelled 'Terre d'Argence'. 'Older vines, for one thing.'

Virgile told me it was only in 1990 that Madame Collard's husband François bottled his first vintage, with serious quantities starting only in 1993, which doesn't suggest great age. However, she explains that the estate was originally bought by her father-in-law back in 1963.

'He never bothered with bottling his wine. He sold it all in bulk to a *négociant* – the old-fashioned way,' she adds, as her Terre d'Argence red follows its sibling. 'Yet in some respects he was very much ahead of his time. He ripped up all his Aramon and replanted with Syrah and Grenache, long before most people. And of course, long before François got involved.'

'Armed with the younger generation's traditional oenology diploma, I assume?'

'Actually, François studied agricultural engineering. Have a look at his *palissage* when you leave,' she laughs. 'It shows! He'll be out there now, making some precision adjustment . . .'

'No, he's not,' says a wiry, energetic-looking figure, entering from the courtyard, in neat navy-blue shorts and a matching polo shirt.

Virgile also mentioned that, for five years after university, François Collard wrote for a wine magazine called *La Vigne*, but he looks more like a military fitness instructor than either journalist or wine-maker.

'Ah, you've reached the "Capitelles",' he notes, as his wife prepares to introduce us to their most prestigious red. 'We first made this in 1998,' he explains. 'From our best, lowest-yielding vines and aged in oak for twelve months.'

He notices that Manu now has his head rather than his glass in his hands.

'You've come from the Feria?' he asks intuitively. 'Everyone's first image of Nîmes! It's why they changed the name from Costières du Gard in 1989, three years after the *appellation*

started. More festive,' he declares, as his wife pours some particularly festive measures.

'I think I want to go home,' whimpers Manu miserably
beside me.

'I don't care how hot it is, you have to come and see the
flowers,' said Virgile's mid-morning summons.

I had been sitting in the only patch of shade by the pool,
trying to persuade myself that the gently tinkling goat bells
on the hill in front of me were sufficiently romantic to compensate for my view of their distinctly unromantic residence.
And surely, I told myself, it couldn't be long before the scent
of the lavender bushes on the terraces leading up to the courtyard behind me was strong enough to drown the farmyard
smells drifting down towards me on the southerly wind.
Maybe the insomniac goat-dog would even stop barking
through the night, when he was a bit more used to living
here.

I had also been struggling to convince myself that the pleasure of plunging into refreshingly cool water would outweigh
the murky greenness of the still unpurified pool. Yet it was
simply too hot to think my way through the challenge of cleaning it.

So Virgile's hectares of glorious blossom promised welcome
relief.

However, as I soon discovered on arrival, there is nothing
heart-stoppingly glorious about a Grenache Noir flower. I am
more than willing to believe its importance in the calendar –
the success of the early summer flowering determining the
potential size of the autumn crop. But it is unlikely to attract
the coachloads of admirers that flock to the bulbfields of
Holland. There is not a petal to be seen – just some tiny clus-
ters of rather dismal-looking yellow stamens around some
equally uninspiring little green pods.

'Isn't the scent amazing?' exclaims Virgile. 'And every grape variety different.'

I thrust my nose deep into the foliage to try to distinguish some sort of perfume.

'This is perfect weather for the flowering,' he enthuses, as he checks on progress farther along. 'Windless and warm. Just as long as it doesn't get any hotter, that is. Or a lot colder or wetter. No, you laugh, but this is really the most critical time of the year. Cold, damp weather could shrivel the infant berries and wind, hail, even heavy rain could destroy them altogether.'

The catalogue of potential disasters is interrupted by the buzzing of the mobile telephone in Virgile's trouser pocket.

'He's accepted my offer,' he says jubilantly when the call is finished. 'Oh, but I haven't told you, have I? I found this amazing load of second-hand equipment. It belonged to a grower, down past Clermont, who's gone bust. The liquidator wanted the whole lot cleared as fast as possible. He's just agreed a ridiculously low price, on condition that I take everything. A pump, a cooling machine . . .'

'Not really your style is it, bric-à-brac?'

'Listen, this is a good deal, even if only a quarter of it works!'

'And if it all works?' I ask unhelpfully. 'Where on earth will you put it?' (It must be the heat that is making me so negative this morning.)

'You're right, I hadn't thought of that.' His features cloud for an instant then brighten again. 'My friend Olivier will have to act as a storage depot,' he declares. 'There's plenty of space at Mas Jullien!'

'Is that where you trained?'

'Immediately before Chile, yes. We've remained good friends, forever swapping ideas and experience.'

'So what does Olivier think about the sales strategy?' I ask, as we return to our vehicles.

Virgile has already told me that a certain Philippe Puech, one of the region's top wholesalers, based in Nîmes, has offered him an attractive price for the whole of his production. The snag, however, is that 'whole' means 'whole'. He insists on one hundred per cent exclusivity, which Virgile is reluctant to give.

'Olivier says it would be a sell-out. He's been courted by Puech himself. Taken out to two magnificent dinners. Thousands of francs worth of wine opened. But he still said "no".'

'He should have said "maybe". There might have been a third dinner!'

'I really can't make up my mind,' worries Virgile. 'It's very tempting – the idea of a single, painless lorry-load taking all my marketing problems away. But would places like Le Pressoir still be willing to buy from Nîmes?'

'And there's my own important order. Not to mention Sarah's,' I tease him.

'I'll try to find a way,' he answers, with a hasty farewell handshake to mask the involuntary twinkle in his eye.

'The weather's not getting any wetter, is it?' puffed Mme Vargas when I met her pushing her wheelbarrow up the lane towards her terraces. It was loaded with a pair of watering cans and I thought at first that she must have been ferrying supplies from their house in the village. The cans, however, were empty. 'We're lucky,' she said. 'We've got a little spring up here. But the trouble is, it's not so fast at this time of year. You have to lean a long way down to reach the water. And you see, that's how Albert lost his balance.'

I had been wondering what new calamity could account for M. Vargas's absence. Now I knew.

'Nothing broken,' she assured me. 'Just a little concussed. I'm sure he'll be up and about by this time next week.'

I offered to help but she wouldn't hear of it. She said I must have quite enough watering problems of my own and, of course, she was absolutely right. I am seldom seen these days without either a hose or a watering can in my hand. The heat has turned irrigation into an almost all-consuming pastime. Indeed, I now walk quite absurd distances to empty half-drunk jugs, even glasses of water, on to whichever roots are currently looking the most desperate.

It has been bad enough over recent weeks, with my round-the-clock life-support system confined to those dangerously late-planted fruit trees. However, the last few days have started to see widespread wilting and even a few fatalities amongst many of the longer-established specimens.

I started the year with the naïve assumption that Uncle Milo would have chosen only plants that would cheerfully survive whatever dearth of rainfall the Languedoc summer might choose to inflict on them. I now realize a little too late that, although they are clearly some of the longest-suffering species known to Europe, they are not designed for the desert.

I ought not to be surprised. After all, I knew from the outset that there were water pipes running everywhere on the more cultivated of Uncle Milo's terraces and they had to be there for a purpose. It's just that I haven't had time to fathom which of the countless taps and valves were supposed to make them work, and every time I experimented it seemed to cut off the house supply for long periods afterwards, so I rather gave up. But now I really ought to try again.

I am having to grapple with other temperature-related changes of routine as well. The mornings are now so hot that, once the sun has risen, even breakfast is unthinkable on the sun-baked balcony outside my bedroom, so I have moved the little table down to the generous shade of one of the cherry trees, which seems at least to catch more breeze than the larger dining table under the main courtyard arcades. In the evenings, even the heartiest red wines need chilling to bring them down to popular conceptions of room temperature. Then at night, it is almost impossible to sleep until the small hours and I wake again as soon as the sun starts rising. Perhaps an afternoon siesta is the only solution.

I am, however, still not waking early enough to get to my apricot trees before Manu. He was there on my doorstep again this morning, with another not especially large basket of slightly underripe fruit.

'It's a very small crop, all across the *département*,' he assured me, as I wondered how long it would be before Mme Gros appeared with another diminutive mustard pot of her 'home-grown' jam.

Then, foolishly, I left my modest share of the harvest to ripen to perfection in a china bowl in the courtyard and returned after an hour or two of watering to find them literally baked by the sunshine.

'I'm not ready,' said Virgile, looking more fraught than I have ever seen him when I arrived at the *cave* in the early afternoon. 'I'm not at all ready. And I've been waiting two hours for this electrician.'

We were supposed, at last, to be bottling the first of his wines but it seems that nothing can proceed without the electrician and, more importantly, his fuse.

'I was worried this morning that the pump on my second-hand bottling machine might be a bit rough – might shake the wine up too much,' he explained, pulling anxiously at his normally neat black curls. 'So the electrician helped me adapt it to use my normal pump instead. Then five minutes after he left, the fuse blew. And it's a very specialist kind of fuse. So I'm stuck here waiting for the electrician to come back.'

'Is it urgent now, the bottling?' I asked.

'Only in the sense that I seem to have wasted the whole week, putting it off with one problem after another. And the minor detail that I need to get some money into my bank account. But every day's getting hotter and this is a job we'll simply have to do with the doors open, for sheer lack of space.'

'But apart from that, how are things?'

'Apart from that, I'm completely overwhelmed. So much grass to be dealt with in the fields. So much spraying needed everywhere . . . I haven't been near my vines at Nébian for a fortnight.'

'Out of sight, out of mind?'

'Exactly. I really ought to be down there now. Instead, I've got Matthieu rolling up any minute to help and no machine.'

The arrival of the other conscript has, however, had slightly more success in diverting Virgile's attention from his troubles. We are still waiting for the electrician but at least we are waiting behind a glass of cold beer at one of Le Pressoir's pavement tables on the other side of the square.

'*Mais, qu'est-ce que c'est?*' asks Pius when he notices that Virgile has set up a brightly painted antique pump and decorative barrel or two outside his cave, as if to attract the attention of potential passing trade. 'Anyone would think you had something to sell!'

It would be fair to say that Pius finds this considerably funnier than Virgile. He continues chuckling away contentedly for some minutes, while Virgile simmers.

Matthieu is far too busy to notice. He is trying to talk Marie-Anne into booking a jazz band that he plays in. (A guitarist first and itinerant cellar assistant second, it seems.) Marie-Anne, however, is only interested in booking a waiter for the evening service.

'Permanently sick, the other one,' she grumbles despairingly, as she joins us. 'But the law says we still have to keep him on. I tell you, you have to be mad to run a business in this country!'

Matthieu suggests the names of a couple of 'resting' musicians that she could try but there are no takers at our table.

'So what about this Puech character?' I ask, in an effort to distract Virgile. 'Are you really going to sell everything to Nîmes?'

'I still can't decide,' he says, conspicuously undistracted. 'At the moment, I'm more against than for. But we'll see . . .'

Eventually, he decides to send Matthieu away until tomorrow, which is just as well, as the church clock is already chiming four when the electrician breezes nonchalantly into the *cave*. He whistles equally unconcernedly as he proceeds to check every fuse and wire in the apparatus. This takes him a considerable time, partly because he is in no discernible hurry and partly because there seem to be enough wires and fuses in this machine for a small sub-station. Virgile remains diplomatically silent but alternate glances at me and his watch are becoming ever more eloquently anxious.

'Twenty-eight degrees,' he reports, having checked on the thermometer that he left outside in a shady corner of the square.

Then, just as the electrician announces to Virgile's dismay that he has put all the wiring back where it originally belonged, thus obliging us to revert to the suspect pump on the machine itself, Pius pops a mischievous head round the door.

'Fifty francs a case,' he says, with the straightest of faces. 'My final offer.'

'That wouldn't even pay for the corks!' Virgile manages to laugh.

Pius has, however, already disappeared, leaving the two of us to discover slowly and depressingly that the electrician's long and complicated efforts have been entirely in vain. The original pump doesn't work. It was the one part of the apparatus that Virgile never tested because he never intended to use it.

'And before you ask, yes, it was part of what you call my bric-à-brac.'

His good humour is starting to crack.

Unperturbed, the electrician launches himself into another jaunty round of whistling, as he contemplates a possible 'Plan C'. Virgile looks more and more tense, his black eyebrows somehow blacker, the birthmark above them more brooding, as he registers an even more depressing external temperature of thirty. Finally, many popular *chansons* later, the electrician finds a way of reconnecting to the superior pump, whilst bypassing the circuitry that was fusing the bottling machine.

'It will be safe, won't it?' asks Virgile cautiously. He is only prepared to suffer so far for his product.

'No problem,' says the electrician, as he waves goodbye, but sadly his words prove over-optimistic. The pump works well enough: no more fuses blowing or anything of that sort. There is a subtler difficulty hidden behind all these pump-related obstacles. The twelve different nozzles on the bottling machine have a regrettable tendency to fill the bottles at twelve different levels. And as Virgile says, customers typically expect each bottle to contain an *exact* seventy-five centilitres, not just an average of that volume, spread across a case.

Half an hour later, the problem is still defeating us. Virgile says he will try again, when it is cooler after dinner, but he is more or less resigning himself to yet another deferral of tomorrow's projected labours, when Marie-Anne appears at the door.

'Are you sure you wouldn't like an evening's waiting work?' she teases. 'Given that you haven't achieved anything else today.'

There is nothing else for it. I shall have to clean the pool. It is too slimy and slippery to be safe, let alone pleasant, yet the weather is now too hot to remain sane for long without it.

However, before I can clean the pool, I need to empty it. I have concluded that this will mean some sort of siphoning arrangement with a hose. But it seems a criminal waste just to pour the water down the hill when I am surrounded by so much thirsty vegetation, clamouring for a passing can. Yet I can think of no other way and am just at the undignified moment of putting the end of the bright green hosepipe to my lips to suck up enough water to get the process working, when Manu appears again.

'I'm not sure you ought to drink that,' he says, with his usual lack of surprise at the eccentricities of the English.

'It's a siphon,' I bristle defensively. 'I'm emptying the pool.'

'Isn't the pump eco-friendly enough?' he laughs.

'What pump?' I ask, after another more determined suck.

'Dear, oh dear,' he sighs and he leads me patiently to a conical fir tree on the far side of the pool, behind which is a little stone enclosure with a little stone roof and under that a pump. 'It pumps the water out of your pool and into your watering system,' says Manu. ' I thought you knew that.'

He remembers that the power switch is handily placed a hundred metres away in the submarine control room (where else?) but sadly he has no clear recollection as to which of several possibilities it might be. So as I run to and fro to monitor the pump's continuing failure to respond, Manu fiddles randomly with switches and levers, leaving me wondering how many of the house's vital functions will have been immobilized in the process. Then at last there is a dull, grinding rumble from the pump, accompanied by a volley of constipated gurglings in all directions, as multiple airlocks are cleared and miscellaneous sprinklers splutter into hesitant life.

Despite prolonged disuse, the system seems to work remarkably well. I shall no doubt be able to target it much more effectively when I have mastered all its various taps and valves. I also suspect that a few hours with a bicycle repair kit will be needed to tackle some of the unintended sprays that must have been caused by winter frosts. But all in all, Uncle Milo seems to have done a remarkably good job.

Except, that is, for one detail.

Well, to be fair, I can hardly hold my ancestor responsible. A man can only foresee so much. And he doubtless had his reasons for installing one of the more vigorous *jets d'eau* immediately beside the principal flowerbed. It is just exceptionally unlucky that Mme Gros should have chosen this particular moment – while Manu and I were otherwise distracted – to set about filling her trug with my lavender crop. There really is no way that Uncle Milo could have predicted just how thoroughly soaked she would appear, as she bears down on me.

But I fear it may be some time before I am forgiven.

I didn't think I had ever seen Virgile looking so happy. He danced a quick, involuntary dance of joy. '*C'est fini! C'est mis en bouteille!*' he whooped ecstatically.

It had been three days' work to produce two thousand bottles of Coteaux du Languedoc, a thousand of Vin de Pays de l'Hérault, and precisely 564 (I had had the job of counting them) of Cartagène. Each bottle was distinctively printed with his flourishing signature, each cork distinctively stamped down its side and all of them had been lovingly fork-lifted to the security of his lock-up garage around the corner.

'But what's happened to the tractor and all the spraying machines?' I had asked when Virgile first opened the unexpectedly empty garage.

'I've moved them. I've managed to borrow a sheep-shed on the edge of the village, from the Poujols brothers. Do you remember? The eighty-year-olds I told you about who made their own wine in bulk for a wholesaler? Well, they own half the village. Far more than they need for their own operation.'

But for all this expansion of Virgile's territory, the bottling process had been resolutely rudimentary, the continuing recalcitrance of last week's machinery necessitating simpler equipment and a hastily assembled chain gang of five.

Virgile himself had been pumping the wine into a funnel at the top of a manually operated bottle-filler, borrowed from his friend Laurent. Arnaud, a lanky young apprentice electrician, filling time before a 'real job', had been energetically unpacking the bottles and loading them on to a ledge located lower down the machine. Régine, a boisterous, belly-laughing amazon from the village, had been squirting the required amounts of wine from the machine's four udder-like nozzles, then passing the bottles down the line to Sandrine, a sylph-like would-be actress, reluctantly 'resting' in Saint Saturnin. Sandrine in turn had been sweeping up the bottles with one outstretched, actressy hand, feeding corks into a separate machine with the other and somehow – through mysterious sleight of hand – finding a third to pass the rapidly finished results back to me. And then I had been grappling with the subtler challenges of juggling them back inside the polythene and cardboard packaging that Arnaud had over-zealously ripped open at the start of the chain.

Whenever the pumping permitted, Virgile had darted across to check the levels in the bottlenecks with a millilitre-accurate measure.

'I don't want to rob my customers,' he laughed, 'but with my cash flow, I can't afford to be generous either!'

But generous is exactly what he seems to be feeling, now that we have scrubbed everything clean.

'Lunchtime,' he announces. 'We're going to a new place in Montpeyroux. L'Horloge, it's called. Jean-Marc, the owner, is going to sell my wine, so he must be good!'

A few minutes later, on a doorstep just across from the Montpeyroux clock tower, after which his establishment is named, the new restaurateur wipes his hands on the food-stained apron that covers his sweat-stained T-shirt and baggy shorts before greeting us one by one. The stresses of restaurant-opening have clearly left no time for shaving for a day or two, but the warmest of smiles shines from his face.

'Just as well we didn't dress up,' whispers Sandrine with a nudge towards the *patron*.

'We're not yet officially open,' Jean-Marc explains as he leads us inside. 'A little technical problem with the safety certificates unfortunately. So I told Virgile he could have either the chef or the waitress.'

Virgile's choice becomes immediately apparent, as an exceptionally glamorous young woman glides mannequin-like down a spiral staircase from the floor above.

'Céline's laid a table for you all upstairs in our little private dining room,' says Jean-Marc. 'It's more discreet,' he emphasizes, with an almost furtive glance towards the street.

The intimate private room is decorated in the same warm ochres and oranges as the larger space downstairs, while here and there some patches of antique blue-and-white wall-tiles appear to be pushing their way out from underneath the painted plaster. The whole effect looks expensively half-finished. It also feels enormously welcoming. The only problem is the heat. Jean-Marc is so concerned that our lunch should go undetected by passing safety inspectors that he insists on closing both the windows and the shutters overlooking the square below.

Jean-Marc is himself, I suspect, the principal sufferer from the heat. With only minimal advance preparation from the absent chef, he is in charge of the kitchen today. He is constantly dashing from there to the table and from the table to the wine cellar, while Céline shimmers round us, as cool as if she were on a catwalk.

'A little ginger-marinated tuna, I thought, to start with,' says Jean-Marc.

As Céline glides sinuously amongst us, distributing plates of glistening raw fish and crisp green salad leaves, our host smiles the beaming smile of a man who has already enjoyed a precautionary portion in the kitchen.

'*Et comme vin?*' Virgile interrupts his contentment.

'*T'as raison. J'arrive,*' says Jean-Marc, as he hurries off down the stairs, leaving Céline to strike a selection of decorative attitudes, while we wait for him to re-ascend with a bottle labelled 'Roucaillat'.

'I thought maybe this rather unusual white? It's a blend of Roussanne and Rolle,' he adds, wiping perspiration from behind his spectacles with the grubby-looking tea-towel permanently draped over one shoulder.

These would certainly be new *cépages* for me but Virgile spotted something that he thinks might be even more interesting on the way in. He is – happily for all of us – apparently incapable of leaving his perfectionism behind in the *cave* and treats us all to four magnificent courses, accompanied by four magnificent wines, each discussed in earnest detail with Jean-Marc before a final decision is taken. The more important the wine the more active Jean-Marc's tea-towel becomes. We can only hope that Céline will be drying the dishes.

Dish-drying would be one explanation of the waitress's periodic lengthy absences from the dining room but another occurs to me, when I notice that most of these disappearances coincide with Virgile's own absences from the table. Céline must be at least a foot taller than him but the last time that he excused himself I'm sure there was a particularly determined twinkle in his eye. And he can't be spending *all* this time negotiating increased overdraft facilities with his bank.

Jean-Marc happily takes over Virgile's place and glass, whenever they are unattended, so there is a considerable pause between our veal with its roasted Mediterranean vegetables and our goat's cheeses with their home-made fig *compôte*. And likewise between those and our *tarte aux abricots* with almond ice-cream.

With each new bottle, the repartee seems to get faster and the local accents more impenetrable, with even Virgile's normally negligible southern intonation starting to defeat me. I have been coping well enough with Arnaud's *'Tum'passesl'ping?'* when he needed some bread and Régine's *'N'yaplusd'ving!'* whenever a wine bottle was empty. But the final hour, over Jean-Marc's on-the-house *digestifs*, must be the severest test for my French since my encounter with Monsieur Mas.

'N'as pigé ri'ing,' laughs Régine, with a bruisingly matey punch to my ribs, as Virgile sketches me a map of a 'secret' route home by minor roads – unknown, he promises, even to the local traffic police.

Returning to the house in the late but still very hot afternoon, I can hardly wait to jump into my newly pristine pool. Without even going round to the courtyard to unlock, I run straight down the steps to the water, undressing as I go, and have already stripped to my underwear when I notice that I am being watched. There is a tall, sinister-looking figure looming behind the bank of blood-red roses that runs along the front of the courtyard.

'Bonsoir,' booms the unmistakable voice of Mme Gros.

Before I can recreate any semblance of decency, she is striding down through the terraces of lavender and rosemary towards the pool to regale me with the news that I have a problem.

'Listen,' she urges, with thinly concealed satisfaction, as I hastily tie my shirt into a makeshift sarong. 'Can't you hear them?'

Well, now that she mentions it, yes there is perhaps some unaccustomed competition for the everyday, omnipresent humming of the cicadas. A deeper, angrier kind of buzzing.

'I meant to mention it when I noticed it last month,' she apologizes unconvincingly. 'But as it is, I'm not sure you'd be wise to go inside.'

I am about to press her for more details when a rapid darkening of the sky provides me with all the explanation I need. A swarm of hundreds – thousands possibly – of bees swoops low above our heads and up through the rosebeds to the point where the roof juts out above my bedroom window. Most of them disappear immediately beneath the rooftiles but suffi-cient remain on the terracotta gutter to turn its shiny green glaze into a dull, pulsating yellow.

'A bees' nest,' says Mme Gros superfluously. 'And from what I can see, your bedroom is full of them. You won't be sleeping there for a while.'

July

'THEY'RE PROTECTED,' warned Mme Gros, when I suggested an insecticide the following morning. 'You'll have to call the beekeeper.'

'They're too far under the roof tiles,' said Monsieur Puylairol, when I persuaded him to come up from the village to take a reluctant look.

Even behind his all-enveloping mask, he seemed far more apprehensive in their company than I was. (The poor man really does need career-counselling.) But he assured me that the difficulty was purely technical.

'There's only a couple of centimetres between the tiles and your bedroom ceiling,' he said. 'It's impossible to remove the nest. You'll have to call the fire brigade.'

'Some people have all the luck,' said Krystina, when two

handsome teenagers leapt from the fire engine with a barrel of insecticide and started propping a ladder up against my bedroom window.

'But I thought they were protected,' I said to the youth who seemed to be in charge. 'I thought I wasn't allowed to kill them.'

'You're not but we are,' he informed me.

'So brave,' sighed Krystina wistfully, as she watched him pull a loose white space-suit over his tight blue uniform.

'Is this your bedroom under here?' asked the senior, more muscular fireboy, as he started drenching the roof with poison and Krystina calculated the plausibility of a second bees' nest in her own bedroom.

'Anywhere else you could spend the night?' asked the number two, as he set off to spray the house from the inside as well. 'They're going to be a bit upset for the next twenty-four hours but after that you'll be left in peace.'

I couldn't face another night in Mme Gros's spare bed but I wasn't sure that I dared face Krystina's invitation to the château either. My safely self-contained 'studio' seemed easily the least of the three available evils – even if every window had to be stiflingly sealed against airborne intruders. But this assessment survived little more than an hour of sweat and suffocation, and at dawn this morning, it is from one of Uncle Milo's threadbare deckchairs beside the pool that I observe Manu tiptoeing past for a little pre-breakfast 'thinning' of my vegetable patch.

I wait until he has gathered almost a basketful of my small, firm courgettes. Then just as he is about to make a start on the runner beans, I trumpet an unexpected *'Bonjour'* from half a metre behind him.

'Nom de Dieu, tu m'as fait sursauter!' he exclaims, as he drops the basket.

His precious pickings tumble over the edge of the terrace but he rapidly recovers his composure. 'I didn't like to wake you. But you see, the thing about courgettes is, the more you pick them, the more they grow. And I said to the wife, if someone doesn't get over there and do a bit of work, he'll have a terrace full of marrows and wonder why I didn't warn him.'

The landscape is changing.

As I drove down to meet Virgile on the edge of Saint Saturnin, I could see that everywhere the once individually discernible vines were merging into continuous rows of greenery. A closer inspection revealed youthful bunches already starting to ripen, as they turned from hard green pellets into something more convincingly grape-like. A few of the individual grapes were even beginning to change colour from green to black. Acidity levels inside them, Virgile explained, would be starting to diminish, with sugar levels rising.

You could be forgiven for thinking that nature rather than man was doing the work at this time of year, but not in Virgile's vineyard. According to him, there were now far too many leaves.

'It would have been better to leave those big outer ones,' he said, trying not to sound too dismayed at my first ten minutes of foliage-thinning.

'I thought we had to aerate the grapes,' I mumbled defensively, wondering why my uncompromising exposure of his youthful Syrah had failed to please. Hadn't he said that too much foliage harboured mildew and other diseases? Didn't he tell me it encouraged butterflies to come and breed their harmful vine worms? Surely, the more I stripped away, the healthier the crop would be.

'The grapes need shade as well as air,' he explained. 'Especially on the far side of the row, where the vine gets all the heat of the afternoon sun. But at least you've left those,' he consoled himself, as he peered over the top of the row.

Only because they were invisible, I thought to myself, as I massaged my aching back.

'Remember, it's sunlight on the leaves that ripens the grapes,' he continued. 'Not sunlight on the grapes. It's the leaves *underneath* the grapes that need to go. And those in the middle, of course. And even more importantly, the side shoots . . .'

So I had another go. Much more expertly, I thought. Plenty of shade. Plenty of material to ripen the grapes.

'But now you've left all these side shoots,' said Virgile, on his second inspection. 'Any shoot growing out from the base of a leaf-stem needs to go.'

'But these have all got grapes on them,' I protested. 'I left them deliberately.'

'They're not grapes, they're *grappillons*,' he said, leaving me little the wiser. 'They'll never ripen. So they need to come off. We have to focus all the energy on the proper bunches.'

The trouble was, the *grappillons* looked so much like grapes. Just a bit farther behind in their growth. So how could I be sure? Maybe anything on a side shoot had to be a *grappillon*.

'*Ça va, Patrick?*' called Régine mischievously from a couple of rows away, where her more experienced efforts had been winning greater approval. '*C'est simple, n'est-ce pas?*' she chuckled, as I braced myself for Virgile's third assessment.

But miraculously, it appears, I have finally got the balance right: well aerated shade and no *grappillons*.

'The butterflies won't like it one bit. They'll go straight to the neighbours!'

He smiles approvingly and we pause for some much-needed mineral water, splashing more of our precious rations than we can really afford over sweat-drenched necks and faces.

There is little sign of the weather cooling. Yesterday some anti-insect candles, left out on my terrace, melted into puddles in the afternoon sunshine. It was far too hot to sleep in the evening and I just sat in the pool with the water up to my chin and counted stars until a hint of a breeze made it possible to think of bed. It was consequently all I could do to keep this rendezvous at nine o'clock – but Virgile and Régine have been hard at work since six.

'I meant to tell you,' he says, as he steers us back to work. 'I've made the big decision. I've sold everything to Puech.'

'Hundred per cent?'

'Unfortunately. It was that or nothing. But the great thing is . . .'

I never learn about the great thing because he is interrupted by his mobile telephone – something that has happened every few minutes throughout the morning. Some of the callers are casual labourers whom he is trying to book for the *vendange* but most are simply suppliers letting him down: in this case, the supplier of his boxes, announcing another fortnight's delay. A compromise alternative design is suggested to speed things up but no, Virgile insists, he wants them to be perfect. He wants his distinctive signature printed on every box, just as it is on every bottle and cork.

'Maybe now you can see why I needed Puech,' he sighs, as he puts the phone back in his pocket. 'I haven't even time for the admin, let alone the sales side of this job.'

'Won't they let you keep anything, not even for friends?' I ask.

'Hardly anything for myself, even. But you and Sarah won't have to go as far as Nîmes. You'll be able to buy from Jean-Marc. His restaurant's a wine shop as well, you know . . .'

Virgile's final words are drowned by a crescendo of counting from Régine. ' . . . *neuf . . . dix . . . ONZE! Voilà, enfin, c'est fini!*'

She started downing tools as soon as Saint Saturnin's church clock started striking, having agreed to work until eleven. She was, however, forgetting a curious eccentricity of many of the local ecclesiastical timepieces. For reasons that no one has been able to explain to me, the clocks are programmed to duplicate the ringing of every hour. The first and second peals are exactly two minutes apart but opinion is divided as to which of them should be taken as the accurate time signal.

'The first is only a warning,' laughs Virgile. 'Still time for one more vine, Régine!'

'Indeed, why not finish the row?' I am starting to suggest, when a resounding '*Ta gueule!*' persuades me that Virgile's assistant will be sticking to the letter of her contract.

There is nothing like a white-knuckled motorway drive with Krystina to induce a sense of nostalgic regret for the days when there were only two ways to leave the Languedoc – either rough seas or stony donkey tracks. For centuries, it was virtually cut off by the surrounding mountains and its wines were more or less unknown outside the region. Or so Krystina has been telling me, as we speed past fields of heavy-headed sunflowers towards Carcassonne and beyond.

Apparently Bordeaux monopolized the Northern European markets from the marriage of Eleanor of Aquitaine to the English King Henry II in 1152 onwards. Meanwhile Burgundy exercised an effective stranglehold on the river route to Paris. There were scarcely any usable roads and the maritime alternative round the coast of Spain was expensive, slow and beset by dangerous storms and pirates. The Languedoc was effectively land-locked.

Until 1666, that is – today's key date – the year when a certain Pierre-Paul Riquet began work on a canal that was to link the Mediterranean to the Atlantic: the Canal des Deux Mers or the Canal du Midi, as it is more commonly known.

'Nothing new in the idea,' says Krystina, as the BMW takes a sudden, skidding turn down a minor road signposted 'Seuil de Narouze'. 'The Romans wanted to do exactly the same. As did Charlemagne. But there was a technical problem. You noticed we were climbing for the last thirty kilometres or so? Well obviously, a canal would have to go up the hill and down the other side.'

'But isn't that why canals have locks?'

'Locks can only get a boat uphill if there's enough water coming down. And here the water needed to be coming down on both sides of the hill.'

Ignoring a no entry sign, Krystina has been racing towards a formidable-looking chain across the track ahead of us. At the very last minute she judges it robust enough to deter her from further acts of civil disobedience and slams on the brakes.

'That's what had defeated everyone,' she explains, as we proceed on foot towards an attraction billed as the 'Partage des Eaux'. 'Until clever Monsieur Riquet spotted a spring up here that could be divided and channelled down in both directions.'

We have reached what looks like a simple T-junction between two canals – the smaller waterway, the leg of the T, feeding the larger horizontal arms, which lead, it seems, respectively eastwards and westwards, towards the Mediterranean and the Atlantic. Riquet's spring has long since disappeared – swamped apparently by the various rivers that he diverted to augment what would otherwise have been a useless trickle.

It all looks so simple and obvious – but the Inland Waterways Association of Great Britain was sufficiently moved to erect a plaque in 1981 as a token of its '*grande admiration*', so I suppose I too should be impressed.

'It must have taken a lifetime to build,' I say to assure Krystina that I am.

'Only fifteen years,' she answers. 'Despite needing tunnels and aqueducts to cross the more difficult terrain.'

A burst of cheerful, heavily Dutch-accented greetings from a passing tourist long-boat, weighed low in the water by its cargo of Gouda, bicycles and sun-cream, prompts a footnote to the effect that the last commercial traffic died in 1989, before a brisk turn on a fashionable heel signals the end of the first part of the visit.

Still on foot, I obediently follow Krystina down a tree-lined avenue towards a stumpy stone obelisk on a rocky plinth.

'Poor old Riquet,' she says at the foot of the obelisk. 'He died just a few months before the canal opened in 1681. And he died completely penniless, having lost the whole of his personal fortune on the project. He'd made his money "farming" Louis XIV's salt taxes. That's how he came to be travelling so much and saw for himself how badly the region needed a better transport system. And the Royal Languedoc Canal, as it was known until the Revolution, fitted nicely into the King's policy of opening up French trade routes. The only snag was, he couldn't afford to contribute very much to justify the "Royal" bit, what with building Versailles and fighting his endless wars. But by this time, it had become a personal obsession for Riquet. Hence the poor man's ruin . . .'

'Krystina . . .' I try to interrupt, having noticed some alarmingly black clouds approaching from the west.

'Vast undertaking though, employing twelve thousand "heads" . . . "Heads", you notice, not people. A man counted as one, but a woman only two-thirds . . . Anyway, a massive step forward. Opened up tremendous economic prospects for the Languedoc. Except for the wine growers.'

She pauses long enough to register a distant peal of thunder but shrugs it off disdainfully.

'Until the late eighteenth century, Languedoc wine still had Bordeaux protectionism to contend with. Heavy taxes, limits on barrel sizes and, cleverest of all, a ban on other regions' wines, except in the weeks immediately after the vintage, when the new wines weren't ready and the old ones had either been drunk or turned to vinegar.'

A dramatic flash of lightning, illuminating the whole of

the westward view, makes scarcely more impression than the thunder.

'Consequently, most of the exports went by sea – from Louis's new port of Sète, at the other end of the canal, on the Bassin de Thau. In fact, maybe we could go there on our way back . . .'

'Krystina, look at that sky!'

Reluctantly, she agrees to head directly for home. Equally reluctantly, she concedes that this might be one of the rare occasions that justifies the erection of the convertible's roof – or rather, might have been, had it not become jammed from lack of use in the sunshine position.

'Don't worry, I'll race the storm home,' she promises, which strikes me as a greater cause for worry than the storm itself.

However, almost true to her word, Krystina gets the BMW to within ten kilometres of the village before the rain catches up with us. Those are, however, ten kilometres too many, and by the time we reach the house, the whole of the courtyard is at least a couple of centimetres deep in water that cannot find anywhere dry enough to run away to. Waterfalls of rain are overflowing all along the normally ample gutters and the splashes bounce so far that even Uncle Milo's deep arcades are inadequate to keep a would-be storm spectator dry today. Not that it matters, as those last ten kilometres have left us about as wet as we could ever be.

We might almost as well join the tree frogs in the pool. When the swimming season first disrupted their routine, they took their stentorian croakings off to the stream, but tonight's climatic conditions appear to have prompted a resoundingly jubilant return.

Almost nothing is visible beyond the roses in the immediate foreground, their huge heads bowed almost to the ground. The valley and the hills on the other side have completely disappeared in the prevailing blackness. Only the romantic pile of rocks, that looks so like a ruined castle on the opposite skyline, stands silhouetted against a single patch of bright, white sky.

'Glass of red wine, I think,' says Krystina buoyantly, emerging from the house with an already opened bottle. 'Warm you up!'

The bottle that she has chanced upon happens, however, to be not just any old bottle. It is one of the tiny run of twelve that Virgile bottled by hand in advance of all the hiccups with last month's mechanical *mise en bouteille*. I have had it for a couple of weeks but was letting it rest a bit before tasting it – something that Krystina's spirited pourings may now be rendering futile.

With glass in hand, I feel like a parent waiting for his child's examination results: I so much want it to be good.

'But this is amazing!' comes Krystina's speedy judgement, before I have more than sniffed the wine. 'Where on earth did you get it?'

I prevaricate a little but Krystina's classroom days gave her plenty of practice at extracting truthful confessions from reluctant lips.

'So that's where you keep disappearing,' she laughs, when the whole story is out. 'I thought it was another woman!'

I have an uneasy sense that life with Virgile will never be quite the same again, but for the moment I'm much more interested in his wine. Because it does indeed seem remarkable: all the complexity and elegance that might be hoped for in a much more lengthily matured wine, yet totally open and accessible poured straight from the bottle, just ten months after the vintage.

'I shall be buying a lot of this,' announces Krystina decisively.

'It may not be quite so simple,' I venture.

'Nonsense,' says Krystina. 'You know me better than that!'

*

'She wants me out of the house,' complained Manu. 'It's a golden opportunity. You can't just stay here hoovering. Especially in these temperatures.'

'But my house is just as deep in confetti as yours,' I grumbled.

'I know. She says I'm dropping it everywhere I go, even this morning. That's why I've been ordered out. It doesn't happen every day, you know!'

'Only the morning after the Lodève carnival,' I granted him, having paused to prevent Uncle Milo's antiquated vacuum cleaner from overheating. 'I bet they don't have this much confetti in Rio de Janeiro!'

I doubted in fact whether many of the elements of the previous night's parade would have been familiar to the average Brazilian carnival-goer – the 'float' contributed by our village being no exception. Perhaps, if the committee had been willing to accept Krystina's offer to underwrite a more ambitious budget, the crudely constructed château scenery might have wobbled on, intact, to the end of the circuit. Or maybe, if the podgy little daughter of the committee chairman had been lighter, her flimsy castle balcony might have supported her all the way to the finish. It would certainly have helped if Manu had put some more fuel in his tractor, before attempting to tow this rapidly disintegrating *tableau vivant* round the town. As it was, our carnival princess found herself mortifyingly immobilized in front of the very revellers who had just witnessed her undignified crash into the puny arms of her infant troubadour.

The ones I really pitied were the majorettes who were next in the cavalcade behind us. They must have been sweltering in their red and silver toy-soldier jackets. But they still had to twirl their batons through every routine in their high-kicking, fishnet-stockinged repertoire, on one of the steepest hills in the Languedoc, while someone fitter than Manu sprinted off to fill a jerry can. Hence the prodigious quantities of confetti, dispensed at this juncture to distract the crowd from an embar-rassing hiatus in the evening's proceedings.

'Is any of this really happening?' a bewildered M. Vargas had asked – only recently recovered from his concussion and understandably suspecting a relapse.

Mme Gros had watched the pageant from the comparative safety of one of the café terraces farther down the route – her place secured an hour or two before the spectacle began and a single Noilly Prat made to last the whole evening. This spared her the worst of both the paper snowstorm and her husband's humiliation but word travelled fast and she has been slow to forgive, which only added to Manu's desperation to escape.

Almost anywhere, it seemed, would do, even my own unfin-ished 'historical business' down on the quays in Sète. Indeed, he was so relieved to have lured me out that he submitted uncomplainingly to my reiteration of the basics hammered home by Krystina on our storm-swept return from the canal.

The most docile of pupils, he heard how the opening of the port in 1670 created important new export routes to England and the Netherlands, even sometimes to Paris, via Gibraltar and the Seine; how the early exports were mainly spirits and liqueurs – travelling better than table wines and commanding higher prices per volume; and how an explosion of planting in the immediate hinterland created a major new market in the sweet Muscat wines to which the location was particularly suited.

'That'll be Muscat de Frontignan – only a stone's throw from Sète,' my passenger hinted hopefully.

'I thought you didn't like sweet wines,' I answered, still obsti-nately determined to see what survived of the seventeenth-century merchants' offices on the waterfront.

'Bawf,' said Manu as a shorthand for 'beggars can't be choosers' and we continued towards Sète.

But then a signpost offered an alternative source of salvation.

'There's always Muscat de Mireval,' he wheedled. 'Smaller, more exclusive really than Frontignan. It's hardly off route. More of a short cut really. We could still be in Sète for lunch. And Muscat would be something new for you . . .'

He was right. I hadn't even begun to explore the region's dessert wines. So I capitulated and followed the signpost.

There is, however, a price to be paid for spontaneity: we have arrived in Mireval with neither appointment nor address, on a morning far too hot for aimless exploration.

'Don't worry, I'll take you to *the* place,' Manu insists. 'Just as soon as the name comes back to me . . .'

We are, I believe, on our third circuit round the village when he notices a placard outside the Domaine de la Capelle, attributing ownership to 'Mme Maraval et Fils'.

'*Eh, voilà finalement!* The Maravals of Mireval,' he chuckles. 'How could I forget?'

Exhausted, I turn into the narrow drive beside the *cave*.

'And look, we're in good company!' He flourishes a leaflet from a pile near the doorbell. 'Supplier to the Elysée Palace, it says. The Ritz as well.' He basks in the glow of his own discernment.

'How did you get to hear of us?' enquires the spry-looking, middle-aged woman who arrives to unlock the *cave*.

'*Ah, par réputation, Madame.*' Manu taps a knowing finger to the side of his nose (presumably persuaded that Maraval *fils* makes the Muscats, while mother minds the shop). 'If a wine is good enough for the President . . .'

'We like to think our limey soil makes the Muscats here more elegant than those of Frontignan next door,' says Madame Maraval, oblivious to flattery, as she unloads an armful of bottles from the fridge at the back of her spacious, efficient-looking cellar. 'More "vivid" maybe. But the truth is, it's only politics that kept us out of the Frontignan *appellation* in 1936, making us wait another twenty-three years for our own! Not that this *is* a Muscat de Mireval,' she cautions, as she pours our first wine. 'It's a Muscat Sec – a Vin de Pays d'Oc that we started in 1998.'

Manu seizes his glass as if it were the last dry white of his drinking career, not just the last of the morning.

'Perfect for aperitifs or asparagus, many would say. But I'd drink this with anything,' Mme Maraval enthuses. 'So much fresher than those other *cépages.'*

No doubt a second glass would have helped Manu weigh the proposition further but Mme Maraval is already introducing us to the classic Vin Doux Naturel.

'Naturally sweet,' she says. 'Or some would argue, unnaturally sweet, thanks to the *mutage* – the adding of alcohol to arrest the fermentation.'

'Like Cartagène?' I ask.

'Similar,' she acknowledges. 'In a Vin Doux Naturel, the juice is partially fermented. So you add less alcohol to get to your required total of fifteen degrees. But the wine still retains a high level of "residual sugar" – a minimum of a hundred and twenty-five grams per litre, in fact, to satisfy the regulations. This one here we make in a light, fresh style, using relatively high acidity grapes and bottling early. Whereas this', she pours another, labelled '*Parcelle 8*', 'is quite different – from our oldest vines, with eighteen months in wood: 1999, only the second year we made it. Much richer but still fresh enough for an aperitif, don't you think? Although I can't say we've quite made up our minds about the use of wood. The Muscat grape's so delicate.'

Each of these Muscats – whether sweet or dry – seems quite simply 'grapier' than anything I have encountered from other varieties. And a very long way from the oxidized wines that must have been shipped from Sète to London.

'Is this the same as the table variety?' I ask.

Manu assumes a collusive 'I ask you!' look to disassociate

himself from my ignorance but this is important. I am thinking now of my own intended plantings.

'No, this is Muscat à Petits Grains,' she explains. 'Much better suited to wine-making, with its smaller grapes and lower yields. You'd normally grow the Alexandria Muscat for the table. Or the black Hamburg variety . . .'

I could usefully hear more but Mme Maraval is already picking up their 1997 experiment, labelled 'Gelée d'Automne'. 'Something completely different,' she emphasizes.

Manu perks up. A blockbuster red perhaps? A crisp, astringent *rosé* even? But no, the deep, straw-like colour in the clear glass bottle tells him this will not be his idea of 'completely different'. However, stoical as ever, he proffers his glass.

'We wanted to make something sweet but without *mutage*,' Mme Maraval elaborates. 'Using late-harvested grapes. And I do mean late – not like most of the so-called *Vendanges Tardives* that you'll find in the Languedoc. The end of November, compared with the first week of October for the Muscat Sec. Only possible in the best autumn weather conditions, when the grapes can dry on the vine, giving super-concentrated juice and potential alcohols around nineteen.'

'Nineteen!' I look warily at my glass.

'I did say potential alcohols. In practice the fermentation stops around fifteen . . .'

'You'll understand better at vintage time,' says Manu condescendingly.

'Again the stopping of the fermentation leaves unfermented residual sugar,' continues Mme Maraval, not noticeably awed by Manu's mastery of these matters. 'But only about fifty-five grams per litre – less than half the amount in a Vin Doux Naturel.'

Manu's nostalgic glance at the Muscat Sec tells me this is still more than ample for him.

'Oh, but maybe you'd like to try this as well.' She takes a last bottle from the fridge with less than her usual enthusiasm. 'Last year's experiment. Another late harvest but this time Chardonnay. "Grains d'Automne", we call it. What do you think? I'm not so sure myself. All right if you like these other *cépages*. But, if you ask me . . .'

'. . . you can't beat a good Muscat.' An affable young man in, I imagine, his early thirties completes her sentence, as he offers us a forearm to shake in lieu of the hand that a hasty wipe on his work-soiled overalls has failed to clean.

'My son, Alexandre.' Mme Maraval smiles and – our tasting completed – she hands us over to the younger generation.

'We really ought to be going,' says Manu, his priority now being lunch.

I was already thinking we had left it too late for Sète – better to make that visit alone some other day. But Manu has never willingly missed a meal and he is anxious to investigate the more limited Mireval options before there is any risk of last orders being taken. Monsieur Maraval, however, seems determined to give us a tour of the *cave*.

'Everything is geared to preserving the freshness of perfectly ripe fruit,' he emphasizes. 'That's why we use only these temperature-controlled, stainless steel vats. We pick everything by hand – with several successive rounds of harvesting in each *parcelle* for maximum ripeness – and then we rush it into the *cave*, using pneumatic presses to extract the juice. But unfortunately I can't show you those,' he apologizes, as we prepare to say our goodbyes. 'We felt there was still a risk of oxidation with the big one that we used to use and the smaller ones on order haven't arrived. If they don't hurry up, everything's going to be *Vendange Tardive* – even the red!'

Manu stops, one foot inside, the other outside the *cave*. He must have misheard. Mme Maraval said nothing about a red.

'The Cabernet Franc,' says Alexandre. 'Our other new experiment. Didn't my mother . . .?'

But his words are lost on my companion. Lunch suddenly forgotten, he is back at the tasting counter.

'Your friend doesn't take "no" for an answer, does she?' says Virgile.

'Krystina, you mean?'

'With a K and a Y,' he confirms, as he pours me a glass of red wine from Jean-Marc's well-chilled decanter.

'She's tracked you down already? Offering fistfuls of cash, no doubt. But you told her "nothing for sale" and sent her here?'

'Oh, I didn't mean "no" for an answer on the wine.' He smiles a little bashfully. 'She accepted that fairly easily. I meant the invitation to dinner at her château.'

'What did you say?' I ask, trying not to sound too obviously delighted at this apparent refocusing of her attentions.

'What do you think?' he answers, frowning at his glass. 'I haven't got time for a social life. I mean, you'd have thought last week's storm would have wiped out a few of my grapes, wouldn't you? But not a bit of it,' he sighs. 'I'm having to employ a couple of people for a *vendange en vert* – stripping the bunches back to my goal of six or seven per vine.'

'But what if there's another storm?' I ask, thinking surely Krystina won't let a little thing like grape-thinning stand in her way. 'What if you end up with too few for the magic three glasses?'

'I'll have to take a chance. If I leave it any later, the vines will have wasted too much energy on the grapes that need to be removed.'

He sniffs the wine doubtfully. It didn't seem so bad to me but he hasn't told me what it is yet.

'You don't recognize this?' he asks.

It does taste familiar but I'll make a fool of myself if I try to guess, and Jean-Marc is too busy rushing between tables to offer me any clues.

With no bookings for the evening, he invited the two of us to join him for a quiet threesome over some interesting bottles. He even shaved for the occasion. But thanks to the weather, Montpeyroux's Place de l'Horloge has been overwhelmed with unexpected customers. There is scarcely an empty place at any of his large, wooden-slatted outdoor tables and even Céline, Virgile's favourite waitress, has had no time for more than strictly professional courtesies.

'It's not as if I haven't enough to do,' Virgile sighs. 'I was out at five-thirty this morning, ploughing up weeds – too much competition for the vines, in this heat. But with so much else to do, I've left it all a bit late.'

I'm impressed but the important thing is, will Krystina be?

'I should really be spraying everything for vine worms – organically, of course, using a special micro-organism that's eaten only by these particular butterflies. There's no harm to other insects. But once inside the butterflies, it starts munching its way through their intestines.' He grins with the vengeful satisfaction of one who has already sweated to annihilate the first and second of the three generations that beset the vines in the course of a summer.

'I don't seem to hear so much about the moon these days,' I remark, still clinging to my faith in Krystina's tenacity.

'Oh don't!' he moans. 'I can't remember when I last even looked at my biodynamic calendar. It's just gathering dust! But next year . . .'

'What do you think?' Jean-Marc interrupts, with a nod towards the wine, as he hurries past with a perilous pile of empty dishes. 'Has our boy done well?'

'He means this is *yours*?' I ask, as I try to reconcile the reticence in my glass with the opulence that was so impressive last week.

'Doesn't taste half as good as the hand-bottled sample, does it? It's gone completely dumb – traumatized by the bottling, I suppose. It'll be fine in a month or so,' he endeavours to per-suade himself. 'But at least, now that Puech's lorry has taken all the bottles away, I can forklift the barrels round to the garage and make a bit of space in the *cave*. I'm miles behind in preparing it for the *vendange*!'

'What else would you like to drink, my friends?' Jean-Marc reappears, mopping sweat from his forehead with the trade-mark tea-towel.

'Or maybe even *eat*?' implores Virgile.

It is nearly ten o'clock and he has to be up at first light to plough another patch of vines before his six o'clock grape-thinners report for duty. Even Krystina, I am beginning to fear, may fail to find space for herself in this schedule.

'Soon,' says Jean-Marc and he darts to the other side of the square to take a dessert order.

'I've had a letter from the co-op,' says Virgile, having pushed his own production aside and selected something himself from the wine racks indoors. 'About the land I'm renting in Saint Saturnin. Serge, the owner, used to take the grapes to the co-operative and the letter says they're refusing to let me vinify my crop independently.'

'Can they do that?'

'It's a term of my lease that my production's outside the co-op. But Serge should have served them with a formal notice. I suddenly remembered the other day and typed up something for him to sign. But I can't remember whether it was two or three months before the *vendange* that it was supposed to be served. If it's two we might be all right.'

'And if it's three?'

'Strictly, it's Serge's problem but in practice it'll be mine as well. At the end of the day, it'll be a question of money. We'll see. I may have been in time and the co-op's letter may just be a bluff.'

'Can't you get some legal advice?'

'The only specialist that I know of is away on holiday.'

'I'd really like to know your opinion of this.' Jean-Marc pauses long enough to deposit two glasses of yet another red wine. Then he vanishes to deliver some bills to the first of his customers who are ready to leave. 'I'll be with you any minute now,' he promises unpersuasively, as he passes back again in search of another table's first courses.

'How about you?' asks Virgile, now ravenous enough to take the law into his own hands and rustle up some bread and olives from the kitchen. 'Are you winning up there?'

'It doesn't feel like it. I thought things would have finished growing by now. Maybe I'm trying to water too much but I can't seem to get it right. If I don't irrigate, things shrivel and die; if I do, they grow faster than I can keep them under control. And of course, the more I clear away the jungle, the larger the area that I have to maintain. The grass on my top terraces is nearly waist-high. In fact, I've borrowed a couple of horses from a cousin of the Vargases.'

'Petrol-free lawnmowers?'

'It seems like my best bet. The machine that Manu persuaded me to spend all that money on is really better suited to a more modest garden like his.'

It is just after midnight when Jean-Marc does at last join us for a bowl of chilled gazpacho, but no sooner is he seated than a customer query calls him away. By the time he returns the soup has 'gone warm', and much to his irritation poor overworked Céline has presumed the dish abandoned and cleared it away. But perhaps this is just as well, as the *patron* now has a series of seemingly endless goodnights to be said.

The village clock is just striking one when the last guest leaves and the plates of chargrilled lamb that are destined for our table finally appear in the restaurant doorway. However, before an almost tearfully weary Céline can deposit them, Jean-Marc suddenly has misgivings about disturbing the villagers if we remain in the square, so we carry everything, including wines and glasses, inside to the discreet upper room where we fêted last month's *mise en bouteille*. Then, just as hope flickers that we might at last enjoy a pleasant half-hour with our host before falling asleep on our plates, he remembers that he has forgotten to stack and padlock the outside furniture.

'Start without me,' he calls, as he disappears back down the staircase.

Sadly we both start and finish without him. Indeed, he is still in the bar, apparently dealing with the sensitive subject of Céline's resignation, when we descend to make our excuses for departure.

'But what about cheese and dessert?' he protests as we edge apologetically towards our vehicles. 'At least a coffee, surely? We've hardly spoken all evening . . .'

I woke very late, feeling curiously disoriented and wondering blearily why the noises from outside my shutters seemed so exaggeratedly near and loud. The usual rasp of Manu's van, for instance, was inexplicably reverberant as it struggled up the track – now rougher than ever since the storm. The familiar rustling from his gardening activities was somehow magnified into a tumultuous and oddly immediate hubbub.

Reluctantly I opened first my eyes and then the shutters. I blinked in the mid-morning sunlight and slowly focused on the fact that I was mistaken. It was neither Manu's van nor his gardening that had penetrated my unconsciousness. It was a huge yellow lorry, completely blocking the entrance to my drive. And on the back of the lorry, rotating from a kind of crane, an enormous mechanical scythe was ripping its way violently through the trees and shrubs beside my entrance-way.

Loath as I was to face the world, there was no escaping the conclusion that one or two questions needed to be asked here

– and asked before rather than after the surrounding vegetation had been entirely razed to the ground. I braced myself for a confrontation.

'It seems the modern goat needs electricity,' said the foreman, pointing towards the new *bergerie* on the nearby hill. 'The supply has to come from here, which means the little wooden post that you've got at the moment won't be big enough. So we're giving you a lovely new one, free of charge.' He gestured down the track towards a second yellow lorry, loaded high with concrete pylons.

'But this is my land. And those are my trees you're hacking down,' I spluttered.

'Oh, I don't think you'll find they're yours,' he said, as he opened a file of papers. 'We've got all the necessary permissions from the owners . . .'

'But I *am* the owner of this little triangle,' I insisted and went to get my copy of the land registry plan.

'Well, even if you're right,' said the foreman after twenty minutes of dogged argument, 'the alternative is, you keep your little wooden post on this little triangle and we put up two more of the big ones over there in front of your house, on land that you certainly don't own. It's the only other way that we can get our cables across the valley.'

'But that would be twice as bad!'

'I knew you'd understand.'

'But it's so big. And so white.'

'It turns a sort of grey eventually.'

'Such a contrast to the trees.'

'We could paint it brown,' the foreman finally offered and despairingly I gave in. I couldn't see a better solution. But ever since Manu first saw the finished result this morning, he has hardly stopped laughing.

'Is that supposed to look like a tree?' he manages to articulate between guffaws.

He's right, of course. The bright shade of russet that consti-
tutes the electricity company's notion of brown is never going
to blend into this or any other treescape – not even in the
autumn, when the leaves are at their reddest. And the gloss
paint has a dependable knack of catching the sunlight at all
sorts of different times of day.

It is another reminder of the extreme fragility of paradise.

August

'I THINK I MUST be the only Frenchman not on holiday,' said Virgile, slumping wearily into his solitary armchair with a homemade after-dinner *tisane*. 'Have you noticed? Even the vines are deserted at this time of year.'

'I thought August holidays were compulsory for the French,' I answered from the sofabed. 'Won't they cancel your citizenship?'

'Others may be ready for the *vendange* but I'm not,' he sighed. 'There's so much weeding I should be doing, plus another round of spraying. And as for the *cave* . . . I need so much more equipment to handle the extra volume this year and I haven't even bought most of it yet!'

'And the legal problem with the co-op?' I asked, wondering whether much of his effort might still be in vain.

'I think we might be all right. There's certainly been nothing in response to our notice.'

'What does Serge say about it all?'

'Luckily, he sees the funny side,' yawned Virgile, rubbing sleep from his eyes. 'He says, if one of us has to go to prison, it ought to be him because I'm productive and he's completely useless. I could certainly have worse landlords.'

I was feeling almost as exhausted as Virgile myself. Whatever the percentage of the English population currently on holiday, much of it seemed to have arrived to share the sunshine at my house. Blithely ignoring the capacity of a three-bedroomed property, improbable numbers of visitors had been determined to demonstrate how much they were missing me and their sense of loss had conveniently climaxed in August.

It was not so much the shopping and cooking that had worn me out. Indeed, many of my visitors were proving keen enough to indulge their favourite Mediterranean fantasies in my kitchen. It was the sheer logistics of juggling bodies between beds, sofas, futons and poolside recliners, borrowed from Krystina – which is why I had asked to spend the night on Virgile's sofabed.

'I saw a friend of yours last night,' he said with a grin.

'Krystina?' I asked, my hopes of rejection suddenly reviving.

'No,' he blushed, 'your neighbour. Monsieur Gros, isn't it? He was down here playing *boules* in the square outside the *cave* but I think he'd had a few too many in Le Pressoir, so his *boules* kept rolling in amongst my *cuves*. You hadn't told him about me, it seems.'

'He's very possessive. I didn't think he'd understand.'

'I don't think he does . . . Understand about my sort of wine-making, I mean. We got talking, you see. He was telling me how I didn't need half my equipment. "A lot of silliness" were his precise words,' Virgile chuckled. 'He said I was nearly as bad as this English neighbour of his, the one that he'd been dragging round the Languedoc all year, trying to teach him a thing or two about wine. That's when I guessed there could only be one of you. But don't worry, he said he'd get your ideas straightened out when you helped him with the *vendange*.'

'He said what?'

'I didn't think you knew about that bit!' Virgile laughed at my look of blank dismay. 'But I'm sure the *vendange* is going to be early this year,' he sighed again. 'The grapes are ripening so fast.'

Then a brighter thought struck him.

He crossed to his little galley kitchen for a large empty gherkin jar. Well, not in fact empty it transpired on closer inspection – the gherkins and their brine had been replaced with water. Or so I thought, until Virgile removed the lid and I smelt the vivid perfume of an *eau de vie*.

'This is my own,' he said, as he poured us each a little. 'We call it *marc*. It's distilled from something that we also call *marc*, just to confuse you – the pips and grape skins left over after the pressing. I'll show you in October.'

I took a sip. It was intensely fruity but uncompromisingly fiery.

'You remember Matthieu?' he asked. 'The part-time guitar-ist who came along to help, that first day we planned to do the bottling? Well, distilling's Matthieu's main work. It was him who made this for me. He does it for practically everyone round here. You ought to go and see him.'

So I did.

'There's not a lot I can show you in August,' says Matthieu, when my car has finished inching its way down one of Montpeyroux's narrowest back alleys to find the borrowed, barn-like garage, where he says he has been 'squatting' for the last year. 'You were lucky to catch me. I'm off on holiday tomorrow. You'll need to come in a couple of months to see the action. But as you're here . . .'

He beckons me out into a chaotically cluttered back garden, where several ancient, rusty-looking distilling contraptions are lurking in the shrubs. If only Manu were here, I think to myself, as he pauses to gather up a crate of oddly assorted lemonade and beer bottles and some tasting glasses.

But then I hear the hoot of a carhorn from the alleyway.

'You forgot your notebook,' calls a familiar voice from a little red van that has somehow managed to follow me. 'I persuaded the wife you'd be distraught.'

I am surprised that the prospect of my distraction cut any ice with Mme Gros. She has been making it abundantly clear that she finds the arrival of the pylon far less amusing than her husband does. Our relationship was never one of easy banter, but on at least three occasions in the last few days her refusal to speak to me has been unambiguous. It was hardly surprising. The shiny red eyesore completely dominated the view from her own garden and she held me responsible. I was no longer to be tolerated beneath her roof for so much as a Coca-Cola. At least, not until the advent of her grandchildren.

The day before they arrived, her pursed lips started to soften. Her gimlet gaze became eerily benign. How charming, I thought, the restorative power of infant society. But the real explanation dawned early this morning, when I and all but my heaviest sleeping guests were woken by shrieks and splashes from the garden. It was perfectly simple: I have a pool and Mme Gros does not. Her grandchildren like to swim (they always swam in Uncle Milo's day, it seems) and clearly a cessation of hostilities was considered diplomatic before an assertion of bathing rights.

'Can't get the youngsters out of your pool,' chuckles Manu, confirming my analysis. 'It's the only thing they wanted to do for the whole fortnight last year! Oh, yes, delighted,' he adds, accepting a glass of *eau de vie*.

Matthieu explains that it was made with *marc* from Sylvain Fadat, the Montpeyroux grower whom I met in January.

'That's really how it started,' he says. 'Most of my work used to be in Burgundy but last year Sylvain was organizing Montpeyroux's Fête des Vins. I was booked to play some 'gypsy jazz'. In the end I never played, but Sylvain heard about my Burgundian *eaux de vie de marc* and he got quite excited by the idea of having his own. So did a lot of the local growers. Not necessarily as a commercial product, maybe just for private enjoyment, or for giving to regular customers.

'By the way, you don't have to finish that,' he adds, extracting a particularly grimy-looking bottle from his crate and pouring us each a second glass. 'I know you're both driving.'

Seeing me about to empty my Domaine d'Aupilhac into a flowerbed, Manu deftly plucks the glass from my hand to juggle three in his two: something which, it has to be said, he is managing commendably well, until a loud snapping of branches startles both of us. Rather as trees are flattened by elephants intent on reaching their waterholes, so, it seems, the surrounding shrubbery is being trampled by someone determined to reach the scene of our tasting. Before Manu can assess the volume of alcohol spilt in this moment of alarm, a well-established pair of oleanders is parted by the emergence of a formidable stomach belonging, we soon learn, to Monsieur Bascou, the owner of the garage and the garden.

'It's *marcs de cépage* that interest me most,' Matthieu continues, having placed a well-filled glass of the second product in the landlord's expectant hand. 'Spirits made from one or maybe two distinctive grape varieties. Like this one – just smell it,' he urges. 'It's Muscat, so grapey . . .'

To spare Manu the challenge of additional glassware, Matthieu leads the party to a rickety garden table, barely visible beneath an assortment of bottles, tools and potted plants competing for space. A guitar in a half-open case occupies one of the rusty chairs. 'You should have seen this place before I tidied up,' he whispers, while the slower-moving M. Bascou catches up.

171

'This is from Virgile's friend, Olivier at Mas Jullien,' Matthieu explains, as Manu squeezes a broad pair of buttocks between the narrow arms of one of the vacant chairs.

M. Bascou, whose girth makes Manu's waistline look almost wasp-like, seems to know from experience that he would be safer finishing his samples at home. He will, after all, have other opportunities to work his way through the range. So with a farewell assault on a group of mahonias, he sets off to wherever he lives at the other end of the undergrowth.

Matthieu meanwhile rummages for a half-hidden flagon beneath an adjacent arbutus, before pouring us something Cognac-coloured, as a contrast to the clear, colourless products that we have sampled up until now.

'It's only the effect of oak,' he explains. 'The tradition began when barrels were the only means of storage and transport. I think stainless steel preserves more individuality but occasionally growers ask for some time in wood.'

'Why don't they simply make their own?' I ask.

'Not allowed to. Not without special licences, which don't make sense for a few hundred litres. Anyone with a vine or a fruit tree used to have the right to distil his own . . .'

'Me included?'

'Absolutely. But the Ricard establishment – you know, the *pastis* manufacturer down near Agde – got the law changed in 1953, wiping out small-scale *eau de vie* production for decades.'

'So how come people like Manu . . .?'

Before I can reconcile the idea of half a century of prohibition with my New Year introduction to my neighbour's home dis-tillation, an immoderate imitation of a man being stung by a passing insect reminds me that this was not supposed to be widely publicized. Better perhaps, in any event, to be on our way while Manu can still rejoin his vehicle unsupported.

'But what if this really catches on?' I ask in parting. 'What if every grower wanted his personal *marc* production?'

'I'd make sure there were lots more distilleries!' he answers emphatically. 'I can't spend all day on this business. *Après tout, je suis musicien!*'

Fortunately for Virgile, one of the few individuals not observing his patriotic duty to be on holiday this month is a man called Monsieur Ferré. I can tell that he is not on holiday because his head is sticking out of a kind of porthole at the far end of Virgile's *cave* and he is singing snatches of *Carmen* at a volume that tends to draw attention to itself.

There are two of these portholes, in fact, but I had scarcely noticed them before, with so much other equipment squeezed into the usable space in front of them. The initial phase of the boiler-suited baritone's endeavours has, however, revealed a pair of concrete fermentation tanks, built behind what I had simply assumed to be the back wall, and M. Ferré is now busy replastering inside the first of them. Each of these *cuves* is about twice the size of Virgile's existing fibreglass alternatives. Together they will give him vital extra space for this year's much increased production and, apparently, all they need is a week of the singing restorer's labours to bring them back into commission.

Meanwhile, in front of the concrete tanks, I can now see a rectangular pit, about a metre deep in the floor. It is equally invaluable for the *vendange*, says Virgile (without exactly explaining how) and equally in line for M. Ferré's reconditioning, it seems, just as soon as he has finished a *reprise* of the 'Toreador Aria'.

Leaving M. Ferré aside, however, I do find myself wondering where everyone can have gone. Every second person that I try to contact is away on holiday – so much so that you might expect the region to be deserted – but, as if in an effort to compensate, an astonishing proportion of the rest of the world's population appears to be vacationing *here*.

The forty-minute drive to the coast can now take most of a weekend and I have to park so far away from the Saturday market that I feel I might as well walk to Lodève from home. And if the postcard queues in the village shop get any worse, Nathalie's baguettes will be stale before I even get to the counter.

I have become quite unreasonably resentful at the disruption of my off-season routines.

Paradoxically, however, the time when so many of the locals are away on holiday seems to be the time when every self-respecting village chooses to have its principal annual festivity. On almost any day, I could choose between half a dozen different *fêtes locales* – except, of course, that the traffic is much too congested to venture farther afield than our own. But anyway, what distant excitements could possibly cap the *Abrivado* here at home?

'What's an *abrivado*?' I asked when I saw the poster in the village café.

'It's Spanish,' said Babette, without enlarging on its meaning.

She was too busy making a trayful of ice-cream sundaes for a table of tourists. From September to June she would revert to her no-choice, foil-wrapped choc ices but it needed only a handful of Americans unfamiliar with the exchange rate to ensure that her more elaborate, high-season *carte des glaces* paid for itself.

'I'm sorry but I think you'll find it's Occitan,' contradicted Monsieur Privat from the corner table that continued to be kept for him, no matter how high the season.

Babette really ought to have remembered that he might know better than her. It was she herself who had told me that he was a retired schoolteacher – of Spanish, no less.

'It means speed,' M. Privat explained, as if still at the *lycée*. 'At least "*abrivada*" does. The "a" at the end of an Occitan word is pronounced like an "o". You'll see the connection at the weekend . . .'

'I hate to disagree,' said Monsieur Puylairol, the beekeeper, as diffident as ever. 'But I always thought it was Languedoc dialect for *"abreuvoir"* – a watering place. In this context, a booze-up. He'll see the connection at the weekend . . .'

In a sense, they were both right. But I had to wait until Sunday to understand why.

On the second Sunday of August, the steep ascent of the main village street is closed to pedestrians. A massive cattle truck is parked just outside the medieval gateway to seal off the bottom end. The entrances to the narrow side alleys are comprehensively blocked with metal crowd barriers and crowds duly gather behind them for a close-up view of the afternoon's sport.

The balcony of La Maison Vargas, being just inside the gateway, must offer an even better aerial vantage point but, happily for me on this occasion, they prefer the excitement at street level and I can look to them for explanations.

The object of the proceedings, they tell me, is to give the more fearless local youth an opportunity to race a succession of bulls through the village. They start from a kind of corral erected up near the café and they chase the beasts down to the truck waiting open-doored at the gate, all the time avoiding the opposite possibility of the bulls chasing them. In fact, the principal aim, which secures the maximum crowd hysteria, is to grab the bulls by the horns and stop them in their tracks but, as the typical bull is considerably larger than even the heartiest village contestant, this is best attempted in teams. So six or seven heroes, eager to prove their testosterone counts, hurl themselves at the animal in a concerted struggle to get a grip on any part of its anatomy, including the tail, that might slow it down. It will not be the most dignified afternoon of the creature's life but, as I know from my visit to Nîmes, there are incontestably worse fates.

This then is the 'speed' element on which M. Privat insisted. M. Puylairol's 'watering', it seems, is largely centred on the village café, where the Vargases tell me Babette is enjoying exceptional trading conditions. In fact, the throng is reported to be dense enough for Manu to have ventured up there, in the hope of infiltrating the bar without being spotted by Mme Gros. Indeed, as soon as the first bull has thundered past us – his pursuers several humiliating metres behind – we see Manu, taking his life in his hands as he hurries down the middle of the street towards us, balancing a tray of beers.

Manu's progress is slowed by the overriding need for periodic checks that his illicit purchases remain undetected but he reaches us just in time to squeeze round the barrier before a second bull gallops heavily past – again unimpeded by the quartet in pursuit.

'No stamina, these boys today,' he scoffs as he hands round the beers.

Exceptionally, he appears to have dug deep into his own dungarees for this round. The unaccustomed *entrée* to Babette's must have gone to his head – or so I imagine, until the Vargases whisper that he can keep the change.

'We'll be happy to share a glass,' they add, leaving Manu happily draining two, as a cheer goes up from the crowd and yet another bull evades its gang of would-be assailants.

'In my day, I'd have managed a two-year-old on my own,' swears Manu. His boasting is, however, rapidly silenced by a contemptuous contralto laugh at his elbow.

'*Ah, te voilà, ma chère*,' says a man whose liberty is about to be forfeit.

'Of course I knew about the local firewaters,' said Krystina, producing a couple of outsized antique balloon glasses. 'Languedoc brandy used to be just as famous as Cognac.'

I took my pick from a well-stocked seventeenth-century-looking drinks cabinet and followed her out on to a starlit terrace.

Virgile's hardness-to-get had unfortunately left me still in the frame. But my house was teeming with sun-seeking families from obscure corners of my address book and Virgile had his brother visiting. So, reluctantly, I was risking alternative refuge in one of the château's sumptuous guest suites, having first discreetly verified that it could be locked from the inside.

'It was even your thirteenth-century friend, da Villanova, down at the Medicine Faculty, who introduced the technique to France,' Krystina explained as she steered me towards a jasmine-scented pergola. 'Admittedly, it was Cognac that established the country's first distillery ages later, in 1624, but it didn't take our local boys long to catch up.'

I was too engrossed in my fruity Marc de Muscat de Frontignan to be over-disconcerted by the proximity enforced by Krystina's tiny stone bench.

'Brandy was a perfect solution for low-quality wine – mainly sold to sailors at first because it took up less space and travelled better than wine. It soon spread ashore though, particularly to the Northern European markets. A hundred thousand hectolitres a year leaving Sète by the end of the seventeenth century. A thousand distilleries . . .'

Languedoc *eaux de vie* might soon have become my mastermind subject, if Krystina had not chosen this unlikely moment to pounce. I should have seen it coming, but I was too enthralled by the stars. I had never seen so many and so bright. And anyway, who would have expected the lunge, when it came, to be so sudden?

The brandy balloon fell from my hand.

'Oh, leave it!' she breathed, no more bothered by the broken goblet than she was by the wasted *marc*.

'No really . . .' I tried to wriggle free. 'I'll get a broom.'

'We were made for better than that,' she panted and tried to pull me closer.

'You could cut yourself,' I persisted until, unwillingly, she accepted that the mood, like the glass, had been shattered.

'Don't bother to wake me in the morning,' she called as she swept from the terrace. 'I've decided not to come to Faugères.'

Matthieu gave me two Faugères addresses to find: two growers spear-heading the revival of an entirely different *eau de vie*, the 'Fine de Faugères' – a distillation of the local wine itself, he told me, as opposed to its grape pressings.

As I arrive at the first, in the heart of the village of Lenthéric, a dusty, dented 50cc motorbike draws up from the opposite direction. By most people's standards, Didier Barral has been enormously successful since he persuaded his father, Léon, to leave the local co-operative in 1993, but he despises what he sees as his profession's usual badges of achievement.

'That's not how I see success,' he says, as he treats me to a parody of the 'modern wine-maker' directing vineyard operations by mobile phone from the wheel of a Range Rover. 'For me, it's a question of happiness in what I'm doing, fulfilling work for the people who help me and a healthy balance of nature on my land.'

From anyone less refreshingly down-to-earth, Didier's aspirations might have sounded pompous, but from him they are both humbling and inspiring: the only possible honourable creed.

He is already offering a glass of straw-coloured white wine before I can explain that I am really on the trail of the Faugères *fine*.

'That's not so easy,' he explains, as he gives the greying stubble on his otherwise youthful cheeks a pensive scratch. 'All in bond, you see – so we don't have to pay the tax until it's had its three years in wood. But that's ninety per cent Terret, what you've got there – the traditional Faugères brandy grape. And like the *fine*, it's aged in wood. That's why there's a slight oxidation in colour and taste. It's a natural product you see.'

I explain that, having sampled the *fine* at Matthieu's, I am not so much hoping to taste it as to find out more about its 'renaissance'. For this, Didier suggests I should try the second of my addresses – but not before I have tasted a formidable selection of his reds.

It seems a shame to have left Manu behind, but ever since one of the grandchildren fell off the grotesque inflatable alligator which now dominates the deep end of the pool, my neighbour has been confined to base for lifeguarding duties. 'Your friends really mustn't feel excluded,' said Mme Gros, when she saw them leaving for the beach this morning. 'The kiddies are very happy to share.'

Didier explains how he usually keeps the individual grape varieties – the Syrah, Grenache, Mourvèdre, Carignan and Cinsault – scrupulously separate until they are blended just before the final bottling, but every sample seems as rewarding as many another grower's finished wines. He also keeps everything for two years before bottling – partly in wood for his top blend but otherwise in stainless steel – which avoids the need for filtering. Natural products again, he emphasizes.

If there is a common characteristic running through all the different *cuvées*, it must be their ripe, fruity intensity. One of the ripest and fruitiest of all is his Mourvèdre – a variety outside the range that I have encountered with Virgile but one that I have heard is notoriously difficult to bring to maturity.

'I never have any problem,' says Didier unapologetically. 'It's all a matter of how you manage the land. The one thing Mourvèdre can't stand is drought, but if your vineyard is a healthy, balanced, natural environment, you'll have all kinds of insects and animals burrowing down into the soil, letting whatever moisture there is get down to the roots. It's simple, natural things like that which make the difference.'

His aim, he summarizes with a modest smile, is to make something irresistible: a bottle of wine that no one would willingly leave unfinished. It sounds so simple and obvious but I suppose the measure of his success must be my own almost Manu-like reluctance to hand in my glass.

At the Château de Fabrègues, a couple of kilometres outside the village, the facts that I was looking for emerge with the speed and precision of a practised publicist who clearly longs to see both the name and the substance of Fine de Faugères on everyone's lips.

'*Appellation Contrôlée* since 1947,' explains Jean-Luc Saur, the dark-green-boiler-suited proprietor of the château and president of the *appellation*. 'Long before the wines got their classification in '82. But ironically, no one was making much *fine* in '47. Demand for spirits was declining and the distillery that had a virtual monopoly was holding massive stocks, up to a hundred years old – so there wasn't much incentive to make any more. In fact, production dried up altogether in the fifties.'

'Until Matthieu?' I ask.

'More or less,' he acknowledges, as he ushers me into a long, tunnel-vaulted tasting room. 'One or two people did experiment but, to qualify for the *appellation*, you have to do all the distilling and maturing in Faugères, as well as simply growing your grapes here. So until Matthieu set himself up inside the boundaries, anything distilled elsewhere ranked as simple Eau de Vie du Languedoc.'

'So last year's was the first authentic *fine* for half a century?'

'Absolutely. With thirteen growers participating.'

'And more than that this year, I assume?'

'Less, I expect. Last year's production will keep most people going for a while. I'm sure we'll make more ourselves, but remember, we've already got five thousand bottles' worth from the last vintage, doing its three years in oak. And I'm not kidding myself that we'll be selling it in cases of six! All of it still in bond, of course, but maybe you'd like to taste our wines,' he offers. 'You'll find them different from most of the Faugères you've tried. 'We don't believe in reds for easy early drinking.'

I am grateful for the warning. I take a tentative sip of the first densely black sample and find it almost overwhelmingly astringent: the bitter taste of tannin, which Virgile has taught me comes from contact with the grapeskins and pips. I am prepared to believe its importance in making slow-maturing, long-lived wines, but for me, it is all too reminiscent of oversteeped tea and I can really only take on trust the idea that something fruitier might be lurking in the background for the future.

Monsieur Saur, meanwhile, is positively relishing the austerity. 'They're tough in their youth but they've great potential,' he promises.

But it is Didier Barral's irresistibility yardstick that comes to mind, as I eye my unfinished glass.

The last of my guests are gone – some more reluctantly than others.

There were those who realized within minutes of arrival that they had made a terrible mistake. Those unfamiliar insects in the showers, the unexpectedly fresh temperature of the freshwater pool, that wildness and unpredictability everywhere, both outside and inside the house, were all so far removed from the sanitized Mediterranean villa of their imaginings. This group tended to console itself by sitting moodily in deckchairs and emptying glasses faster than I could open bottles.

Others, however, embraced both the pleasures and the challenges of a life beyond chlorine and air-conditioning. They found such inspiration in my inexhaustible fig tree that they begged to monopolize the kitchen at mealtimes. They saw such charm in my picturesquely impractical granite sink that they fought for the privilege of washing up. They then harnessed themselves to my strimmer for the rest of the day to work up an appetite for the next round.

Some were so enamoured that they now want to buy houses of their own here. One or two, indeed, want to buy *my* house here but I think I have convinced them that it is not for sale. I have yet to work out how I shall find either the time or the money, after this year, to keep it going in the manner which it deserves but it is emphatically not for sale.

So yes, the last of my guests have finally gone. The last of the breakages is replaced and the depleted foodstores are replenished. At least, they will be, as soon as I have driven home from the Wednesday morning Clermont l'Hérault market.

I ought to be speeding straight back with the more perishable purchases but it seems ages since I last saw Virgile, so I decide to make the small diversion to Saint Saturnin, to ask him when the long-awaited assault on the grape harvest might be likely to start. He asked me to be on stand-by for active service from the end of the month but I've not heard from him since.

The familiar white Mercedes van is parked in its usual place beside the church but the *cave* is locked and there is no answer to my knock at the door of his flat. Pius spots me from the Le Pressoir terrace and beckons me over for a briefing.

'He's ill,' he says with a frown. 'Taken to his bed with a fever. A virus, he says, but more like simple exhaustion, if you ask me. Well, you know as well as I do the hours he's been working.'

'I couldn't make him hear,' I explain.

'He doesn't want to see anyone,' says Pius, shaking his head.

'But what about the *vendange*?' I ask, in the hope of reassurance.

'I'd say, it doesn't look very promising,' is Pius's grim-faced reply.

September

'THIS IS THE most important decision of the year,' said Virgile, when he finally called me from his sickbed. 'To start or not to start the *vendange*.' He was still feeling feverish but he had managed to drag himself out to do a round of the vines, to monitor the state of play. 'I've taken some sample pickings,' he explained, 'to check on the sugar levels. I reckon I should be starting on Monday. The trouble is, there's so much preparation that I ought to be doing in the *cave*.'

'You'll manage,' I tried to reassure him. 'You always do. Much better to get some rest.'

'At least it should stay fine,' he consoled himself through the muffling of his duvet. 'Set fair until the next new moon, I hope, around the middle of the month. So we've a bit of time to play with. You know, I didn't even start until that time last year but everything's so much more advanced . . . I really must get the equipment sterilized.'

'Get some rest,' I urged him again. 'But is there anything I can bring you? Some grapes, perhaps?'

'Very funny,' he said. 'I'll see you on Monday.'

But when Monday came, Virgile had only half his team available. A couple of Polish girls who helped him last year had telephoned to say that their train from Warsaw was going to take them three days and Régine had defected at the last minute to his friend Olivier at Mas Jullien. So, pragmatically, he persuaded himself that a further delay would do no harm and said he would call me as soon as he was ready to push the button. By Friday, I was beginning to wonder what else could have gone wrong, but it was only when he finally rang on Sunday to say that my phone had been out of order for half the week that I realized I had missed the first three days.

He sounded far too excited by the quality of the harvest to mind about my absent pair of hands. He had started on Thursday with his earliest ripening variety, the Grenache Noir, then followed with the Syrah from Jonquières on Friday and his Cinsault down at Nébian on Saturday.

'The grapes are so healthy,' he marvelled. 'Such concentrated sugar. Amazing potential alcohols! Well, thirteen and a half for Syrah, that's not so unusual. But fifteen for the Grenache and, you'll never believe it, twenty for the Cinsault! That's not wine,' he laughed, 'it's *confiture*! The kind of vintage you dream about!'

So I could hardly wait to be part of a dream.

There is, however, nothing more likely to ensure the return of a sharp sense of reality than a Monday morning bent double, rummaging amongst the greenery for the grapes and cursing the fact that the Saint Saturnin Syrah is the one *parcelle* where Virgile decided to take a chance and go easy on the leaf-and-bunch-thinning. It is not so bad for the Polish girls, Magda and Margherita. They are short enough not to have to stoop so much and anyway, the others have all had three days to acclimatize. Even Arnaud, the lanky young electrician, still waiting for the 'real job', bows uncomplainingly to his task. But for me, as the morning advances, an all-consuming craving to stretch myself anywhere flat on my back – even in the stoniest space between the vines – eclipses even my hunger pangs.

'And all for just three glasses per vine,' I keep thinking.

The bunches have been collected in small plastic crates – only about thirty centimetres deep to avoid putting too much pressure on the grapes – and Virgile wants to take a trailer-load back to base at midday.

'Please, please let me be picked for trailer-loading duties,' I think to myself, as I try to catch Virgile's eye with a surge of what I hope will be convincingly muscular-looking grape-snipping. 'I don't care how heavy the crates are – anything for a change of posture.'

But Virgile already knows the sinewy zeal that Arnaud will bring to the task and I am condemned to carry on crouching until lunchtime.

Tiring as the work is, there is never a moment's slackening of the team's attention to detail. Even when Virgile absents himself briefly for a spot of troubleshooting elsewhere, a lingering sense of his quiet, perfectionist authority somehow keeps everyone motivated.

'Did you ever see such healthy grapes?' enthuses Florent, an incongruously stylish journalist friend of Virgile's younger brother, who is 'between newspapers' but clearly needs a regular income to finance the expensively cut, floppy-fringed hairstyle that refuses to stay out of his eyes as he bends for the next bunch.

'Not where I am,' grumbles Gérard, the final member of the team, a neurotic-looking Northerner of indeterminate age who, as far as I can gather, has come to live with his mother in the Languedoc in the hope of forgetting a broken marriage. 'Just my luck to chose a row with so many rotten grapes,' he whines, as if nature were conspiring with his former wife to make his misery complete.

'Careful,' says Virgile, intervening. 'Most of those grapes

you're cutting out from those bunches are just a bit dry. It's only actual rot that needs to go.' Unseen by Virgile, Gérard pulls a face, half-despairing, half-mutinous. I know how he feels – the two conditions look so similar.

As if to rub salt in our weary wounds, we seem to be surrounded by neighbouring growers with huge mechanical harvesting machines, which are busy piling effortlessly indiscriminate mountains of grapes into enormous open trailers. No fastidious grape selection over there.

'All destined for my friends at the co-op,' says Virgile, with a wink, as he reads my thoughts. 'Actually, I've decided it's the only option for my unwanted Grenache Blanc. It's going to be machine-picked tomorrow and taken down to Gignac, where at least I know the co-op won't make a fuss if I change my mind next year. But I still wish I didn't have to do it mechanically. It isn't just a question of picking perfect grapes,' he explains, as he shows me some bedraggled stalks from which a neighbour's fruit has just been rudely ripped. 'You see what it does to the vine. Leaves it confused, thinking there's something still to be fed, instead of building up energy for the winter. But talking of food . . .'

Saint Saturnin's clock has now twice gladdened our hearts with a twelfth stroke.

We return to the flat to find Virgile's once fastidiously tidy kitchen looking as if it has been vandalized. More dishes than I thought he possessed are piled high on every surface. Domesticity is obviously alien to the Polish girls, who are 'camping' in the allegedly uninhabitable accommodation above the *cave* (the height of luxury, they say, after last year's tent). Domestic order is presumably equally foreign to Florent, who has spent the last few nights even closer to the chaos, on the sofabed. But at least he can cook. Admittedly, seven ravenous grapepickers who have been hard at work since 7.45 may not be the most exacting gastronomes but awesome quantities

186

of Florent's hastily assembled pasta dish seem to disappear within minutes of being served.

Such conversation as is managed between mouthfuls lurches around in a confusing mix of languages. Margherita speaks no French, almost no English but excellent German, so Gérard uses his reasonable German to monopolize Margherita in a way that he fondly imagines is highly seductive. Magda – visibly delighted to be free of Gérard's attentions – speaks little French, no German but passable English. Consequently, to communicate with the Polish girls at all, Virgile has been forced to reveal more competence in my language than he would ever admit to me before – and he seems to be rather enjoying it. Meanwhile, Florent and Arnaud speak only French and they speak it even to those who plainly do not understand.

The afternoon picking is essentially 'more of the same'. It finishes around five o'clock, when everyone disperses except Virgile, Arnaud and myself who then try to summon up the energy for what Virgile, with his new-found delight in the English language, describes as '*zuh rrrreal worrrrk*'.

The equivalent of four trailer-loads of Syrah grapes, all waiting in tall stacks of plastic crates, now have to be heaved into the gaping mouth of the *érafloir* – the formidable-looking destemming machine, currently occupying most of the usable space in the middle of the *cave*. A huge hose pipe, about fifteen centimetres in diameter, stretches from this to the top of an empty fibreglass *cuve*.

'It's a very clever machine,' shouts Virgile, reverting more comprehensibly to French above the rattle of machinery. 'It removes the stalks and lightly breaks the skins, without crushing the pips, which would make the wine bitter.'

The machine is spewing the stalks into a larger crate at the back, leaving just the juice and skins and pips to shoot up the pipe.

'Remember, the juice itself is white,' explains Virgile. 'Very few red grapes have red juice. As I explained for my pink Cartagène, it's contact with the skins that gives a wine its colour.'

He leaves the *érafloir* and dashes up a ladder to pour a carefully measured quantity of colourless liquid into the top of the fast-filling *cuve*.

'You won't be able to taste this,' he promises. 'It's sulphur dioxide. The amount I use is way below the permitted maximum, even for organic wines. But it's absolutely essential for disinfection. It prevents oxidation and kills the bacteria, which would otherwise kill the fermentation.'

He jumps nimbly down again for a further check on progress.

'Are you two sleeping over there?' he jokes, as he whisks away a brimming crate of stalks and substitutes an empty one.

However, far from slumbering, Arnaud has been tirelessly feeding the insatiable mouth of the *érafloir* with roughly three crates of grapes to every one of mine.

Lack of space forces us to work with the double doors wide open and our combined activities have quickly been adopted as something of a spectator sport – not only for the early diners on Le Pressoir's terrace but also for numerous would-be winemakers in the village. Stéphane, for instance, the son of Serge, the owner of most of Virgile's Saint Saturnin vines, is familiar enough with grape growing. He grows them on other family land but he delivers them all to the co-operative, which is where he says goodbye to them.

'I'm thinking of breaking away myself,' he keeps telling anyone who will listen. 'Maybe next year . . .'

But as Virgile's whisper cynically explains, the co-operative has a vested interest in ensuring that its growers learn as little as possible about wine-making.

'Dad says your Grenache is already fermenting,' says Stéphane in amazement.

'Well, yes,' says Virgile, confirming the most natural thing in the world.

'But what did you do to start it?' asks the only man in Saint Saturnin who seems to know less about wine-making than I do.

'Nothing,' laughs Virgile. 'No magic, no spells and no prayers. The only strange thing would be, if it didn't start. Have a look at the Syrah in those crates. You see a slight bloom on the skin? Well, those are the yeasts. They're alive, and as they come into contact with the juice, they feed on the sugar content, which enables them to multiply, whilst converting the sugar into alcohol.'

Stéphane scratches his head incredulously. 'Maybe the year after next,' he seems to be thinking.

When eventually the last of the crates has been emptied into the *érafloir*, Virgile puts Arnaud on clearing-up duties and asks me to clamber up the ladder to join him on the 'roof' of the pair of newly refurbished concrete tanks. He unclamps one of the wide circular trapdoors and shows me the fermenting Grenache down below.

'Have a smell,' he says, as I wriggle forwards in the metre-high gap between *cuve*-top and ceiling. But then I recoil so fast from the sharp prick of gas that I bang my head on a beam. 'Carbon dioxide,' he says, 'the other by-product of the fermentation process, replacing all the oxygen. Fall in and you're dead!' he adds encouragingly.

A crab-like shuffle back towards the ladder strikes me as the most health-enhancing strategy at this point but Virgile quickly dispels any such thoughts.

'You're going to do a *remontage*,' he announces. 'Pumping the juice from the bottom back up to the top. How do you say? *Teck zees owe-zuh.*'

He looks very pleased with himself as he thrusts a hose into my hand and disappears down the ladder.

'*Verrrry carrrre-fool . . . I sweetch on zuh pomp.*'

As the pump whirrs into action, the juice from the tap down below starts gushing out at my end to water the surface of the mixture that is brewing in the darkness of the vat beneath me. After Virgile's words of warning, I dare not lean in too far to see what effect I am having. However, he explains that the object of the exercise is to introduce more oxygen and mix the contents thoroughly, otherwise all the fermentation activity will be concentrated in the semi-solid 'cap' at the top.

I have to crouch there waggling the heavy hose for half an hour to ensure an even distribution. The continuing procession of spectators acknowledges me tentatively, as if anyone passing his evening wedged between a concrete tank and a ceiling must be a little mad.

'*C'est qui là-haut?*' asks one of them.

'*C'est Patrick,*' explains Virgile.

'*C'est qui ça?*'

'*Un ami anglais.*'

'*Ah bon,*' says the questioner, having all the explanation he needs.

To relieve the monotony, Virgile passes me up a tasting sample of the slightly effervescent half-juice, half-wine that we are pumping and follows it with some of the Syrah that we picked today.

'Look how red it is already!' he exclaims with delight.

'I'll have to take your word for it,' I answer from my shadowy niche, but the taste is so intensely, deliciously fruity, it seems almost a shame to let the yeasts do their work.

Virgile meanwhile has filled a large, flat-based, test-tube-like vessel with more of the Syrah and is closely examining what appears to be a thermometer, floating vertically in the juice. He is measuring the sugar density, not the temperature, he explains. It tells him the potential alcohol, which at 13.5 per cent shows that his decision not to thin the bunches has not resulted in any loss of concentration.

'*Do you want eeeat wizz us?*' Virgile asks me, as he checks on Arnaud's purification of the crates with the high-pressure water jet.

It is almost nine o'clock and the prospect of simply rolling over to Le Pressoir is considerably more appealing than driving home and cooking. So I say 'yes' with alacrity, only to discover that we shall in fact be 'self-catering' again, *chez* Virgile. We stagger up to the flat to find that Florent, the chef, seems to have devoted all of the intervening three or four hours to washing his hair, with disappointing results on the food preparation front.

'We'll help,' offers Magda cheerfully as she and Margherita squeeze into the overcrowded galley kitchen. They are full of energy after their rest but their inexpert assistance keeps slowing Florent down as he deserts his post to consult me on the English for things like 'turn down the gas, you'll ruin the meat'.

'Have a beer,' suggests Virgile, as he waves aside my own offer to assist. 'Make yourself comfortable. You're the guest.'

I help myself to a bottle from the fridge but would prefer to do anything which might improve our chances of eating before midnight. Once again, I am reminded how much Virgile needs a wife.

'Not much of a crop,' says Krystina, reluctantly helping me gather up the almonds that have fallen to the ground, their smooth exterior husks already curling back to expose the roughness of the inner shells.

I excused myself from today's *vendange* on grounds of urgent almond husbandry, but the truth is, I was just too exhausted. When Krystina dropped by in the middle of the morning to ask me to translate the instructions for her latest electrical beauty aid, she found me still asleep.

'Very disappointing,' I grant her. 'I'll be lucky to fill a second basket, even with what's left on the trees. And for once, I can't blame Manu. He says they give him indigestion.'

The embarrassments of our disastrous encounter on the starlit château terrace have never since been mentioned. Her dealings with me have, however, changed. While not exactly cool, they are now straightforwardly, schoolteacherly brisk, which is an enormous relief.

'Your olives are even more of a failure!' she says with her usual brutal honesty, as she arms herself with a trug and transfers her efforts to lavender-picking – an activity more in harmony with her romantic notions of rural life.

'It's the same throughout the *département*,' I answer defensively. 'For some reason, the olive trees – especially the famous Lucques – didn't flower properly this year. And then the August drought put paid to most of what few olives there might have been. It's a real disaster, a *"crise"*, according to the Vargases. Well, Madame Vargas, anyway. Monsieur has twisted his ankle and can't even get down the stairs. She says there's going to be a massive shortage. But at least the trees are healthy. It's not another 1956.'

'I don't know why these people get so excited about 1956,' says Krystina dismissively. (For some reason she has never had a great deal of time for the Vargases, nor much sympathy for their ever-disintegrating health.) '1956 was nothing compared to 1709.'

How effortlessly she steers the conversation back to her own territory, as she starts assembling some artfully casual-looking lavender bunches to scent my house for the winter.

'The frosts of 1709 wiped out most of France's vineyards, as well as its olive trees – except, as luck would have it, in the Languedoc. The snooty Parisians were reduced to buying Saint Chinian and Corbières, so demand simply soared – especially with a broader range of society beginning to drink the stuff. You see, until this period, wine had only been produced in relatively limited quantities. Food shortages had been an almost constant problem and vines had been seen as a threat to vital cereal production. But suddenly the eighteenth century saw a fever of opportunistic plantings sweeping down to even the most unsuitably fertile land in the plains. Every little land-owner had his patch of vines – especially after the Revolution, when the vast estates of the Church and the nobility were broken up.'

'But quality?' I ask, as I stretch to reach the last recalcitrant almonds from the top of my ladder.

'Mainly dire,' she summarizes crisply. 'Traditional methods with traditionally poor results. Not much advance in two thousand years!'

I am late but I hope Virgile will understand. I had a crisis to cope with at home. The Vargases' cousin's horses had escaped.

It was very unfortunate. They had been making such an encouraging impact on the grass, with never a hint of delinquency in their good-natured munchings. But just as I was carrying my early breakfast into the courtyard this morning, a wave of unexpectedly robust expletives broke over me from Mme Gros's side of the stream. The horses, it appeared, had extended their flattening of the hay to a flattening of the fence that divides my land from her husband's vines.

I tore across the bridge, expecting to witness an implacable defence of her boundaries, but found instead a figure racked with paralysing doubt. The incursion had, I realized, presented Mme Gros with a serious dilemma. An unchecked equine rampage offered the tempting prospect of a catastrophic reduction in her husband's hectolitres for possibly years to come. Yet that would place her too profoundly in my debt. And anyway, there were sovereign rights of territoriality to be upheld here ... But before she could agonize further, Manu's panic-stricken arrival ensured a decisive vote in favour of expulsion.

'*Oh, putain de merde, quel bordel!*' he observed hysterically. '*Mais quelle espèce d'imbécile . . .?*' he shot an accusing glance in my direction and then turned his attention to the animals. '*Eh, foutez-moi le camp, alors!*' he bellowed, as he flapped his arms breathlessly to reinforce the message.

The damage to the vines was, in fact, negligible but it still took considerably longer than Virgile is likely to believe for the three of us to drive the horses back to where they belonged – and for me to draw on deeper reserves of diplomacy than I knew I possessed.

So it is nearly eleven o'clock when I finally arrive in Saint Saturnin to find a big, rectangular machine, which I have not seen before, parked in a pool of shade outside the *cave*. It looks a bit like a battered air-conditioning plant on wheels. A frowning Virgile is standing beside it, banging an illuminated numerical display with the flat of his hand. The number displayed is apparently not to his liking.

'The Grenache is too hot,' he announces. 'Already twenty-seven degrees, and if it gets as high as thirty-two, the fermentation will stop. Even slightly below that, there's a risk of boiling away the subtlety.' He gives the machine a vigorous shake. 'The trouble is, I've no idea what temperature it is inside this thing. The thermostat's all over the place and I'm afraid of overchilling the wine. Because anything below twenty-three will stop the fermentation too. If only I could find the repairman's number . . .'

'Second-hand?' I ask superfluously.

'Part of my bric-à-brac,' he admits. 'But don't forget how little I paid. It would be so much easier if I could put it inside where it's cooler, but how can I do that with the *érafloir* in the way all the time?'

A supervisory check on the morning picking campaign is now well overdue. The Saint Saturnin Cinsault was polished off yesterday and the Jonquières Carignan should be finished by lunchtime, so Virgile decides he will have to entrust the cooling operation to me. He shows me how to take the Grenache's temperature, using the test-tube-like container and a conventional thermometer.

'But whatever you do, don't let it go below twenty-three,' he warns me, as he climbs up into the tractor-cabin. 'Not that there's much hope of that!'

For a few minutes, I just stare at the machine and the pump and the concrete *cuve*, too nervous to lay a finger on any of them. Then, eventually, I summon up the courage to open the tap. A rapid stream of Grenache gushes down into the pit and, as soon as it is about a quarter full, I switch on the pump. With a greedy gurgle, the wine is sucked up and forced on out through a succession of pipes to the cooling machine in the square, then back inside to the top of the tank again.

So far so good, but I am supposed to be monitoring the temperature as well. It takes me a few minutes to get myself organized but not long enough to explain an initial reading of 24 degrees. Another, fractionally later, is even less plausibly 23.5. I am obviously misreading the scale. It was supposed to take much longer. But now a third reading looks dangerously close to 23. I quickly turn off the tap and the pump, preferring to wait until Virgile can show me what I'm doing wrong.

'I don't believe it!' he cries, returning with the trailerful of Carignan.

His tone says unmistakably, 'Can't you be trusted with anything?' and the vanful of pickers, driven back by Arnaud, gathers round inquisitively to see what disaster has struck in the master's absence.

'But you're absolutely right!' he rejoices, when his own rapid test confirms the same 23 degrees. 'And so quickly! What a relief!'

He is in fact sufficiently relieved to release the team for the rest of the day. One more full day, he thinks, should finish the

Saint Saturnin Carignan, which is all that now remains, and Gérard seizes the opportunity to invite the girls to his mother's house for the afternoon and evening. His mother has Polish ancestors, he says, and she is crazy about all things Polish – but it is all too clearly Magda who will be seeing the most of Maman, while Gérard's irresistible Germanic seduction strategies are targeted on Margherita.

Virgile intends to use the time to concentrate on his cellar work, but unfortunately his relief is such that he fails to see the impossibility of the 'quick lunch' that he proposes for the two of us at Jean-Marc's.

'Just a glass,' Virgile says abstemiously, as Jean-Marc shows us to a table near the bar at the front of the restaurant. However, for once something other than our wine order is uppermost in our host's priorities.

'Do you recognize this man?' he asks as he hands us a copy of the latest edition of a quarterly magazine devoted to the local wines.

It is open at a photograph of an impeccably dressed, immaculately coiffured, clean-shaven man of about Jean-Marc's age, smiling from behind a bar. Beside him is a strikingly tall and attractive young woman, looking remarkably like Céline, whose departure from this very restaurant Virgile is still lamenting. In fact, surely, it is Céline? Surely it is Jean-Marc's bar?

'Do you think they've caught my best side?' asks Jean-Marc, as we marvel at the hours that must have been sacrificed to personal grooming in order to create this moment of unrecognizable spruceness. 'Not a bad little write-up, for a place that opened in July,' he adds. 'But more importantly . . .' He turns to a feature devoted to rising Languedoc wine stars, where the photoshoot has confined itself to portraits of the relevant bottles. Prominent amongst these is a distinctively flourishing serigraphic signature. 'Here's an even better write-up for something bottled in June.' He beams with almost fatherly pride.

Jean-Marc does eventually focus on our order but it is much later than Virgile hoped when we return to tackle the *remontages du jour* – the two tanks of Syrah and the main tank of Cinsault.

The smaller, super-concentrated Cinsault, with the twenty per cent potential alcohol, he will leave for another day. He has yet to decide what to do with it. The yeasts, he explains, would normally keep going until all the grape sugar was converted into alcohol and there was nothing left for them to feed on. However, in cases like this, with exceptionally high sugar levels, the fermentation will almost certainly stop around fifteen per cent, because the yeasts will be killed by the strength of the alcohol, which they themselves have created. So the wine will probably end up as a semi-sweet, red 'curiosity'.

'Like a *Vendange Tardive*?' I ask, remembering a little of Mme Maraval's arrested fermentations and residual sugars, down in Mireval.

'Exactly. Something perhaps to accompany *foie gras* . . . Or possibly desserts . . . But would it sell?' he worries.

As usual, with the *érafloir* monopolizing most of the usable space, the doors of the *cave* remain open for maximum manoeuvrability. 'I can't wait to get that machine out of here,' Virgile grumbles at frequent intervals. 'In fact, I can't wait to get to the final day!' he adds almost as often.

The open-door operation is, as always, attracting plenty of idle curiosity. Luc, the truffle baron, lingers only long enough to be satisfied that the wheeler-dealer's vocation offers more repose, while Stéphane, the would-be *particulier*, slowly scratches his close-cropped head in bewilderment, as the dream of a break from the co-op slips back by another two years. There is even an encouraging number of interested purchasers.

The only snag is the absence of anything for sale.

'You can buy it in the next village, Montpeyroux,' says Virgile hopefully, knowing all too well that they will probably succumb to some alternative *vente directe* on the way. 'But what else can I do?' he asks me. 'With seven and half hectares and all this cellar-work, I can't do everything. I have to delegate something and selling's the one thing that doesn't impact on quality.'

Despite the late hour, he manages to make time for everyone, not least a succession of tiny, uncomprehending village children who never fail to distract him for a joke or a cuddle. He would make a natural father but, as he has often lamented, Saint Saturnin remains a village of bachelors.

And a business deal forced Sarah to cancel her summer visit.

'This isn't an aristocratic house,' says Count Henri de Colbert, the owner of the Château de Flaugergues since 1972, as he leads me up the monumental eighteenth-century staircase, occupying almost a third of this otherwise elegantly simple building. 'Like all the so-called "Montpellier Folies", it belonged to one of the newly-rich financial people, the Montpellier Mafia, if you like.' He pauses halfway up to show me one of the staircase's famous, gravity-defying key vaults. 'Etienne de Flaugergues,' he continues past some magnificent tapestries, 'a Councillor at Montpellier's Court of Revenue, Grants and Finance, bought the place in 1696. An ordinary farm, it was then. It took him until 1740 to turn it into what you see today.'

'But it was already a wine estate?' I ask.

'It was a vineyard in Roman times,' says the Count, as if a mere three hundred years of tradition might be beneath his contempt. 'But remember, there was very little monoculture anywhere until the nineteenth century. Still, we mustn't get bogged down in history. This is a living place – the only "Folie" which is an operating wine estate and open to the public and permanently lived in.' (I have already seen the subtle clues of occupation in the bulge of the Count's folded pyjamas under the covers and the Kerouac novel on the bedside table, in an otherwise faithfully nineteenth-century bedroom.) 'They're called "Folies" because they were built "in the foliage", not because they were acts of madness – although some were madder than others. They were mostly summer residences.'

'This close to the city?' I query.

The Château de Flaugergues is certainly close to Montpellier. It is effectively *in* Montpellier, just three kilometres from the city centre and completely surrounded by offices, hyper-markets and ring roads. The post office knows it more prosaically as 1744 Avenue Albert Einstein. Incredibly, however, here amongst all the tarmac and concrete, are thirty hectares of vine-yard. In the hands of anyone less determined, they too might have been swallowed up by the urban sprawl which now fills almost every metre between the city and the sea.

'What interests you most about Flaugergues?' asks Count Henri, as we head outside to the terrace dotted with citrus bushes. 'Wine or culture?'

I have not really thought about it. With neither of my 'minders' at my side – Manu being preoccupied with prepara-tions for his own *vendange* and Krystina away for a few days, pampering herself at a health spa – life seems altogether less polarized.

'Both, I suppose,' I hesitate.

'Good,' he replies decisively. 'For me they're inseparable. The house was built for pleasure and it's our aim to share that pleasure.' He gives each of the statues of Peace and Plenty guarding the front door an affectionate pat on the head. 'Did you see the sundial on your way in? You win a bottle of wine if you know the meaning of the motto: "*Jam non tua*" . . . No? It means "No longer yours". Time, that is. As soon as you've looked at the clock, the moment's passed. We have to make the most of every second, every good thing. So why don't we taste some wine while we talk some more?'

He leads me down through the lovingly restored geometry of the formal French garden, created, he explains, with ten thousand box trees gathered by the family on Sunday afternoons in the *garrigue*.

'We finished the *vendange* yesterday,' he says, as we reach the *cave*. 'So the pressure's very slightly off. Except, oh dear, I've a coachful from Denmark arriving. I might have to leave you to my oenologist. He'll tell you how much better the wines could be, if I'd only spend money on air-conditioning for the *cave*. Well, maybe one day . . . But here's a challenge.' He pours me a glass of his 'Cuvée Sommelière'. 'Our best seller in Britain, this. But how many months in oak, would you say? A last chance to win the bottle of wine.'

'Three?' I suggest cautiously.

'None at all.' He smiles delightedly. 'Just an exceptionally long fermentation. Fools a lot of experienced critics . . . But you'll have to excuse me, they're here,' he apologizes, and I watch him gathering his party round the sundial's motto and ebulliently offering that unclaimed bottle to any Danish Latin scholar who shares his own sense of how to get the most out of life.

I have not missed the last day after all. Yesterday's Carignan was more plentiful than Virgile had thought and required more elimination of individual, sub-standard grapes. Another morning's work remains.

'We're going to finish on the very day that we started last year,' says Virgile delightedly. 'My mother's come up from Montpellier to make us a celebration lunch but goodness knows where we'll have it. The flat's far too small.'

Anyone who has had the briefest involvement with the harvest appears to have been invited. An hour or so's work and it seems you're in, so a picnic would be best, if only the wind would die down. But none of Mme Joly's exasperated appearances in the *cave* has succeeded in clarifying her son's plans for either venue or menu. He has other priorities.

'A completely different fermentation technique,' he promises, as he rinses one of the last two empty fibreglass tanks. 'A *macération carbonique*. No more destemming.' He gestures towards the detested, space-consuming *érafloir*, which is still outstaying its welcome. 'Just whole, uncrushed bunches, piled on top of each other in the *cuve*. We can make a start with the leftover crates from yesterday. But first some DIY.'

He winks as he carries a length of lightweight plastic tubing and a roll of sticky tape up to the top of the concrete vats.

'We need to borrow some carbon dioxide,' he explains, as he improvises a pipe to funnel the gas from the tank of Grenache across to the empty *cuve*. 'Some people rely on the gas produced by the fermentation of the bottom bunches, as their skins start breaking under the weight of those above, but this is more effective. Either way, by surrounding the grapes with carbon dioxide, you deprive the yeasts of the oxygen they need for a traditional fermentation.'

'So what happens instead?' I ask, as I struggle to pass the first crate up to him at the top of the ladder that he has propped beside the *cuve*.

'A yeast-free intra-cellular fermentation inside the grapes.' He sees me looking puzzled. 'The important thing to understand is the difference in the resulting wine – brighter-coloured and fruitier. It works particularly well for Carignan.'

'Virgile, I'm going shopping,' calls a maternal voice from the square outside. 'You'll have to trust me. *A bientôt!*'

I clamber back over the obstacles for another crate. The back of the tiny *cave* has never seemed so depressingly far removed from the front, as I mentally multiply the distance between the van and the ladder by the quantity of crates remaining to be emptied. However, before these dispiriting calculations can be completed, in slouches Luc with a friend of his to ask what we're up to.

'Waiting for you two to help us,' answers Virgile, as Luc and his equally exercise-averse sidekick find themselves unexpectedly conscripted into a human chain.

With three pairs of arm muscles – even with Luc's scrawny biceps reluctantly responsible for the final upward push – the task seems to take about a tenth of the time. We are almost congratulating ourselves on clearing the backlog when Virgile's tractor rumbles up with a trailer which must contain easily twice the quantity that has just been emptied into the *cuve*. But at least we now have Arnaud's limitless energies at our disposal – indeed, such is his whirlwind of energy that Luc and his friend are able to sacrifice the lunch invitation for which they have just qualified and slink away for a few days' rest.

The remainder of the picking gang returns in Gerard's car with jubilant tales of celebratory grape fights. Gerard's peeved expression and grape-stained shirt cannot, I feel, be unconnected with Margherita looking so spotlessly pleased with herself. Magda too seems suspiciously gratified by the spectacle of Florent's stickily matted locks, requiring heaven knows how many hours of shampooing in the shower. They disappear to clean themselves up, leaving Arnaud and me to ferry the final crates into Virgile's waiting arms.

The morning harvest is almost too much for the *cuve*. Indeed, I wish more had been wasted in the grape fight, as Virgile clings to the top of the ladder, trying to juggle the final bunches into the last remaining cubic centimetres. But then, at last, the assembly of the *macération carbonique*, and with it the whole of the *vendange*, is finished.

'The end!' whispers Virgile, looking almost disbelievingly round at all the different fermentations that he has set in motion over the past few days: nine well-filled *cuves* and one deliberately left empty to allow for future rackings.

'I'm not sure I'd have believed all this back in January,' I tell him, genuinely humbled by the achievement.

'*Si tu veux, tu peux*.' He gives a modest shrug.

'If you want, you can,' I repeat to myself quietly, thinking there are worse philosophies than this.

'But not quite the end,' Virgile briskly returns to the fray. 'It's washing-up time, Arnaud.'

He starts to strip to his boxer shorts, which seems an unnecessarily radical approach to the cleaning of the crates. But then he puts his ladder up against a *cuve* of Syrah and starts clambering into it. The high-pressure hosing is, as usual, Arnaud's department. Virgile has what he calls a *pigeage* to do.

'Excuse me, there are people over here trying not to be put off their food,' calls Pius from Le Pressoir's terrace, where Virgile's semi-nudity is apparently visible through the ever-open doors.

'Make the most of it. I'll be charging a fee from next week,' replies Virgile, before explaining to me what he is up to.

The half-solid 'cap' of skins and pips needs to be submerged in the juice to stop it drying out. It also needs plenty of general agitation to extract maximum colour and flavour. Of course, many would achieve these things less picturesquely with a pole, he admits as he hauls his purple-stained body out of the Syrah and into the main tank of Cinsault and I utter a silent prayer that Manu falls into the latter, less folkloric category.

'Let no one deny that he puts a lot of himself into his wine,' quips Arnaud.

'Old joke,' puffs Virgile, clinging to the side, as far from the dreaded carbon dioxide fumes as possible. 'You wouldn't believe how hard this cap is,' he adds, although I would in fact, because it almost supported his weight when he started.

'Are you going to be long in there?' asks a long-suffering Mme Joly, come to tell him that everyone else is ready and waiting.

'We're using Stéphane's garden,' says Virgile. 'I phoned him while you were out. It's the last on the right, as you leave the village. You take everyone down there and I'll be along in a quarter of an hour.'

Mme Joly frowns the frown of a mother who has experienced Virgile's quarters of an hour before. 'Well, don't forget, you're bringing the wine,' she says, disappearing.

I excuse myself for a shower and return to the *cave* to find Virgile on his third – and he promises me final – *pigeage*. 'Just five minutes,' he assures me unconvincingly, as I head on down to the picnic ground.

'Incredible!' I gasp at the sight of the abundant pastoral banquet with which Mme Joly is busy anchoring two large tablecloths on the windswept lawn.

It seems inconceivable that she could have sliced all these tomatoes, beetroots and radishes in so little time – or grated all this carrot; or chopped all this fruit; or even managed to unwrap the profusion of pâtés, hams and cheeses that are jostling one another for space. And yet there is more: sausages and chicken pieces are already sizzling on a barbecue.

'And all from that tiny kitchen!' I marvel.

She gives my compliment a modest shrug.

'It's amazing,' I insist. 'Just like Virgile's miracles in his tiny *cave*.'

'*Si tu veux, tu peux.*' She smiles as she tosses an overflowing bowl of salad leaves. 'But you think his wine's all right?' she adds, sincerely seeking reassurance.

'All right?' I laugh in disbelief.

'I'll take that as a "yes",' she says, returning her attention to the barbecue. 'But you realize, he only got inside that *cave* a week before last year's harvest? He was tending his vines all year, with nowhere to go. Then just at the last minute, he found this place. It took him all of the first week to get rid of the animal smells. "I'll never be able to take my grapes in there," he kept saying. But he managed.'

'*Si tu veux, tu peux,*' I echo, more impressed than ever.

What Virgile has not managed, however, is his own arrival with the wine. The single bottle contributed by Florent has long since been drained and the pickers are growing restless, so I make an emergency sprint back to the *cave*.

'It's in the storeroom, under the stairs leading up to the flat,' says Virgile, who has emerged from the *cuve* and is drying himself with a very red-stained towel. 'The key's on a hook over there by the fuse-box. I just need to shower and send a quick fax to the analysis laboratory. Then I'll be there. Promise.'

As he hurries out into the square with the towel round his waist, I notice a postcard sellotaped to the front of the fuse-box. It features a photograph of Che Guevara, overprinted with a catchphrase. '*Soyons réalistes,*' it says. '*Exigeons l'impossible!*' (Let's be realistic – Demand the impossible!)

It could be Virgile's own motto, I reflect, as I take the key.

Five or six of the branches on the plum trees have snapped, which is hardly surprising. The weight must have been intolerable. Nature's niggardliness with the cherries and apricots has been absurdly over-compensated by a plum crop of epic proportions. Even the insects, which appear to have systematically punctured almost every pear and apple in the orchard, have given the plum trees an inexplicably wide berth.

Ludicrously, as soon as Virgile's *vendange* was over, I compounded the problem by mounting an almost twenty-four-hour guard. Too late, the full enormity of the potential harvest has borne in on me and, just when a dawn raid from Manu would be the greatest blessing imaginable, Mme Gros has been refusing to accept anything more than the daintiest of punnets.

'Please don't worry about us,' she bristled, with the deeply affronted air of one who would sooner see her husband drink himself to oblivion than allow him anywhere near my plums.

I have been making enough jam to fill a market stall. I have bottled some of the fruit in alcohol for the winter and pickled more in vinegar. I have filled every spare centimetre of the freezer, given bulging carrier bags to anyone in the area who I thought would let me and even borrowed a prune-making machine from the Vargases. But still the trees are heavily laden.

A hearty casserole in the shelter of the village café's reinstated plastic windbreak has brought temporary cheer but no solutions. I am just beginning to wonder whether I should humble myself to beg for Manu's intervention, when Babette arrives with an enormous slice of tart, heaped high with what are unmistakably the plums that she had from me.

'What a treat!' I gulp, as I fight back the tide of nausea.

'Nobody blames your uncle,' says Mme Gros, as her penetrating stare unequivocally accuses me. 'No one expects a dying man to worry about potholes in the drive. And we know you've had a lot on your own plate. But we were rather hoping by now . . .'

We are standing on opposite sides of one of the deeper chasms in the track that leads up from the post boxes to our respective properties. We share the use of at least a hundred and ninety of its two hundred metres and, fondly imagining that the cost of its upkeep would be similarly shared, I have in fact, for a number of weeks, been looking for a tactful opportunity to broach the subject of a joint repair bill. But Mme Gros has saved me the trouble by coming straight to the point. The drive, she insists, belongs to me and me alone and, with it, the responsibility for maintenance. Her *notaire* was quite clear on the point.

'It's been bad enough all summer,' her reproaches continue, as we stand aside to let the wheels of a little red, grape-laden van spin deeper into the remaining gravel. 'But with all this coming and going for the *vendange*, it's a nightmare,' she grumbles, as she stumps off to the village to purchase one of the Languedoc's less munificent harvest lunches.

Manu's picking began only a couple of days ago. The ripening of the grapes is always relatively late up here because we are so much higher than villages like Virgile's, but this year most of the local growers were able to start earlier than usual, at the beginning of last week. However, the timing of Manu's grape-gathering is always geared to the four or five days of sick-leave taken by his sons and, oddly, this seems to require a degree of co-ordinated pre-planning. So it is a vanload of somewhat overripe fruit that finally lurches out of its rut and up the hill to the semi-derelict lean-to that serves as the family *cave*.

Rather to my surprise, I have seen very little of either Manu or the sons. The notion that I was to be favoured with a place in their picking team seems to have been quietly forgotten. I imagine they are all far too suspicious of fancy ideas picked up in Saint Saturnin to let me anywhere near the scene of their vinicultural crimes. But notwithstanding the rather mushy-looking grapes, Manu still seems quietly confident that he can maintain his customary quality levels.

'Quantity might be down though,' he warned me last night. 'I might have to ration you next year.'

October

V IRGILE'S *VENDANGE* IS not in fact quite over. During the last
two weeks, Magda and Margherita have seen active
service with a variety of other growers who, for various
reasons, had later harvests than Virgile. Yesterday, however,
they were called back to base for a final campaign because
Virgile had not yet made his beloved pink Cartagène.

He originally planned to do the same as last year and make
it with a blend of Syrah and Grenache Noir. However, this year
the grapes were so ripe and the skins so richly pigmented that
the juice was already deeply coloured before it even left the
érafloir. So were the Carignan and Cinsault. Too deeply
coloured, he reluctantly decided, to achieve the delicate, pale
rosé that he wanted.

At first, having sent all his Grenache Blanc to the Gignac co-operative, he could see no alternative. But then he remembered some slightly later-ripening varieties of white table grapes that came with one of his rented 'job lots'.

'But how will you make it pink?' I asked, as I joined Arnaud and the Polish girls for a positively last session with the secateurs.

'I still haven't worked that one out,' he admitted unconcernedly. 'There's a tiny bit of Grenache Noir that we overlooked before.'

'You mean, this time, the *rosé* really will be a blend of white and red?'

'Time will tell,' he replied.

We stripped the field of every last Chasselas grape but still we needed more. Reluctantly, Virgile accepted the sacrifice of most of his precious Servent, the variety he had hoped would be keeping his table supplied until the end of the year. It was, however, a few kilometres away, so he and Arnaud went ahead in the van, while I followed behind with the '*ladeez*'.

We had just reached the relevant vines and I was about to pull up beside the van when I smelt something burning. On closer analysis, I could see something burning. There was smoke coming from the window of Virgile's van, and as he jumped out, gasping, from the cabin, it billowed from underneath the steering wheel.

'Drive away!' screamed Magda, as Virgile started ripping out his dashboard to get access to the burning wires. 'Get the car away from the fire!' she shrieked again, as Margherita gave voice to what I took to be similar sentiments in hysterical Polish.

Arnaud, stumbling from the other side of the cabin, yelled something unintelligible from lungs choked with the acrid smoke. 'Disconnect the battery!' he tried again.

'It's in the back!' shouted Virgile, still wrestling beneath the steering wheel, where flames had started to flicker.

'For god's sake, drive away!' was still the preferred option for Magda and Margherita, and it struck me they did have a point. It would hardly be constructive to fuel the fire with a second vehicle. So, feeling less than heroic, I followed their recommendation and drove to the opposite corner of the field. By the time we ran back, we found that Arnaud the electrician had saved the day. The drama, like the fire, had fizzled out with the isolation of the battery.

The girls were by now in tears. They had been close to tears ever since discovering the night before that all the buses back to Poland were full for the next two weeks, which meant they would have to face another three-day train journey. The self-ignition of the van was the last straw.

Virgile, on the other hand, seemed as cheerful and focused on the work in hand as ever. 'Thought we'd be roasting the Chasselas for a minute, there,' he observed wryly, as he started distributing the empty crates for the final gathering of Servent.

He did, however, have a problem. His van was immobilized and he needed a lift from me to pick up his tractor as the only other means of delivering the grapes to the *cave*, and a mobile phone call *en route* confirmed his suspicion that his 'minimum insurance' did not extend to fire damage. The business plan blessed by his bank was going to need a bit of adjustment. Likewise his plans for the rest of the day, while he tried to find a competent repairman who could also lend him a car. The Cartagène would have to wait for twenty-four hours.

'But I still haven't decided how I'm going to make it pink,' he confesses this morning, as he takes off his shoes and socks and rolls up the legs of his jeans past the knee. Saint Saturnin is about to be treated to a display of the dying art of foot treading, which the space constraints of the *cave* require him to stage in the square outside.

The awkward metal bulk of the *érafloir* has at last been banished to the garage but its place has been taken by the almost equally sizeable wooden wine press, which I last saw in January – now borrowed back, it seems, from whoever lent it for last year's operations. It is the old-fashioned, hand-operated variety, shaped like an enormous drum, with slatted sides, through which the juice will escape as a wooden lid pushes gradually down on the grapes. Arnaud has almost finished scrubbing it ready for action but first come the gentler preliminaries from Virgile, as he rinses his feet in a bucket and steps into the first of a line of crates which I have been organizing on the cobbles.

'Don't we get to see the boxer-shorts today?' calls Marie-Anne from outside Le Pressoir, as Virgile hitches up his jeans and advances to the next crate, like a seaside paddler stepping from one rock pool to another.

'No chance,' he shouts, as Arnaud and I begin to fill the drum with the first of the freshly trodden grapes.

'What's your price?' chimes in Pius.

'Take every wine but mine off your list!' comes Virgile's first and final offer, which predictably puts an end to the negotiations.

The first of the juice is already streaming through the wooden slats as Arnaud – a tower of stamina and strength, as always – fits the lid and starts the strenuous, steady rocking backwards and forwards of the long, sideways-projecting lever that slowly forces the lid down.

'I've cracked it!' proclaims Virgile, still squelching about in the final crate, as the level of frothy white juice in our plastic collecting tub rises. 'I've figured out how to make it pink.'

Climbing swiftly out of the grape pulp, he pauses only for the briefest of rinses before starting to organize his pump. The inward pipe he rests in the nearly brimming tub, while the outward one is hung over the top of a recently emptied *cuve* – or rather, not quite emptied, as Virgile explains. It still contains the skins and pips from one of his Syrahs, which should have been emptied out for distillation yesterday, when the wine was drawn off. But the problems with the van left a lot of things undone.

'This should give a touch of Syrah flavour, as well as the bit of colour,' he explains, as he starts to pump the pure white grape juice over the *marc*. 'Mustn't leave it too long though. Maybe a couple of hours.'

The juice from the second load of pulp undergoes the same process, except that it is already subtly pink from the small amount of forgotten Grenache Noir that was rustled up for the purpose. Even before the pumping is complete, Virgile runs off a sample from the bottom of the *cuve* and finds to his dismay that, less than half an hour after the infusion began, the colour is already too dark – a proof, if any were needed, of the incredible concentration of this vintage.

'There go my Christmas table grapes,' he sighs resignedly. 'I'm going to need every last bunch of Servent to make this pale enough again.'

'I am *not* going trainspotting,' I told Krystina, in a rare moment of self-assertion. 'I don't care how enormous the impact of the railways on the nineteenth-century wine world was, I don't need a field trip to grasp the point.'

There were trees to be pruned – ludicrously tall and straggly fruit trees in desperate need of my saw.

'*C'est un peu tard, quand même,*' said the Vargases – both, for once, as fit as they are ever likely to be – when I announced my plans last week. 'Summer's the time for pruning, if you want any fruit next year. Otherwise you risk diseases. Still, beggars can't be choosers . . .'

I persuaded myself this morning, however, that it was nearly as warm as an average July in the Cotswolds so I may just get away with it.

Krystina has grudgingly appeared in a kind of *haute couture* safari suit, which is apparently the closest that she gets to gardening clothes. But her sulky demeanour as she steadies my ladder tells me it could take some while to jolly her back into full pedagogic gear.

'Give me a date,' I coax, as I tackle the last of the ridiculously high branches on an apricot.

'1855,' she mumbles grumpily.

'The year of what?' I prompt, as the branch begins to topple.

'The first train from Montpellier to Paris,' she admits unwillingly.

'But I thought the Parisians were already drinking our stuff,' I encourage her, exchanging the pruning saw for secateurs with the aim of shaping the remaining growth into something more recognizably tree-like.

'Only when they had to,' comes the reflex correction. She may be about to weaken.

'It wasn't so much a question of likes and dislikes, more a matter of price and durability,' she starts again, then checks herself, agonizes for a second and finally throws grouchiness to the wind.

'You see, the railways cut the cost of transport by eighty per cent. And they were so much faster than the canals – even the lighter, more perishable wines could travel. The vineyards round Paris, with their much less favourable climates, simply couldn't compete and were quickly turned over to cereals . . .'

Krystina, predictably, has nearly as many 'Tales from the Railway Bank' as I have apricot trees, but as I diversify to the almonds, so she broadens her own theme. 'The railways were only a part of a wider industrial revolution,' she explains, still anchoring my rickety wooden ladder. 'The urban population explosion brought enormously expanded demand at the cheaper end of the market. Hérault wine production nearly quadrupled between 1850 and 1870, as more and more vines spilled down to the plains and grapes like Aramon and Terret yielded dramatically higher volumes . . .'

I am no longer really concentrating, feeling suddenly over-whelmed by the chaos of severed timber that needs to be tidied up in the little remaining daylight. Small for the outdoor bonfire, large for the hearth indoors was the kind of thing that I had in mind but Krystina has no patience with such fastidi-ous segregation. She hurls everything in sight towards a for-midable unlit pyre near the stream. It is already almost as big as a bonfire safely can be. In fact, it is starting to look like some sort of defensive barrier between me and my neighbours.

'You realize that bonfires are illegal until the First of November, don't you?' calls Mme Gros with evident satisfac-tion from the opposite side. 'Especially with your drive impassable to fire engines!'

'Just the Carignans left to do,' says Virgile, as he opens a tap.

The traditionally fermented version immediately gushes out from its *cuve* and into the handily perforated crate, which is suspended as an improvised sieve across the freshly scrubbed pit in the cellar floor. He catches a little for a swift appraisal of colour, smell and taste and passes it to me. (It is already sur-prisingly drinkable – firm and fairly one-dimensional, yes, but not at all 'difficult'.) An activation of the pump sends it gurg-ling on through a series of hosepipes to an empty *cuve* on the opposite side of the cellar, leaving only the wine-soaked *marc* in the original. He opens the porthole at the bottom and starts shovelling out the *marc* by hand. A dozen or so bucket-loads – perhaps half the total amount to be processed – and the waiting wine press is full.

'Arnaud's favourite,' jokes Virgile, as the taller and slimmer of the two young men applies himself to the rhythmic pushing and pulling of the metal lever that slowly forces the residual wine from the skins to the chain of waiting buckets. 'Hogs all the best jobs for himself,' he teases, as the skins get drier and Arnaud's puffing gets louder.

Virgile's efforts are needed on the other side of the press, constantly tasting the bright purple-red liquid that is flowing increasingly slowly from the broad metal spout. At a certain point he decides that the wine is losing finesse. 'See for yourself,' he says, as he offers the glass. 'It's harder and greener-tasting.' So the remaining bucket-loads are consigned to a separate *cuve* of mixed variety *vin de presse*, already started in the earlier sessions. I ask about its fate and he says he'll wait and see.

'It may give extra weight to the principal blend,' he suggests. 'Or I might make something completely separate. It depends how things develop . . . And on my mood . . .'

Duplicate quantities from a second press-full complete the procedure and then there is the little matter of filling the tractor-trailer with the newly compacted skins. Virgile and I manage to heave the four substantial crates from today's operations unaided, while the tireless Arnaud starts what promises to be a couple of hours of cleaning up. However, the dozen or so crates from the previous days, which have been gathering flies on a patch of wasteland outside the borrowed sheep-shed on the edge of the village, need the strength of all three of us because they have, unfortunately, been gathering rainwater as well. This not only makes them almost impossibly heavy, it also leaves a blood-red trail dripping all the way through the village as Virgile drives off.

'You're going to be popular,' I say when I draw in behind him at our destination.

But I need hardly have worried, as most of the other tractor-loads queuing behind us are oozing in a similar fashion. It is one of the busiest afternoons of the year in Saint André de Sangonis, a village about ten kilometres from Saint Saturnin and home to one of the *département*'s largest distilleries.

'A bit different from Matthieu's place, eh?' laughs Virgile, as I blink incredulously at the purple mountains of grape-pressings awaiting treatment, and the three towering cranes rotating above them to shift huge mechanical grab-loads into the massive processing pits in the courtyard. 'I have to surrender ten per cent of all the alcohol I make to the state,' he explains.

'Like a tithe?' I ask, amazed at the existence of such a medieval-sounding imposition.

'Exactly,' he confirms, as he registers his *marc* with the office and puts a small sample into a numbered plastic sandwich box which is issued to him. 'I'm hoping I'll get enough from this to cover my obligations. I certainly don't want to give them any of my wine. Nor do I want to lose any of the serious stuff that Matthieu is making for me.'

'But what do they do with the sample?' I ask, as the contents of Virgile's trailer start their undignified slide into one of the pits. 'Surely it's too late for testing, now that it's mixed in with everybody else's?'

'The sample tells them how much alcohol they'll get from a kilo,' explains Virgile. 'Did you notice? That was a giant weighing machine that I was parked on. All we have to do now is stop there again, so they can compare the before and after weights and calculate my entitlement. Then I'll get Matthieu to show you some "real distilling",' he adds, as he shakes his head at the sight of a workman dousing the skins with water to make an unappetizing pseudo-wine for distillation.

'Virgile's right,' says Matthieu, when we arrive in Montpeyroux. 'There's absolutely no need to add water, except maybe a tiny bit at the bottom to stop it sticking. All you have to do is "cook" the *marc* as it is.'

The rusty stills that I last saw resting in the August sunshine are all now belching smoke into the autumnal garden and Matthieu is busy stoking the fires underneath them with wood.

'How's your chemistry?' he asks, as he lifts the lid of the nearest dustbin-like heating compartment to check its contents.

'Assume total ignorance,' I reply, having only the haziest

idea how the odd-looking contraption in front of me is proposing to turn the mound of steaming *marc* inside it into *eau de vie*.

'All you really need to understand is that alcohol and water evaporate at different temperatures,' he says. 'Seventy-eight degrees for alcohol and a hundred for water – so the vaporized alcohol is drawn off first. It re-condenses in the form of alcohol as it passes through here.' He points to an arching pipe that rises from the 'dustbin-lid' and descends to a smaller receptacle on the other side. 'In fact, it goes through twice to achieve sufficient purity and strength but that's basically all there is to it.'

'Is this mine?' calls Virgile from the garage, where he is lifting the lid of an immaculately gleaming stainless steel container.

Matthieu nods affirmatively and, scooping a little out in a glass, Virgile explains that it's a blend of Syrah and Grenache. It was made from the best of his *marcs*, delivered last week and already finished.

'Except that it's eighty per cent alcohol,' he warns, and he laughs at my sharp intake of breath as I taste it. 'It has to be watered down for normal consumption.'

'And aged for about three years to round it out,' adds Matthieu. 'But fortunately for his cash flow, he only pays the tax when he takes it away.'

'Otherwise I'd be broke,' says Virgile. 'With two hundred litres in here and another fifty from last year!'

Matthieu is just proposing a modest diminution of the fifty for comparison, when the telephone interrupts him.

'A couple of minutes,' he assures the caller. 'Promise,' he adds and replaces the receiver. 'That's why I told you in August that I'm not going to get too big,' he says, as he reaches for his coat and his keys. 'If my son says he's home from school early, I want to be there.'

*

'I don't believe this,' fumes Krystina in front of the third pair of firmly locked gates since our morning espresso.

It all began at a sunlit café on Béziers's broadest boulevard. She was explaining how the city had changed beyond all recognition on the back of its early nineteenth-century brandy wealth, with a hundred and fifty distillers and a weekly *eau de vie* market which was one of the most important in France. Then, it seems, around the middle of the century, the brandy wealth had adroitly turned itself into wine wealth as demand for wine and competition from other spirits, especially Cognac, both increased. Finally, the resulting fortunes had been channelled into château-building: a remarkable hundred or more springing up within fifty kilometres of Béziers.

Unfortunately, however, they are proving rather less accessible to the public than Krystina confidently assumed when she insisted on a day's deferral of my apple-tree pruning. They encompass, she assures me, just about every style you can think of – even an oddly English Neo-Gothic – but their gates (and we have now failed to get past a fourth pair) are tending to look very much the same.

'The Languedoc nobility built very few grand houses under the *Ancien Régime*,' says Krystina, putting on her bravest face, as we drive on to number five. 'Not just because they were relatively hard up but because they were far enough from Court to avoid the ruinous royal progresses that forced so many of their northern colleagues into expensive building programmes. These are all "new money",' she explains, as she rings fruitlessly at another bell. 'Either directly from brandy and wine or indirectly from ancillary trades like barrel-making.'

With a last despairing tug on the bell chain, even Krystina knows she is beaten, but the sun is shining, the leaves of the autumn vines are glowing red and gold and, most important of all, we have a picnic in the boot of the BMW.

A break for lunch, however, implies no break in the history lesson.

'They weren't just investing in bricks and mortar,' she continues seamlessly, whilst I unpack an elaborate suite of picnic furniture. 'They were also spending money on experimental crossbreeds and improved technology. Not what you'd think of as modern, of course. More a matter of horse-drawn ploughs replacing mattocks, that kind of thing. But quality and keeping potentials were genuinely improving.'

'A golden age?' I ask, wondering whether we really need the second parasol.

'Until disaster struck,' she confirms, with a peremptory signal that we do. 'Ironically, it was all a result of that international crossbreeding activity. First came powdery mildew, from North America – oïdium, as your friend Virgile would call it.' Her tone implies the abandonment of all ambition to make him *her* friend, as does the savagery with which she stabs the parasol spike into the ground. 'The wretched fungus reduced the Hérault crop by sixty per cent within three years of its arrival in 1851.'

'But surely oïdium was treatable with sulphur?'

'So they discovered after three or four years of crisis,' she grants me. 'But almost as soon as they'd done so, a second calamity threatened to wipe out every vineyard in Europe.'

'The phylloxera fungus?' I ask, determined to win what few points I can on botanical health hazards.

'It wasn't a fungus,' snaps Krystina, impatiently watching me struggle with her absurdly heavy hamper. 'It was a parasitic aphid, about a millimetre long, which fed on vine roots and eventually killed them. But it also came from North America.'

She pulls a luxurious-looking bottle of champagne from the hamper.

'It arrived in the Hérault in 1867 and by 1881 the whole *département* was infected. At first, nobody understood why the

219

vines were withering. Growers blamed the weather, the exhaustion of the soil, even divine retribution! By the time the real cause was recognized, it was out of control.'

She spoons a family-size jar of caviar between two plates.

'The official response was hesitant and slow. They tried flooding the vines to kill the eggs but that was expensive, short-term and only possible in the plains. They also tried insecticide but that killed all the other insects and sometimes the vines themselves. The only solution that worked – the expensive grafting of European vines on to phylloxera-resistant US rootstocks – was long resisted. Understandably perhaps, when all these problems were seen as America's fault in the first place.'

Alternate mouthfuls of Krug and caviar are making the discourse less intelligible.

'When they finally tried it, they found a lot of the imported rootstocks were infected with *downy* mildew.'

'But surely that was treatable with lime and copper sulphate?' I try to reassert my expertise in these matters.

'So they discovered – eventually. But by then, a lot of smaller growers had been driven out of business. The vineyard area more than halved in ten years and many of the better vineyards on the hillsides were never replanted. That's why you find so many abandoned "ghost villages" up near us. Yet the region over here, around Béziers, got off relatively lightly. Phylloxera didn't arrive until 1878, enabling the rich local growers to get richer, while prices quadrupled. So they were much better placed than most to reconstitute their vineyards . . .

'Not to mention building their châteaux,' she adds, with the ominous emphasis of a woman determined to penetrate at least one of them before allowing me to go home.

The horses will have to go. It's a pity because I've grown fond of them. But they have started damaging the supporting terrace walls, as their success in devouring the more accessible expanses of hay has forced them into less obvious corners of the land. And now that the autumn rains have made the soil so much softer, the scope for more widespread destruction decisively outweighs any potential benefits from continuing hospitality.

More agreeably, the wet weather has brought a permanent return to the pool of the syncopated croaking of the tree frogs, without yet achieving the Wagnerian volume of the early summer broadcasts.

It has also encouraged the sprouting of a perplexing assortment of unidentifiable wild mushrooms. There are some luridly bright and, to my untutored eye, unashamedly toxic-looking orange ones around the roots of some of the olive trees, while those in the orchard look innocuous enough for the table. Yet how can I be sure that nature isn't tricking me with false clues?

The book that guided me so authoritatively through the world of *fouine* droppings covers only a handful of examples, and Manu uncharacteristically disclaims any expert knowledge in this territory. 'The wife's department,' he informed me. Yet something in Mme Gros's poisonous look when she last lamented the state of the drive told me it might be tempting fate to ask her advice. So, rather unadventurously, I am resorting to a purchase in the drizzly Clermont l'Hérault market.

'Why not try the *trompettes de mort*?' suggests the wizened, elf-like mushroom salesman, half-hidden by the rainshield that he is improvising with the local newspaper. '*Délicieuses avec un peu de persil et de l'ail.*'

But somehow that look from Mme Gros has diminished the appeal of these sinister-looking, jet-black delicacies and I opt for some dependably innocent *cèpes*.

'*Vendange* still going strong?' asks the stallholder, having noticed my dark-purple-stained hands, which uncountable scrubbings have failed to whiten.

'All over,' I assure him, adding, 'I was doing a *décuvage* on a *macération carbonique*', then instantly feel ashamed of my slide into cellarspeak obscurities.

'Well, *bonne continuation*!' is my salesman's baffled valediction.

I do, however, feel strangely proprietorial about the *macération* – perhaps because Virgile and I dealt with it on our own, without the aid of Arnaud, who had disobligingly gone to an interview for an electrician's post.

It was clear as soon as the tap was turned that this was going to be quite unlike the traditional fermentations. So little juice emerged that I assumed there must be a blockage but Virgile explained that most of the wine was locked inside the grapes. Indeed, when he opened the porthole, it was clear that the grapes on most of the bunches piled high inside the *cuve* were more or less intact, looking almost perfect enough to eat. We tried them. They were little explodable capsules of rich, slightly effervescent winey juice. Every bunch had to be dragged out by hand, hence my arms being purple up past the elbows. We put four or five loads into the winepress and took it in turns to give each an exhausting double pressing. Then finally we tasted the results: immensely drinkable, intensely fruity, 'red-fruity' to be specific, but smaller in quantity, Virgile tells me, than if the grapes had been conventionally fermented.

'Oh well, *tant pis*!' say my aching arms. 'You can have too much of a good thing.'

I have learned something important very late.

I now know that Uncle Milo's house is only twenty minutes' drive from what has ever since last night been my favourite restaurant.

But as I said, this life-changing discovery has come painfully late, for today Le Mimosa will be callously closing its menus for a five-month *fermeture annuelle*. The New Zealand cook and her Welsh wine-waiting husband will be paying monstrously self-centred visits to distant families and otherwise indulging unreasonable winter wanderlust, leaving me bereft. To make matters worse, the belated discovery was made in Saint Guiraud of all places – a village that I must have driven through two or three times every week since January, on my way to Virgile's. And most sickening of all, I owe my introduction not to Virgile but to Mme Gros.

In a moment of madness, I had invited her to a birthday dinner in *her* favourite restaurant. (Well, all right, there was a modicum of method as well: given my extended absences next year, it was clearly in my interest to leave her feeling loved.) But Le Mimosa was not, of course, her 'favourite' restaurant. She had never been there either. However, she had, I suspect, heard sufficient to know that it would be prudent to save it for an occasion when the bill would not be paid by Manu. (Perhaps, on reflection, the extended *fermeture* is not such a bad thing after all.) Anyway, so determined was Mme Gros to allow my generosity free rein that she allowed us to order the six-course '*menu capricieux*', invented daily by Bridget Pugh according to the inspirations of the market place. She even sanctioned the '*dégustation*' of six accompanying wines, selected by David according to the inspirations of his wife's dishes.

'I don't believe that woman eats her own food,' whispered Mme Gros suspiciously, as soon as Bridget took our order. Her advance intelligence had not encompassed the proprietors' overseas origins and she was suddenly doubtful of the wisdom of her choice. 'In fact, I don't believe she eats at all,' she persisted, watching Bridget's slim and graceful form return to an open-plan kitchen, which was surely smaller than my own. 'Hardly what you expect in a cook,' she snorted.

However, by the time our delicately presented first course arrived, we had learned that cooking was only the second of Bridget's career accomplishments. Her first – unmistakable in her rigidly straight-backed poise, as soon as we knew – was that of a ballerina, the two of them having met when David was pursuing his own first profession as a violinist with the Royal Ballet in England.

'*Mon dieu*,' whispered Mme Gros, as if foreign restaurateurs were bad enough, without them being *artistic*.

'I'm doing something special tonight,' said David with infectious enthusiasm, as he brought us the first of our wines. 'All six will be from one of the best of our neighbours, Mas Jullien in Jonquières.'

'Only a little for my wife,' cautioned Manu, no doubt hopeful that his own six pourings might be correspondingly enhanced.

The name of Olivier Jullien evidently meant nothing to either of my guests but hardly a week has passed this year without some express or implied acknowledgement from Virgile of Olivier's importance as friend and mentor. So a tasting of two different whites, a *rosé*, two reds and a late-harvested dessert wine, all of his making, was a treat that felt long overdue.

It also helped to distract me from the evening's embarrassments – like Mme Gros diluting her wines with mineral water. ('Very nineteenth century,' said David, with scarcely a flinch. 'Disinfecting the water with wine.') Or Manu greeting the biggest selection of cheeses that I have ever seen with a confession that he was '*très, très amateur du fromage*' and wanted to sample them all. ('Two plates would have been more honest,' said David dryly.)

More importantly, the tasting left little doubt about where the Renault should be pointed this morning.

Unusually there is no sign of either Manu or Mme Gros. Maybe they are both the worse for wear or maybe they are writing their thank-you letters. Either way, I am able to get away alone. However, in my haste to do so, I forget to telephone to see whether a visit would be convenient, and although Olivier's greeting is as warm as I could wish, it is clear from the level of activity in his *cave* that my timing could have been better. I fumble an explanation about the Mimosa and my consequent resolution to effect a significant depletion of his stocks but he shakes his head and smiles, as if at my innocence.

'Nothing left at this time of year,' he apologizes. 'You'd need to come back after Easter. But you've come all this way and I need some coffee, so why don't you join me?'

Olivier looks to me like restless energy personified and the notion that he is accustomed to coffee breaks seems profoundly unlikely but it would be churlish to refuse.

'Once organic, always organic,' he says with a grin, as he empties the dregs from his breakfast cafetière into a kitchen pot plant.

I ask whether I could at least reserve some of each of the wines that I enjoyed last night.

'Out of the question,' he replies but then smiles and explains that he no longer makes the majority of them. 'Take the reds,' he continues, as he passes me a mug. 'The two you tasted were deliberately different, from contrasting soils. "Depierre" and "Cailloutis", I used to call them. But then I got so sick of customers saying, "Oh, you've only got Depierre when I so wanted Cailloutis" or the other way round. So now I'm blending it all into one, called simply Coteaux du Languedoc.'

He tells much the same story for his whites. 'Les Vignes Oubliées' (The Forgotten Vines), which David served us, used to be made from some of the older grape varieties of the Languedoc, like Carignan Blanc, which had almost disappeared. It represented a balance between tradition and experiment and it summed up a lot of what Olivier stood for. But his customers started caring less about the contents of the glass than the romance of the concept. It had become a straitjacket. He felt typecast. So now he is trying to recover some autonomy by slimming down to one 'basic' red and one 'basic' white – each free to blend different grape varieties from different soils and each free to seek its own version of perfection from vintage to vintage.

Olivier says that he will, however, continue with one additional red wine. He calls it 'Les États d'Âme' (literally, states of mind or, more precisely, soul) and, as the name suggests, it is an improvisation. It reflects his mood of the moment and defies description precisely because it explores a different direction every year: an emblem, it strikes me, of the modern Languedoc's restless spirit.

Like Virgile, Olivier is interested in the biodynamic approach but last year he learned the hard way the dangers of embracing it too literally. He allowed the frosts to kill some newly planted vines, instead of taking avoiding action earlier. He now believes that, if there are eight factors to be taken into account, the biodynamic calendar should always be the eighth. Otherwise it simply paralyses.

'You can wait for ever for the ideal moment that never comes,' he says ruefully.

It is easy to see why he has been such a source of inspiration to Virgile and yet I am sure he does not see himself as any kind of leader. He is much too individualistic and mercurial for disciples. But he does have a strong sense of his 'role'. If he were in Burgundy, he explains, he would have a totally different responsibility: to follow time-honoured traditions and bring out the best from a particular patch of land in a single, traditional grape variety. But what is the function of Mas Jullien in the Languedoc?

He pauses thoughtfully.

'Not to meet people's expectations,' he says emphatically. 'Rather to surprise. Sometimes even to disappoint. But always to stimulate.'

He pauses again, as if in search of another way of defining his aims.

'You know, in my grandfather's day, the Languedoc was a simple, self-sufficient paradise,' he says wistfully. 'Still substantially a land of "polyculture", with olives, fruits and cereals grown alongside the grapes. A bit cut off by the mountains but able to grow almost everything its people needed – nearly all the wine for local consumption and nearly all consumed within the year . . . Well, my responsibility is to transfer something of that lost quality of life back into the quality of my wine.'

'Can you believe this weather?' says Virgile, rolling up his shirtsleeves in the courtyard garden behind Le Pressoir.

We have just completed a hot and sticky visit to his local tax office. Every month, it seems, he has to make a tediously complicated declaration of any comings and goings of alcohol in his *cave*: on this occasion, for instance, the arrival of the pure alcohol that he has been adding to the Cartagène. Even more tediously, he then has to pay the related duties.

However, at least he does not have to go far for these periodic brushes with bureaucracy. The tax office doubles as the reception desk at Saint Saturnin's co-operative – or vice versa, depending on your perspective. The customs clerk leads a parallel life as the co-op's receptionist and telephonist, in return for free accommodation. Even more bizarrely, she also runs the village *tabac* through the same small, sliding glass window. Most of her filing cabinets are incongruously filled with stamps and cigarettes instead of tax returns and it was largely the volume of the morning's tobacco sales that made the taxation formalities so prolonged – well, that and the fact that the clerk had to keep on telephoning the co-operative's chief accountant to pick his brains on the correct completion of her forms.

'A whole hour inside the enemy camp!' I reflect, as we wait for our aperitifs.

'That's honestly not how I see the co-op,' says Virgile.

'After all the grief they've given you?' I ask, in genuine surprise.

'We're not in competition; we're *complimentary*,' he insists. 'I just wish they'd see it that way themselves. Different products, different roles. You see, for me, a healthy market means a lot of people drinking wine on a regular basis. And that means a lot of decent quality, affordable wine for everyday consumption, rubbing shoulders with the best. Which is not to say that the co-op doesn't make some very good wines . . .' The arrival of our glasses of Cartagène relieves him of any further struggle to be fair.

'Anyway, the weather's done wonders for the wine – *tous entrés dans le malo!*' He notices that this means nothing to me. 'The malolactic fermentation,' he elaborates. (Still nothing.) 'A separate, second stage in the fermentation process,' he explains. 'Activated by bacteria, about two weeks after the alcoholic fermentation. It converts the sharper "malic" acid that you find in apples into softer, rounder "lactic" acid – like in milk. Makes the wine less grapey, more . . . "winey", for want of a better word. You'll see for yourself soon.'

Virgile takes another sip of Cartagène. It comes from Mas Jullien and I notice a frown replacing the smile. 'Have I told you about Olivier?' he asks. 'How we've stopped discussing wine-making? He saw my signing up with Puech as a betrayal. We're still friends. We'll still go hunting together, I'm sure. But no more exchanging of ideas and experiences,' he sighs with a powerful sense of his loss. 'Olivier has very high ideals.'

November

'DID YOU HAVE many snakes this summer?' asked Mme Gros casually a couple of weeks ago.

'Snakes?' I queried.

'In your spare bedroom,' she clarified. 'Always their favourite in your uncle's day. Never could work out how they got there.'

'Well, no . . .' I was happy to confirm. I had never noticed so much as a distant rustling in the grass.

'You do look under the beds, don't you?' she pressed. 'Not that they're poisonous, of course. Just a bit big to trip over if you're getting up in the dark.'

Uncle Milo's trusty nature book was a little more detailed on the subject of the region's indigenous serpent, if not entirely reassuring. The *Couleuvre de Montpellier* did not, apparently, 'normally' attack humans. It just had this off-putting tendency to rear up like a cobra when irritated. But the principal consolation, given the time of year, seemed to be that sightings were generally confined to the months of March to September – a time-frame endorsed by Mme Gros, as she made gratuitously clear on Sarah's long-deferred return, a couple of days ago.

'Just as well you didn't come back in the summer,' she said with unconvincing solicitude. 'You wouldn't want to be woken up like Milo was once, by a snake tapping its head on the window.'

The reason for Mme Gros's coolness towards Sarah is not entirely obvious – unless it could be her reluctance to share the substantial kiwi crop, which is coming up to ripeness against one of my terrace walls, with more of us than is strictly necessary, especially with someone who has now come twice in a year to get more than her fair entitlement.

Sarah has, however, been lucky to coincide with some unseasonably mild, almost summery weather to make up for any lack of warmth from across the stream.

Even Monsieur Mas, the tractor-man, was wearing a vest and shorts when he came up yesterday to plough the gently sloping rectangle where I am planning to put my vines. He seemed to be saying that it was too hot for planting. But then again, he might have been saying it was the heat that was making his hearing aid whistle. Until the French dental profession comes up with a set of false teeth to make his accent more penetrable, I shall never know.

At Virgile's suggestion, I am planning to experiment with some newly developed hybrid vines that will not need constant spraying during next year's absences. In an ideal world, I would have been out acquiring them during these last few days but my conscience made me take advantage of the sunshine to see whether a coat or two of paint on my window frames might increase their chances of surviving another winter.

I have not seen Virgile since our lunch but the fact that most of Sarah's excursions have deviated through Saint Saturnin has enabled me to shadow him by proxy. I feel I am up to date with every gurgle of his malolactic fermentations, without ever putting down my paintbrush. Yesterday evening, however, just a few minutes after the return of Sarah's Range Rover – loaded surely with Jean-Marc's entire stock of Virgile's Coteaux du Languedoc – I dropped my brush with a start at the sound of a scream from Sarah's bedroom.

I ran in from the courtyard and up the stairs to find her standing on a chair. It was the only time I had ever seen her looking less than composed. She was pointing at the ground in terror.

'It's a snake!' she whispered, as if further screaming might provoke it.

'Where?' I asked from the safety of the corridor. I couldn't see anything.

'It was a snake,' insisted Sarah, still balancing on her chair, but she could no longer see anything either.

We searched cautiously but thoroughly, not just in Sarah's room but everywhere, yet we found nothing snake-like. She knew that I thought she had imagined it, no doubt prompted by Mme Gros's welcome speech. It was, after all, much too late in the year. So we said nothing more about it.

Until this morning.

Sarah wanted to make an early start for her great drive north to the Channel and she offered me a lift to the village, so that I could take advantage of the fine weather to walk home again with my bread. And we are just at the bottom of the drive, turning the Range Rover past the post boxes, when a sizeable bird of prey – a buzzard, I shall assume until I can check with the nature book – swoops low across the track, no more than twenty metres ahead of us. Evidently, something in the hedgerow has aroused too much interest for it to worry about the approaching engine noise. And then we see precisely what.

Wings beating vigorously, the buzzard rises vertically to hover for a moment in our direct line of vision and there, in glorious, sunlit close-up, clamped firmly in the predator's beak, is a fiercely wriggling, metre-and-a-half-long snake.

'I win!' says Sarah, as she waves goodbye.

Virgile's *cave* was locked and deserted and so, I soon established, were both the flat and the nearby garage. The doors of the sheep-shed on the edge of the village, however, proved to be open. A radical clearout was in progress. The grassy area outside looked like a scrap dealer's forecourt and sounds of strenuous physical activity were coming from within. All I could see in the darkness inside was the shadowy outline of the tractor and its trailer. The latter was piled perilously high with what I judged from the smell to be the sheep-droppings of earlier centuries and every few seconds I heard a grunt, as an invisible Virgile hacked another shovelful from the dung-mountain behind the tractor.

It was, however, Arnaud, not Virgile, who answered my call of greeting and emerged to get his breath back in the cleaner air outside. Everything had to be cleared before Virgile could move his barrels in, he explained, but Virgile had disappeared to check something with the sheep-shed's owners – the Poujols, he thought Virgile had said. Then the two of them were going muck-spreading in Virgile's vineyards. He should have been back long ago. Half an hour, at the most, he had said. It would be dark, if he didn't hurry . . . But Arnaud's explanations were interrupted by the sound of footsteps running up the alley.

'STOP!' shouted Virgile, as he took a shortcut up a grassy bank to join us amongst the piles of rusting metal.

'Too late,' said Arnaud with a nod towards the overspilling trailer.

'*Zut!*' said Virgile, more moderately than the occasion

merited. 'They've changed their minds, would you believe! Or at least, they can't make up their minds. Two hours I've spent with the four of them and still they can't decide! The eighty-year-old brothers are bad enough but the sons are even worse. "We might want the manure for our own vines," they say. "No problem," I say, "as long as I can get rid of it." "But we've nothing to transport it in," they say. "Don't worry, I'll sort it," I say. "But it'd need a second person," they say. "Don't worry, I'll find one," I say. "But we'd have to decide which vines to put it on," they say. And two hours later, they're still deliberating. They'll let me know tomorrow.'

But tomorrow has come and there is still no news, no decision from the house of Poujols. The family committee is still *in camera.*

'There I was, hoping for a formal tenancy,' sighed Virgile despondently, when I dropped by. 'Then I could organize some electricity and water. But if they can't agree about a heap of sheep-shit, how are they ever going to reach an agreement on a lease?'

Virgile has had a second, almost equally frustrating day. He has been trailing round the local bars, drinking more beer than he cares to, in a search for six stainless steel beer barrels for storing his *eau de vie*.

'I can't afford new ones,' he explains, on the drive across to Matthieu's. 'But if I offer the bar-keepers the equivalent of their lost deposits – and down enough beer to empty the barrels – they can sometimes be persuaded to let go of them. But what do I find when I get home? Only three will open. The others – the ones that cost me the most – are factory-sealed. I'll have to find a wholesaler who'll exchange them. But goodness knows how much more beer that'll cost me!'

He shudders, as the first of the usable three rattles across the stone floor to join the rest of Matthieu's chaos.

'This'll cheer you up!' promises the master distiller, laying down his guitar to hand us each a glass. 'Can you guess?' He sniffs a third appreciatively himself. 'I made it last week. From fruit.'

Before I can hazard anything foolish, the familiar, well-filled stomach of the *atelier*'s owner enters from the darkness of the back garden, followed closely by the man himself. Matthieu swiftly pours him a fourth glass of the mystery spirit.

'Is it our special?' asks Virgile cautiously.

'Just so,' confirms Matthieu. 'Fig and grape,' he adds for the benefit of me and M. Bascou. 'Using Virgile's Grenache Blanc for the grapes – picked just before the co-op moved in.'

'And for the figs?' I ask.

'Just figs,' he shrugs and I realize too late that here, all along, was the solution for my surplus plums. Then, suddenly, Matthieu's normally easy-going countenance looks aghast.

His landlord enjoys a cigarette with his *eau de vie* and ordinarily no one would wish to mar the man's enjoyment less than his tenant. But just at M. Bascou's ankles – entirely obscured from view by the protuberant stomach – is a substantial funnel, through which Matthieu is carefully filtering the precious Marc de Merlot of one of Montpeyroux's most perfectionist growers, still at its undiluted eighty per cent strength. Fearing that the funnel is about to be confused with an ashtray and faced with the twin disasters of pollution and conflagration, Matthieu reluctantly decides to intervene.

The expression of contentment on M. Bascou's rosy cheeks as he sampled Matthieu's latest experiment suggested a man who relished nothing more than a new experience. This impression is, however, swiftly dispelled as he learns how quickly a smouldering *Gauloise* can be extinguished in a bucket of water.

In the circumstances, it seems tactful for Virgile and me to withdraw, leaving Matthieu to see whether a few more glasses of his excellent fig and grape can stave off an impromptu rent review.

'Looks sleepy enough, doesn't it?' says Krystina, as we watch the last of the plane leaves falling on the Place du Vendangeur in the village of Argeliers in the Minervois wine district. But she steers me towards a rough expanse of wall between numbers 13 and 15, where a plaque records that it was here (perhaps at the ostensibly vanished number 14) that the so-called Wine War of 1907 began.

It was led, so the plaque attests, by a winegrower called Marcelin Albert and it started, so Krystina informs me, with a local village protest, a refusal to pay taxes. But it rapidly escalated into a whole summer season of wine-related rallies and riots across the region, until five men were killed and fifteen seriously injured in a demonstration of 700,000 in Narbonne. The Government sent in 10,000 troops but many were sons of local *vignerons*, who promptly deserted, while half the region's mayors resigned in sympathy.

'So, what was all the fuss about?' asks Krystina rhetorically, as we stroll outside the village through the vineyards, where the leaves, having finished changing colour, are already starting to fall.

'Fraud,' she answers immediately. 'Artificial wines made with imported raisins and sugar – initially to make up post-phylloxera shortages but continuing long after supplies of the genuine article returned to normal at the end of the century. Wine prices plummeted, hitting smaller growers hardest. To listen to the protests, you'd have thought this concocted competition was the only cause. "Down with poisoners; long live natural wine", went the slogan. But in reality, there were two other fundamental problems – hugely expanded imports from Algeria and massive overproduction here in the Languedoc.

The region was making forty-four per cent of the country's wine from only twenty-three per cent of its vineyard area. It was selling on price not quality. But nobody in 1907 seemed to focus much on any of this. Adulteration was the big issue. The government tried tackling it with increased sugar taxes and anti-fraud inspectors. But you'll never guess their master weapon. An official definition of "wine". The first ever . . . Well, you have to remember how much phoney stuff was abusing the name,' she adds defensively, as she finds the quote in her filofax.

'Astound me,' I challenge her.

' "The product of the alcoholic fermentation of fresh grapes or of the juice of fresh grapes",' she reads lamely.

I am not astounded.

'Some of our customers will only deal with my husband,' says Patricia Boyer, half-heartedly tidying her wind-tangled hair, as she closes the *cave* door against another gust. With Daniel Domergue, the absent spouse, she co-owns Virgile's recommended Minervois wine estate – the Clos Centeilles, about twenty kilometres west of Argeliers – and, although I think the look behind her somewhat fierce-looking spectacles is more amused than affronted by her clients' sexism, I am happy that Mme Gros's chiropody appointment has prevented Manu from putting this to the test.

'*Tant pis* for them,' shrugs Madame Boyer, as we survey her exceptionally large stocks maturing in bottle – unusually, it seems that they are never released until ready for drinking. 'Daniel's hardly ever here. Not during the week.' (I remember Virgile mentioning his viticulture professorship at Béziers.) 'He adores the practical side of wine-making but he'd go mad if he were here all the time,' she laughs, still pondering the precise whereabouts of her intended selection. 'That or burst a blood vessel. Like this morning when Jérome, our tractor man, put hydraulic oil in the tractor! A few neurones missing, I'm afraid. I mean, you don't need many neurones as a *tractoriste* but you do need some! . . . Here, I've got a bad back – can you climb up to that one?'

She indicates the uppermost of three crates of bottles, each about a metre cubed.

'You have to be a monkey, to taste our wines!' she laughs, as I search for a foothold on the bottom crate. 'In theory, you see, it's me that's responsible for cellarwork and marketing. Not forgetting the endless paperwork. That's me too. The vineyard activity's meant to be Daniel but with the state demanding more and more time from its teachers . . .'

'Do you have much help?' I ask, clinging desperately to the top crate with my fingernails.

'A boy in the *cave* who needs constant supervision,' she replies. 'No super-abundance of neurones there either! But I'm fed up with brilliant apprentices who disappear to found their own domaines as soon as we've taught them anything.'

I have to keep reminding myself that this is the patient half of the marriage.

'But what have you got there?' she calls, when I successfully stretch my hand through a crack to touch glass at last.

'I've no idea,' I say, as I inch my way downward with an unlabelled bottle.

'What does it say on the cork?' she asks.

'1995,' I manage to read at my awkward angle.

'No, put it back,' she says. 'I must have got the crates muddled. It's '96 we want. Much more forward than '95 for Pinot Noir, so we'll sell it first. Try the next one along,' she suggests, as I struggle back up again.

After more gymnastic activity than my limbs have known in a decade, we finally assemble the precise six bottles that she had in mind and retreat across the windswept courtyard to a smart little tasting room at the top of a short staircase on the side of the house. We sit on cold metal chairs at a café-style table and Mme Boyer pulls her sheepskin coat more tightly round her. The room is not significantly cosier than the *cave*. It is sparely decorated but a poster on a freshly painted wall underlines the fact that the Clos Centeilles forms part of a recently recognized, superior sub-section of the Minervois, called La Livinière.

'I'm happy to belong,' says Mme Boyer. 'But you have to appreciate, these *Appellation Contrôlée* rules aren't about making wine *good*. They're just about making it *less bad*!'

She cites the minimum planting densities, which have been puzzling me since someone mentioned them earlier in the year. I could understand a maximum but why a minimum?

'A crude way of limiting yields,' she explains. 'Close planting makes the vines struggle a bit, reducing their yields. So setting a minimum makes up for growers too lazy or ignorant to prune as hard and debud as thoroughly as they should. But take my word for it, the vines' suffering always shows . . .'

Happily, Mme Boyer's reservations about the regulatory framework are not interfering with her bottle-openings. I already have a glass of 1998 'Capitelle de Centeilles', made exclusively, she tells me, from Cinsault – the variety which, according to Daniel, made the Languedoc's reputation in the seventeenth and eighteenth centuries. Into a second, she is pouring a 1999 'Carignanissime', made exclusively, as its name suggests, from Carignan.

'Ironic really,' she admits. 'Daniel's advice to his pupils has always been, "Rip up your Carignan and start again – don't tinker around trying to redeem its deficiencies with *cépages améliorateurs*." Pretty iconoclastic stuff in the seventies. The traditionalists practically threw him out of his teaching post, forgetting that Carignan was unknown here until after phylloxera. But now, of course, with every second *vigneron* making his hundred per cent Syrah, they simply shrug their shoulders and tell him "*c'est normal*"! It makes him apoplectic.'

'But presumably he didn't . . . practise what he preached?' I venture, as I lift my glass of Carignanissime.

'It's a long story,' she says. 'Daniel's original four hectares, about ten kilometres away, were all replanted by the end of the seventies, well before most of his imitators. Syrah, Mourvèdre and Pinot Noir, he used – traditional Languedoc *cépages*, he insisted, from the days before phylloxera. Even this Pinot Noir,' she adds, as she pours me the so-called 'Guigniers de Centeilles' that cost me so much muscle-ache to extract from its crate.

'Then in the summer of 1990, we suddenly lost the use of the *cave* we were renting over there – I say "we" because I'd also appeared on the scene by this time. So we had absolutely nowhere to vinify the harvest. Talk about panic! But right at the last minute, some other purchaser backed out of buying this place. We loved it as soon as we saw it but the house was semi-derelict, the *cave* only just about usable and it came with an additional ten hectares of Grenache Noir, Cinsault and Carignan, all in urgent need of picking. With only primitive cellar equipment, we were so desperate we thought we'd have to sell everything in bulk for a song. We didn't even dare to taste the wines until the spring. And then we suddenly discovered how rich and concentrated the Cinsault was.'

'But the Carignan?' I prompt.

'Ah yes, the Carignan.' Mme Boyer pulls a face, which is difficult to reconcile with the attractive, fruity wine in the glass. 'It left us pretty cold, to be honest, seventy-year-old vines or no seventy-year-old vines. Heavy tannins, no aroma and a tendency to dry out as it aged. But we couldn't eliminate it all at once because of the time involved – not just the ripping up and replanting but the wait while alternatives established themselves. So I suppose we got used to it. We certainly came to despise it less. We learned, for instance, that we could soften the tannins and enhance the aroma with a *macération carbonique*.'

'And the ageing problem?'

'Drink it young,' she laughs, as she completes my somewhat bewildering row of samples with her top wine – a Syrah, Grenache and Mourvèdre blend called 'Clos de Centeilles'.

Before she can elaborate, there is an ominous-sounding crash from the direction of the *cave* and she rises quickly to her feet.

'I'd better leave you to it. I told you about the low neurone count out there.' But then she pauses with one foot halfway out of the door. 'You have to understand why we went into wine-making. We loved fine wines, Burgundy especially in Daniel's case – hence the passion for Pinot Noir. Unlike most growers who never touch a drop from outside their own domaines, let alone outside their regions.'

Another crash.

'You know, sometimes I'm not sure the combined IQs of the *tractoriste* and the cellar boy add up to treble figures,' she sighs, looking despairingly down the stairs, but still she lingers a moment longer. 'We weren't interested in being the biggest or the best or the most expensive,' she says. 'We wanted to make wine that people would *enjoy*. That's what we believe wine is for.'

Yet another crash.

'Maybe not even *double* figures,' she calls, as she speeds down to the *cave*.

'Close that door!' orders Virgile, when I linger for a moment in the entrance to the *cave*. 'I'm trying to keep the cold out. There are three electric heaters in here. It's warmer than my flat.'

It seems such a short time since it was the heat that we were doing everything we could to keep out – almost as short indeed as the interval since ice buckets were rudely chilling the same red wines that we now nurse up to 'room temperature' in carefully cupped hands. But the swift return of colder weather has left Virgile with a temperature-related

problem on his hands. While most of his malolactic fermentations have obligingly finished, with every last drop of malic
acid eliminated, the cooler temperatures have encouraged
two of them – the Grenache and one of his Syrahs – to stop
halfway.

'If the heaters don't get them going, they'll stay like this until
the spring,' he says.

'And would that be serious?' I ask.

'It would be inconvenient,' he says, preparing to lock up,
'not being able to finish with a process and move on. It would
also mean I couldn't give them any more sulphur dioxide,
exposing them to bacteria over the winter. I'd certainly sleep
easier if they started up again. The Syrah, I think, may already
be under way – you can hear a bit of bubbling, if you put your
ear to the *cuve* – but I'm not sure about the Grenache. I'm
waiting for a fax with the latest analyses. I think the concrete
may be insulating it too well but I'm afraid there's just too
much of it for me to move it out into the only fibreglass *cuve*
that's empty.'

'And the sheep-shed?' I enquire, as we abandon the snug-
ness of the *cave* for the chilly square outside. 'Still waiting to
hear from the Poujols?'

'They rang me this morning.'

'To say "yes"?'

'To say they haven't managed to meet yet.'

'Tous pour chacun; chacun pour tous,' muses Manu at the sight of
the combative slogan set in stone on the façade of the
Maraussan Cave Coopérative, between Béziers and the
Minervois. All for each and each for all.

'They needed a fighting spirit in 1901,' says the aptly named
Michel Bataille, the co-operative's energetic-looking young
President.

'To found this place, you mean?' Manu slowly latches on to

the significance of the bright centenary posters in the entrance-
way.

'Correct,' says the President, as he takes us into a rather soul-
less meeting room lined with fading black-and-white photographs of the pioneering participants. 'Remember, the turn of
the century was a time of crisis. Wine wars and all that . . . But
Maraussan's initiative was a bit more positive.'

'Was this the country's first wine co-op?' asks Manu, still
worrying away at the message on the posters.

'Correct again. You see, the Languedoc wine trade was dominated by two extremely wealthy groups – the major châteaux
and the powerful *négociants*, the middlemen, who had such a
stranglehold on pricing, they could buy up the wines of the
smaller growers for next to nothing. That is, until Elie Cathala, a
socialist lemonade-maker of all people, had the bright idea of
cutting the middlemen out. He saw an opportunity to sell
directly to the numerous purchasing co-operatives that the fast-
expanding working populations of Paris were already establishing. Provided, that is, that the growers could achieve a sufficient
critical mass and be seen to be sufficiently socialist themselves.'

Manu could not have chosen a better moment for a listless
wander down the room and a myopic squint at a well-preserved coloured chart hanging between the photographs. M.
Bataille explains that this is an early graphic explanation of the
establishment's original principles, produced for the benefit of
the Ministry of Agriculture, where I suspect official eyebrows
may have been raised as high as Manu's are this afternoon.

'Twenty per cent of the profits went on proletarian propa-
ganda,' the President elaborates. 'A further five per cent to the
central co-operative movement, twenty-five per cent to other
workers' organizations and only the remaining fifty divided
between the co-op's actual members. And divided, what's
more, in equal shares, regardless of contribution . . . But it
worked,' he responds to Manu's involuntary shudder. 'By

1905, they had over two hundred and thirty members in a village of only four hundred families. They had their own railway trucks and soon they established a network of over thirty distribution centres round the country. They were shifting fifty thousand hectolitres a year at a time when many of their neighbours were pouring last year's wine into the river to make way for the next vintage.'

'And all made here?' I ask, as we follow him into a cavernous *cave*, lined with gigantic wooden barrels.

'Not at all,' he replies. 'Not at first. These earliest collective efforts were more about marketing than wine-making. And even when they got this building up in 1905, it couldn't handle more than fifteen per cent of the volume they were selling. Until it was extended, the rest was made and stored at members' homes.'

I am surprised how little activity there is today. Even allowing for the fact that this is a relatively quiet period, the *cave* has a neglected air that is hard to reconcile with all the certificates for wine fair medals adorning the walls. But M. Bataille anticipates my thoughts. In 1995, he tells us, Maraussan banded together with half a dozen neighbouring co-operatives to form the Vignerons du Pays d'Ensérune – the largest co-operative wine enterprise in France, with 1,880 members and nearly fifty salaried staff – enabling them to concentrate production in the three most modern sites.

'But we haven't forgotten those fundamental values,' he insists, turning back to one of the centenary posters and its quotation from the co-operative supremo for the *département*, extolling the virtues of 'solidarity, equity, the sharing of knowledge, means and risks . . . the collective struggle in the service of the individual and against individualism . . .'

Manu winces more convulsively than before.

'We no longer reward everyone equally,' M. Bataille reassures him. 'You could do that with a single product, the one anonymous *vin de table*. But now, with more than twenty different wines, at widely different prices, we have to have different rates, based on quality as well as quantity.'

At the age of forty-two, Michel Bataille has been elected President of the Ensérune umbrella structure, as well as that of Maraussan, for each of the last four years. He rushed back this afternoon, in his city suit, from a conference in Montpellier, where he had been discussing falling market shares with opposite numbers. This evening, he says it will be pullover and jeans for an emergency meeting to rally the uncomprehending troops in the face of ever-strengthening New World competition.

'You see, they were promised a good return in the eighties,' he explains. 'They were told that all they had to do was rip up their Carignans and replant with Syrahs and Cabernets. So they can't understand that it's not that simple any more. The trouble is, a lot of them take no interest at all in the way a wine is made . . . You think I'm joking but some of them are barely interested in drinking it. Grapes are just a crop to them. They might almost as well be growing potatoes! We have to change all that – get them to understand why we're telling them to thin the bunches, not just blindly follow instructions. And all the time, all I really want to do is go home and prune my own vines.' He sighs regretfully. 'I only ever see them at weekends and even then my wife complains, so I delegate most of the work.'

'So why do you do it?' I ask.

'Well, someone has to,' he answers with a smile. 'And I guess I've persuaded myself I'm less of an idiot than some of the others. But we can't afford to get this wrong.' The smile fades. 'Amidst all these jolly centenary celebrations, we've got serious problems. The whole region, I mean. Not just us. This is the worst crisis in Languedoc wine for twenty, maybe forty years – with only two years at the most to crack it!'

I can hardly believe what I'm hearing. To go from Virgile –

apparently capable of selling his wines several times over, at prices he hardly dreamed of – to Michel Bataille in Maraussan, convinced that the region's production needs to be reduced by four million hectolitres, maybe even double that if there's no public subsidy: it just doesn't seem possible.

Then I remember a vague impression of gathering protest throughout the summer, an undercurrent of simmering violence, reported in the local papers. There was a story in July, for instance, of a hundred and fifty *vignerons* forcibly clearing foreign wines from hypermarket shelves; an editorial recalling the notorious 1976 riots at Montredon, near Carcassonne, in which both a grower and a policeman died; another co-operative president insisting, 'It's a choice between being well regarded and dead or badly regarded and alive.'

'It's the same old story,' says M. Bataille, 'falling consumption and overproduction – some say, even fraud. But now there's the extra factor of competition from the southern hemisphere. A third of the area's vines may have to be destroyed. We can only hope it's the quality hillside sites that are spared this time. When subsidies for ripping out were last on offer in the eighties, it was mostly the lower-quality, easy options in the plains that survived.

'But we don't help ourselves with our ridiculous over-regulation,' he complains. 'The Australians grow German Riesling, Californian Zinfandel, whatever they like, but here they're illegal. And while the rest of the world slims down to simpler product branding for international markets, what do we do in France, with our four hundred and fifty *Appellations Contrôlées* and goodness knows how many *vins de pays* – only a handful of which anybody can remember? . . . We create more!'

As I drew back my bathroom curtains a pair of partridges scuttled self-protectively away through the gaunt, black, dead-looking silhouettes of the almond trees: the first of the trees to lose their leaves, just as they were the first to unfold them in February. There used to be four of them – the partridges, that is – paying regular group visits to the house, but the hunting season started a couple of months ago and I fear the other two were early casualties.

On every Saturday and Sunday since early September, the nearby lanes have been dotted with huddles of hunters, dressed like sinister mercenaries in khaki, planning their next assault on whatever wildlife has hitherto escaped them. This morning, however, I am sweeping fallen leaves from the court-yard at the front of the house when I spot a small but aggres-sively gun-toting battalion striding confidently up the drive. Their yapping dogs look set to race ahead and savage the first living flesh – almost certainly mine – that they can lay their fangs on, but at the very last minute the contingent turns sharply away and saunters nonchalantly through my neigh-bours' habitually open front gates.

I know that both of them are out – away indeed, paying another of their six-monthly visits to the teetotal sister-in-law – because I happened to hear Manu's heart-rending pro-tests falling on deaf ears yesterday morning. And maybe the invaders know this too. Certainly, their swaggering progress up through Manu's little vegetable patch appears to be free of any scruple that their trampling of his onion sets might be unwelcome. But then I see that the entire platoon is heading unmistakably for the bramble-tangled fence that marks the boundary between Manu's festering compost heap and the point where my own upper terraces loop round behind his.

Fortunately, the expected incursion is sufficiently inhibited by the combination of compost and brambles for the last of them still to be straddling the fence when I have crossed the stream and run up to confront them. The steepness of the

climb, however, ensures that little of my indignation successfully bypasses my breathlessness.

'*Propriété privée*,' I pant almost unintelligibly.

'There's no sign,' they chorus in what is clearly their stan-
dard defence.

I have, of course, carelessly overlooked the necessity for
signs to keep my neighbours inside their private property and
outside my own and, were it not for the painful heaving of my
lungs, some pithy riposte to this effect would already have
stunned them. But as it is, I am forced to content myself with
the fact that only modest additional carnage is inflicted
between here and their exit by the back gate.

At the foot of the village memorial, devoted to both the World
Wars, were a few bedraggled floral wreaths that had been
decaying there since Armistice Day.

It was the first time that I had studied the roll of villagers
morts pour la France but anyone who did so was bound to notice
the extraordinary number of Vargases carved in the granite –
considerably more than any other family. There was a smatter-
ing of other familiar names as well but not a single Gros.

'Funny that,' said Krystina. 'Obviously the ancestors were as
war-shy as Manu is work-shy.'

'Maybe the Groses were just "survivors",' I protested, wondering why I felt obliged to defend my neighbour's forebears.

Before she could argue further, a chill gust of wind convinced Krystina that a table in front of the café's wood-burning
stove would be a more congenial setting for the rest of the
morning's tutorial. To her great indignation, however, the
table that she had in mind has proved to be occupied.

'What's he doing there?' she protests, when she sees that
Monsieur Privat has abandoned his habitual place in the
corner for this warmer alternative. 'He shouldn't be here at all
yet. It's not even lunchtime!'

M. Privat's smile, as he catches my eye, suggests that he has followed rather more of Krystina's English than she assumed.

'You saw how that first war decimated the labour force,' Krystina resumes, having reorganized the remaining café furniture to sit as close to the stove as the competition permits. 'A million and a quarter soldiers killed out of eight million mobilized. Twenty per cent of the male population between twenty and forty-five wiped out in four years. Not to mention the other three-quarters of a million permanently injured.'

Babette appears with a small carafe of *rosé* for M. Privat. Krystina unilaterally orders hot chocolate for both of us and returns to August 1914.

'The amazing thing was the incredibly positive mood . . .'

'Even the village priest joined up,' M. Privat contributes unexpectedly in impeccable English. 'He fought alongside my father. But of course, he was not expecting to miss so many services. The same with the wine-workers. They were all expecting to be home for the harvest . . .'

'Certainly everyone on both sides expected a short decisive campaign,' Krystina reasserts herself primly. 'But they were wrong. The whole thing turned into a long war of attrition.'

'The *vendange* was left to the women and children and the old men,' M. Privat joins in again, more animatedly. 'So my mother used to tell me. Well, obviously, the shortage of labour was a problem everywhere. Just the fact that the . . . *comment dit?* . . . breadwinner was away – or dead – that was a big problem. But lack of man-power was especially difficult for making the wine. It was still so labour-intensive, you see. And horses – they were still the main form of transportation but most of them had disappeared to the front as well. And as for important supplies like copper sulphate . . .'

Krystina opens her mouth to reaffirm her usual ascendancy but no sound emerges, so M. Privat fills the vacuum.

'The 1914 vintage was I think you say . . . a "bumper", no?

But the Languedoc growers had a clever idea to get rid of it. They gave two hundred thousand hectolitres to the military hospitals. *Rouge*, of course – more masculine!' He chuckles as he glances at his quarter litre of *rosé*.

'Anyone can *give* their wine away,' Krystina quibbles, unaccustomed to this supporting role.

'Anyone but Manu,' I add and M. Privat laughs as if he too has known the Cuvée Emmanuel Gros.

'No, the medicine was so popular,' he explains, 'the government was soon buying huge quantities for regular distribution. The soldiers' daily rations started at a quarter of a litre, if I remember correctly, increasing to half as the going got rougher.'

Krystina, unable to get a word in, contents herself with adding extra logs to the stove to heat our more distant table.

'By the end, officers were authorized to raise this to three-quarters and then the men themselves were allowed to purchase a further quarter at special rates. I don't know the English word but my father's job was organizing the supplies, you see. He told my mother in his letters how he was commandeering wine from all over France but still he couldn't keep up with demand. So he'd have to . . . what's the word . . . "fob" them off with Spanish and Italian imports.'

Krystina has had enough. With Babette busy serving M. Privat his chicken liver salad, she pushes a large denomination banknote under her cup and prepares to leave. M. Privat, too carried away to notice even the arrival of his food, continues innocently unaware.

'By the end of the war, the returning soldiers had acquired a taste for their daily litre. Marvellous for continuing demand but the problem was, so many *didn't* return. The loss of all those young men created a glut . . .'

Krystina exits without even a goodbye and M. Privat pulls a face, as if to ask: 'Was it something I said?'

We sit in silence for a moment.

'What happened to your father?' I ask eventually.

'I never knew him,' says M. Privat, turning his attention to his chicken livers. 'He's out there on the monument, amongst the Ps.'

December

'YOU WEREN'T JOKING were you?'
Virgile winked as Babette brought us each a plate of *coq aux olives*. (It had seemed only fair to warn him about her limited repertoire before he made the journey up from Saint Saturnin.)

'It usually tastes better than it looks,' I encouraged him, as he pushed aside the chaos of paper spread around us.

'It does,' he confirmed. 'But we haven't made much progress, have we?'

The hastily tidied piles of papers were why we were there: Virgile had offered to buy me lunch if I spared a couple of hours to help him with the paperwork that he had to sort out for the *Appellation Contrôlée* authorities. More information than anyone would have thought they could possibly find interesting had to be collated into some sort of intelligible order. He should have done it months ago but he hadn't been able to decide how best to organize the material. It was all there somewhere, he assured me, but scattered across whatever scraps of stationery had come most quickly to hand at earlier stages of the year.

I knew that I ought to be back at Les Sources, making a final land-reclaiming push before the end of the year. With almost every autumn leaf now fallen, the extent of the challenges remaining had become depressingly unambiguous. Yet the postman's news of early-morning ice on the plateau behind the village somehow sapped my motivation for outdoor activity before I had even finished sharpening the chainsaw.

'I'm sure they meant well,' said Virgile.

'Who?' I asked, preoccupied with thoughts of secateurs and strimmers.

'The *Appellation Contrôlée* authorities – when they first dreamed up all this bureaucracy in 1935. Sometimes I think it was a good thing that they took nearly fifty years before they bothered very much with the wines down here. I mean, nobody sympathizes more with focusing people on quality instead of quantity. But look where we've ended up!'

He scowled at the heap of papers and poured us each some more of the best he had been able to find on the undistinguished café wine list. (Babette had not taken kindly to his request to 'bring his own' next time.)

'The *vignerons* suffered badly between the wars,' he

continued. 'My grandfather never stops telling me. Both internal and external markets were severely damaged – especially Germany and Russia, surprise, surprise. The general economic depression made things even worse. No wonder village after village embraced the relative financial security of the co-operative movement. I read somewhere, there were about four hundred co-ops in the Languedoc-Roussillon by 1940 – nearly all producing cheap, indifferent plonk.'

'The dreaded three-starred litres of my youth,' I reminisced.

'But after all the efforts of the last twenty years, she still comes up with this!' Virgile whispered, as he peered disbelievingly at the label on Babette's 'top of the range'. 'Mind you, for all the EC subsidies on offer in the eighties – both for ripping out vines and distilling surpluses into industrial alcohol – we still had the winelakes. But then again, consumption was falling. People were drinking less but better. And drinking more mineral water, even tap water as the quality of that improved. One way or another, the traditional glass of *rouge* was dying. Hundreds of thousands of corner cafés were closing. My grandfather never stops complaining.'

'I know,' I said, as I toyed with the last of my cockerel bones. 'Manu says there used to be five in this little village. But this is the sole survivor . . . Isn't that right, Babette?'

'*C'est exacte,*' confirmed a husky voice behind a cloud of cigarette smoke. 'Your young friend there doesn't know how lucky he is!'

'People forget,' says Samuel Guibert, checking the last of his e-mails and spinning his swivel chair to give me his full attention. 'When my parents bought this place in 1970, it was quite an achievement just to sell a Languedoc wine in a bottle, let alone make a "Daumas Gassac". But then, when they came here, there were no thoughts of making wine at all.'

'It wasn't a wine estate?'

'No, you see, my father was a leather-goods manufacturer up in Millau – the family company had supplied gloves to the British Royal Family for three hundred years – and my mother was studying Irish Celtic ethnology in Montpellier, where she teaches now. They'd recently married, in my father's case for the second time – he was already in his mid-forties. They needed somewhere halfway between the two towns . . . Well, maybe not halfway,' he laughs. 'My mother did well there!'

The Mas de Daumas Gassac, on the outskirts of the village of Aniane, must be about thirty kilometres west of Montpellier and at least three times that distance from Millau.

'They both fell in love with the place. Well, who wouldn't?' He gestures towards the mellow stone farmhouse and unspoilt landscape, visible through the window of his crisply modern, predominantly white office. 'That's why we'll never expand our vines beyond the present forty hectares. We want to pre-serve its charm as a place to live and also maintain a healthy balance with the surrounding *garrigue*. Respect for nature, you see.'

It is easy to believe that Samuel, aged somewhere in his late twenties, has recently returned from six years in New Zealand. It is not just his faultless English. It is something less tangible in his well-travelled confidence. He has been working mainly, he explains, for the giant Montana winery but concentrating on imports and exports rather than the more obvious learning curve of New World wine-making technology. And although he is quick to emphasize that there are no such narrowly defined roles here at home, it is marketing which continues, for the time being, to be his principal focus within Daumas Gassac.

'Gassac's the name of the local stream,' he explains. 'And Daumas is the name of the family that was farming here. Old-style, struggling polyculture.'

'A bit of everything?'

'Yes. A few vines but mostly abandoned. My parents wanted

to bring the land back to life with something but they'd probably have settled for sweetcorn – even olives – if they hadn't come across this guy from my father's native Aveyron.

'Henri Enjalbert, the geography professor at Bordeaux University, convinced them that this was an exceptional *terroir* for wine-making. All the conditions were right. The soil was well drained, rich in minerals – especially copper, iron and gold – and very poor in organic matter, to push the vines to their limits. And there's a cooler microclimate in this narrow part of the valley. Ten degrees at night in summer when Aniane, just over there, is registering twenty. It gives us longer growing seasons and later, richer harvests. Enjalbert was very excited. "You could make a *grand cru* to rival Lafite and Latour," he said. "If you're mad enough to try." '

'So, tell me, *monsieur*, do I look like a madman?' says an older voice from behind me.

Guibert *père* invites me to join him in his own rather cosier, lamp-lit office, while Samuel, more at home behind his streamlined workstation, loses no time in reconnecting to the Internet.

Still strikingly handsome, Aimé Guibert must, I calculate, have reached his late seventies but I can see at a glance that he has lost little, if any, of the energy, determination and fastidious perfectionism that first made Daumas Gassac great. It was, he modestly acknowledges, an ambitious project by any standards but especially so for a couple with absolutely no wine-making experience. He read exceptionally widely (the broad, wooden antique table that serves as his desk is piled with books today) but, more crucially and very much against the odds, he persuaded a second distinguished Bordeaux professor to take an interest.

Emile Peynaud, who held the chair of oenology, was no stranger to extra-curricular hand-holding but it was usually confined to the starriest of the claret châteaux. On this occasion, however, something – maybe the novel challenge of a 'virgin' start – enticed him to step outside his norm. He made it clear that actual visits to the Languedoc would be once a year at most but he volunteered an invaluable telephonic 'helpline', provided all calls were made at 9 p.m.

'Is it thanks to him that you're so opposed to cloning?' I ask, having heard from Samuel how virtually all the vines here derive from different, individually selected cuttings.

'That's more the result of my experience in the leather trade,' he answers. 'Seeing the damage done when science interferes with nature – crossbreeding and inbreeding destroying some of the world's finest species. But I'm convinced it's our single most important quality factor. Complexity from diversity. As well as naturally lower yields – we never need a *vendange en vert*. Respect for nature, you see.'

'And the choice of Cabernet Sauvignon?' I ask, having also learned from Samuel that this classic Bordeaux variety has always dominated their production. 'Was that Professor Peynaud's influence?'

'Not at all. It was simply what I knew,' he explains. 'My father had a cellar full of fine Bordeaux. But remember, it's only eighty per cent Cabernet. Fifteen other *cépages* – some of them pretty obscure – make up the balance. It's the same story with the white. Mainly Chardonnay from Burgundy, Viognier from the Rhône and Petit Manseng from Jurançon but mixed with tiny quantities of a dozen different oddments.'

'For complexity again?' I ask.

'It's like the chef's tiny pinch of spice,' confirms Monsieur Guibert. 'The pepper on a strawberry. The exact balance of the recipe changes every year. It depends on what nature gives us. So does the precise approach to the wine-making. A different response to the challenges and opportunities of each vintage. No hard and fast rules. Respect for nature again. A bastion against the savourless, "technical" homogeneity of the modern world. A museum of Old Europe!'

'But not exactly traditional Languedoc wines either?' I suggest.

'No. And in the early days, that certainly didn't make them easy to sell,' he remembers wryly. 'Henri Enjalbert had warned us that it might take two hundred years to get recognition and it's true that nobody took us seriously at first. Well, you could see their point. A total novice's unknown "country wine" from a joke wine region . . .' (Samuel has already explained that, even after the arrival of the Coteaux du Languedoc *appellation* in 1985, anything made with Cabernet could only be labelled as *vin de pays*.) 'A serious price and not even made for easy, early drinking – needing up to a decade in bottle to show its best. In 1978, our first vintage, we found ourselves with eighteen thousand bottles, which nobody wanted to touch. Only when we finally got it into a couple of Paris restaurants did word start spreading.'

'And now?' I prompt.

'We get three thousand visitors a year and sell ninety-five per cent of our sixteen thousand cases before it's even bottled.'

'Could I make that ninety-five point nought one for next year?' I ask and resign myself to leaving empty-handed.

'I'm not trying to catch you out,' I explained, as I took the foil-wrapped bottle from the fridge and poured Virgile a glass. 'I just want to know what you think.' I poured myself a glass and tasted it myself. I already knew what I thought. I thought it was wonderful. But I wanted to see what Virgile thought. I wanted to see whether I could change his mind.

'Languedoc, I assume?' he asked.

'Close,' I said. 'It's Roussillon.'

'A bit remote for you, isn't it? Have you been exploring farther afield? It seems so long since I last saw you.'

'I found it in a restaurant in Narbonne and managed to buy a bottle in the wine shop next door. You don't have to guess.

It's just that I thought of you when they told me about this. It reminded me of something you said . . . But anyway, what have you been up to? How did the *Salon* go?'

The *Salon* had been a mammoth Montpellier trade fair, dominating the whole of Virgile's last week. It was not an event for wine-marketing – that would dominate another week in the spring. It was an occasion for all the ancillary businesses, the barrel-makers and bottle-blowers, to market themselves to the *vignerons*, and Virgile had suddenly found himself in urgent need of label-printers. After all the agonizing over his serigraphic labelling back in March, Puech had ruled it out as a style that belonged in the supermarket. It would have to be replaced with something more conventional before the second half of the 2000 Coteaux du Languedoc was bottled in the spring.

'Didn't I tell you?' he beamed, with surely more excitement than mere label-choosing could inspire. 'It was right at the end, on the last day. I bumped into Jean-Pierre, Olivier Jullien's father. He told me he was selling a couple of hectares of Grenache Noir. The advert was going to appear in the paper the next day.'

'You don't mean you were tempted?' I asked, deferring all discussion of the mystery wine.

'I hardly slept all night. Then I got up early and went to have a look at the vines the next morning. They were just amazing. They'd been lent to Olivier for a number of years, so they'd been really immaculately tended as part of Mas Jullien. The most beautiful wooden supports for the *palissage*, you wouldn't believe it! And for some reason, Olivier no longer needs them. Maybe he's bought something better. Or changed his blend. As you know, we no longer have that kind of conversation. But anyway, Jean-Pierre doesn't need them either. So I made an offer. There and then, before anyone could read the paper. And just as well, because there were loads of other offers.'

'So you actually *own* some vines now?' I congratulated him, as he turned his attention to the puzzle in his glass.

'I'm expecting to sign next week. But it isn't just the question of ownership. It gives me a much better balance of grapes. I won't have to declassify so much, on account of excess Carignan. Maybe nothing at all. But you know, the bank would never have let me do this without the Puech deal,' he added defensively. 'Do you know, he brought a party of fourteen the other day to taste the 2000 Coteaux du Languedoc that's still in barrel? All squeezed into the *cave*, they were – Americans, Japanese . . .'

'And were they pleased?' I asked, still trying to read Virgile's reaction to the wine in his glass.

'Delighted,' he said. 'Except for the quantity. As one of the Japanese remarked, if they each took five cases, it would all be gone! "You need another twenty hectares, kid," said one of the Americans. "And *fast*!" ' He giggled at his barely recognizable American accent. 'You must taste it yourself before the end of the year.'

'And the sheep-shed?' I risked enquiring.

'Don't ask!' he sighed. 'Well, actually you can ask. We did clear the manure in the end but it took me and Arnaud two whole days. They kept changing their minds about exactly where they wanted it spread. The final load was supposed to be for the garden of one of the sons but . . .' Virgile snarled the next bit through gritted teeth. '*He hadn't quite finished his autumn clearing, had he?* "Couldn't I just leave it in the sheep-shed for another month or so?" he wanted to know. "After all, it was only a few *barrels* I wanted to move there, wasn't it?" '

He looked for a moment as if he might do violence to the glass in his fist but the moment passed. The wine had all his attention again.

'I could enjoy a lot of this,' he murmured.

'You should make some yourself then.' I stifled a grin.

'But you know my white wine problem. I've only got the Grenache Blanc.'

'You could make this.'

'I don't follow.'

'It's pure Grenache Blanc. From the Domaine de la Rectorie in Banyuls. You said you weren't convinced it could work. But I thought, when I tasted this in Narbonne . . .'

'We must go and see these people.'

'It does work, doesn't it?' I pressed him.

'The bank won't like it,' Virgile answered indirectly. 'I'll need some new equipment for a white wine. But somehow I don't think next year's Grenache Blanc will be going to the co-op.'

'Je ne suis pas d'accord,' said Monsieur Vargas.

I could hardly believe it. It was rare enough for him and his wife not to speak, quite literally, as one. But to find them in actual disagreement was, for me, a first. And on their wedding anniversary too.

'It was me who'd been called up,' he reminded us to assert the primacy of his own recollections. 'Me and the five million others.'

They had invited me over *'pour un petit apéritif'* to honour their sixty-one harmonious years. *'Que nous trois,'* they had warned. 'The children live so far away now.'

It was my first visit to the Vargases' narrow little house at the bottom of the village street but I saw at once that very little could have changed in all their six decades of marriage. Even the ancient television set, blocking most of the light from the window, must have arrived around the mid-point.

The nature of the anniversary had led quickly to an explanation that this should in fact have been their sixty-second. However, Germany's invasion of Poland in September 1939 and France's declaration of war two days later had put paid to their wedding plans for that autumn.

'We wouldn't have minded so much, if it hadn't been followed by all those months of phoney war,' they reminisced, as M. Vargas carefully untwisted the wire securing his champagne cork. (He clearly didn't do this very often.) '*Un drôle de guerre*, they called it, didn't they? Hardly any different from peacetime. Certainly, none of the excitement and enthusiasm that our parents felt at the start of the *Grande Guerre*,' they both agreed, as the cork finally popped.

However, quite exceptionally, they were less united as to *why* there had been so little will to fight. Mme Vargas blamed defeatism – a sense that the Germans were unbeatable – while Monsieur attributed it to over-confidence: a conviction that the war could be won by economic blockades, without the need for battle. Hence those unprecedented words: '*Je ne suis pas d'accord.*'

M. Vargas himself seemed as shocked by their echo as any of us.

'Whatever the reason . . .' he began hastily, so anxious to dispel any note of dissension that he spilled the champagne. 'Whatever the reason,' he tried again, as he dabbed at the drinks table with a handkerchief, 'we just sat there waiting for something to happen. We scarcely did anything to help the Poles. Just hid behind the concrete defences of the Maginot Line.'

'And the *vendange*?' I asked, remembering that the Vargas family made wine in those days. This was the second time in little more than a generation that a war had been declared in the run-up to the harvest and I wondered whether it had all been left to the women and children again.

'For once the government got its priorities right,' answered Mme Vargas, raising her glass to toast us both. (She had already explained how she had married into the Languedoc from a Burgundian wine-making family – although I would never have guessed from the quarter-filled glass that she insisted was '*déjà trop*'.) 'This time, they let the *vignerons* get their grapes in before calling them up or requisitioning their horses. But of course, afterwards, production suffered badly, not just from loss of manpower but from lack of vineyard supplies and so on.'

'It took all of us by surprise, when it finally came, the May 1940 invasion,' said M. Vargas, apparently keener to resume the military side of the history. 'Even the British in Northern France. A *Blitzkrieg*, the Germans called it, didn't they? Well, we neither of us had the right kind of tanks to resist it, you see. The British were driven out at Dunkirk and we were driven back to Paris. Just six weeks after the first German offensive, we were defeated.'

I had known for a long time that defeat was followed by division – the division of France into occupied and unoccupied zones. But as usual, I owed the detail to Krystina. She had told me how the armistice signed by the new French government led by Marshal Pétain at the end of June 1940 provided for the German occupation of three-fifths of the country, the German retention of nearly two million prisoners of war and an unlimited French obligation to finance the German war effort until a peace was concluded. They were harsh-sounding terms but, as Krystina had emphasized, no one at the time expected peace to be very far away. With Britain left alone, a German victory seemed both imminent and inevitable and, by doing what he thought was only a short-term bad deal, the eighty-three-year-old Pétain hoped to secure a better negotiating position in the aftermath.

'It was all the richer parts of France, in the west and the north and the east, that went to Germany,' said the Vargases, once more in their characteristic unison.

'All the top wine districts too,' M. Vargas added. 'Bordeaux, Champagne, Alsace, the Loire . . .'

'With a special kink in the demarcation line to take in the

expensive end of Burgundy,' his wife completed the list with feeling. 'My parents started walling up their wines to hide them from the Germans.'

'It was bad enough when they requisitioned the stuff to drink it,' said M. Vargas. 'But we minded even more when it was earmarked for distillation into fuel or industrial alcohol for things like antifreeze and explosives. Meanwhile Pétain and his cronies up in Vichy were doing everything they could to stretch supplies. When they weren't just wittering on about *"Travail, Famille, Patrie"*, that is. They relaxed half the quality controls that had just been put in place between the wars. Previously outlawed varieties were suddenly permitted again, minimum alcohol levels were lowered . . .'

This was already by far the longest solo speech that I had ever heard from M. Vargas, and his wife clearly thought it too long. She intervened with a little dish of last year's home-grown Lucques, expecting her husband to join her, as he normally would, in a short hymn of praise for their favourite herb and lemon-peel marinade. But Monsieur was still in 1940.

'It wasn't just the wine, of course. The Germans' systematic seizure of most of our raw materials and manufactured goods was creating desperate shortages – clothing, fuel and most especially food. Then to cap it all, the 1940 harvest was a disaster.'

'You should have seen our wedding that winter,' said Mme Vargas. '*C'était pitoyable!*' she added in a way that tried to sound like the last word on the subject – but failed.

'People were literally starving,' her husband continued. 'Especially in the towns. Béziers and Montpellier were two of the worst fed in France.'

A small plate of biscuits spread with *tapenade*, a homemade olive paste, had no more success than the Lucques in re-routing the conversation.

'I was back here by the autumn of 1940, you see. It was a term of the armistice that the army was demobilized. I was glad I hadn't joined the navy. That was supposed to have been de-mobilized as well but Admiral Darlan was determined to hold on to it.'

'How did we get on to all this?' Mme Vargas protested more directly.

'There were still thousands missing as prisoners of war,' Monsieur pressed on regardless. 'But the dominant feeling here in the south was relief that the Germans hadn't invaded this far. There was very little interest in De Gaulle's "Free France" activities over in London and not a lot in the *Résistance*. What really changed things was the German occupation of the south.'

'You don't think our guest might like to talk about something more cheerful?' Mme Vargas tried again with a bowl of pistachios.

'In November 1942, the British and the Americans invaded North Africa and the Germans immediately invaded the rest of France. Within a few days they were marching into Montpellier.'

'*Ecoute, Albert* . . .' Some crisps had no more success.

'We were now experiencing for ourselves what the people in the north had been suffering for the last eighteen months. Thanks to an artificial exchange rate, the German soldiers were able to go through our shops like plagues of locusts, leaving us to do the best we could on the black market. Prices and wages were all controlled by the Germans but their demands for "occupation costs" continued to rise. Meanwhile hundreds of thousands of men were being conscripted to work in Germany.'

'*Sérieusement, Albert* . . .' This was not at all the way Madame had planned their *petit apéritif*.

'People were finally beginning to think an allied victory might not be a bad thing after all. And when Lodève was liberated on 22 August 1944 . . .'

'*Albert, c'est trop!*' Madame Vargas raised what little voice she had for the very first time in our year's acquaintance.

'I really don't mind,' I said. 'It's interesting.'

'*C'est passionnant*,' said M. Vargas.

'*Je ne suis pas d'accord*,' said Madame, embarrassed at her outburst.

A big, bold municipal sign pointing encouragingly eastwards from the main road south of Aniane might imply to the passing devotee that the Domaine de la Grange des Pères is going to be every bit as accessible as Daumas Gassac, which is equally clearly arrowed down the same route. From this point on, however, there is very little hope of locating Laurent Vaillé's *cave* without further and better directions. And even if you found your way to his door, you still might not find your way inside.

'He doesn't normally do visits,' said Le Mimosa's David Pugh, when I pleaded with him to put in a word for me. 'Partly because he's got nothing to sell – all snapped up long ago – and partly because his time is limited and he'd rather give no visit than half of one.'

But David did, it seems, put in the right word. The last lap of the route has been duly vouchsafed and Laurent Vaillé is extending a hand of welcome.

I am once again without Manu. Urgent fairy-light hanging duties have come between my neighbour and the climax of the year's tastings. The imminent return of the grandchildren for Christmas has prompted an unexpectedly festive departure from Mme Gros's normally dour domestic decorative policy. Twinkling, multi-coloured lanterns are about to adorn the façade of her cottage. The lamps were actually Uncle Milo's and I had been thinking of using them to garland a cherry tree or two myself.

'But it would be a shame to waste them,' said Manu when

Mme Gros despatched him to persuade me that my own pro-
posal might imperil the next season's crop.

Laurent Vaillé's *cave* is barn-like yet distinctly ecclesiastical-
looking. It once belonged to the monks of nearby Aniane, the
eponymous 'Granary of the Fathers', he explains.

Inside it, four enormous, immaculately gleaming stainless
steel *cuves* dominate the far end but make surprisingly little
impression on an otherwise almost empty area. There must
be enough unoccupied space for maybe three times Virgile's
total operation. Yet for all the apparent under-utilized capacity
– not to mention the legendary scarcity of the product –
Laurent says there are no plans to expand beyond the
present fourteen hectares. He is quite content with the luxury
of space.

He refuses, however, to say how many bottles he makes. I
sense he has enough difficulty reconciling disappointed customers to their limited pre-sold allocations, without them
being able to translate these into precise percentages.

'I do keep a bit back for friends,' he admits. 'And for my *bon
viveur* builder. And for those picnics, when everyone says,
we'll bring the food, you bring the wine!'

No doubt he knows that I know that almost everyone in the
region regards him as the best but he says all this with a total
lack of self-congratulation. He is altogether more good-
humoured than I had expected and yet the natural expression
into which his strongly chiselled features periodically relax is
one of uncompromising determination.

Everything around us is spotless. Even the assortment of
overalls hanging neatly on a row of pegs looks pristine. A
large, well-scrubbed worktable is empty except for a wooden
case of wine, stamped 'Domaine de Trévallon'.

'I started my training over there,' Laurent explains, 'in
Provence. Then with that name behind me, I managed stints
with Chave in the Rhône and Comtes Lafon in Burgundy as

well.' (David Pugh recounted how much interest this pedigree managed to generate, before the first vintage – the 1992 – had even flowered.) 'But you've not come to listen to my life story,' he laughs, as he heads for the stairs to his subterranean cellars. Then he checks himself halfway down to ask one of the year's more superfluous questions. 'You *would* like to taste?' he verifies.

'Excavated by me and my father. And absolutely essential in this climate,' he says, as we emerge in the first of several smoothly plastered, well-lit chambers below, where long rows of expensive-looking barrels stretch, apparently indistinguishably, ahead of us. 'We make just the two wines,' he explains, as he heads unerringly for the cask that he has in mind. 'White and red. You'll find some places founding all their reputation on some minute quantity of whatever they regard as their top *cuvée*, putting all their effort into that and neglecting the rest. Well, here everything we make is the best!'

So far my direction-changing New Year bottle of red has remained my only taste of La Grange des Pères. The white, with which Laurent is deftly filling a large pipette, is completely unknown to me. I watch him share it between two glasses, before thoughtfully sniffing his own. The piercing dark eyes under his intensely black eyebrows register approval. I taste it myself. It is only a couple of months old but already surprisingly complex – indeed, I have seldom felt more disappointed to be offered a spittoon, in this case a red bucket – yet he tells me that it has not even started its malolactic fermentation.

'Maybe in the spring, maybe in the summer,' he speculates. Unlike Virgile, he seems utterly relaxed on the subject.

'We made this first in 1995. It's normally eighty per cent Roussanne, ten per cent Marsanne – both traditional Rhône grapes – with ten per cent Burgundian Chardonnay. But this year we had almost no Chardonnay. It's the first variety to ripen, and last spring, when there was little else going, some hungry wild boar simply scoffed the lot,' he laughed, again utterly relaxed at the thwarting of his plans.

The white from the 2000 harvest has completed its malolactic and is consequently richer, more complete, more 'winey', in fact, just as Virgile said. Like the 2001, it is still in barrel and Laurent explains that all his whites are matured in this way for two full years. Indeed, they are even fermented in the barrels as well. Yet, remarkably, they smell and taste only very subtly of oak.

'Is that because it's such a long, slow process?' I ask. 'Is that the secret?'

'There are no secrets,' he says with a smile, as we move to another vault where the reds are resting.

Here the individual varieties – roughly forty per cent Syrah, forty Mourvèdre and twenty Cabernet Sauvignon – are kept in separate barrels until just before bottling. Laurent takes me through each of the 2000s. The 2001s are untastable, he says, having just begun their 'malos', but the 1999 vintage has just been blended for imminent bottling and we can quickly taste that as well.

'But there's not much time before dark, if you want to see the vines,' he gently hurries me.

Reluctantly I follow his example and empty the remains of my sample back into the barrel, but once upstairs, it seems there is just enough time for the 1999 white, which is also waiting for bottling in one of the stainless steel *cuves*. It has a power and persistence that seem to eclipse even the reds but there is no time to consider further. Laurent is turning out the lights.

'You weren't thinking of going in that, were you?' he laughs at the sight of my modest Renault. 'Assuming, that is, you were hoping to drive it home again.'

I clamber obediently into his four-wheel drive.

'The family land down here in the valley wasn't suitable for vines,' he explains, as we climb a winding road into the hills. 'At least, not for quality vines. My father had farmed it for the co-op but we ripped everything up, planting grain instead. We searched for a year before we found what we needed,' he continues, abruptly abandoning the road for a steep and rugged track, which he tells me they carved through the limestone with dynamite and bulldozers. (He was right, of course, there are potholes and ditches on this ascent in which the Renault might almost have disappeared.)

'Incredibly infertile,' he beams contentedly, as we emerge on to the spectacularly barren-looking plateau at the top. 'We found a few vestiges of nineteenth-century vines and olive trees, but basically nothing but scrub had grown up here for well over a hundred years.'

The land is also incredibly stony, the density of the round white pebbles looking almost snow-like in the pink evening light. There is not another vineyard in sight. The sense of quiet and isolation seems very nearly tangible.

'It must be the highest in the area,' I suggest in hushed, almost reverent tones.

'Nearly three hundred metres,' confirms Laurent more matter-of-factly. 'You can make out the Pyrenees in better light. But you see that hill over there? That's where the famous Robert Mondavi was hoping to buy.'

The Mondavi story is one that has been on a lot of lips this year. The local socialist mayor had agreed to let the Californian wine-maker acquire and clear about fifty hectares of woodland in return for much-needed support for the underfunded, underachieving village co-operative and the deal had bitterly divided opinion. Many, including Laurent Vaillé himself, argued that Mondavi's arrival would give the Languedoc invaluable publicity, which it could never afford by itself. Others, like the Guiberts at Daumas Gassac, thought it inexcusable to destroy a forest when there were plenty of perfectly good vineyards for sale around the region – ignoring, of course, American efficiency's insistence that everything should be conveniently contiguous. In the end, the newly elected Communist Mayor of Aniane simply reversed the deal – as he had always pledged to do in his election campaign – and Mondavi, unamused, was reported to be severing every last link with France. The co-operative would be unlikely to find another saviour.

The sense of bareness up here is perhaps exaggerated by the fact that all the vines appear to be grown exceptionally close to the ground. Unlike Virgile's and every other vineyard that I have seen this year, they have no central trunk. Laurent believes the method must once have been traditional in the region because it can be found in the very oldest vineyards.

'Is that the secret?' I ask him, but he merely smiles and assures me once again that there are none.

Looking closer, I see that he has already started his pruning – a painful kneeling operation, I imagine, at the height of those vines.

'I started at the end of November,' he confirms. 'I'd been doing so much work in the *cave*, I just had to get out of doors! It always lifts my spirits, to come up here. Same with my brother.' He points to a tractor doing a pre-prune in the distance. 'He always prefers to work in the fields.'

'I didn't know you had a brother,' I say. Most people have talked about La Grange des Pères as if it were Laurent and Laurent alone, and he is clearly the public face for what little public contact there is.

'People say I hide him because he knows the secrets,' he laughs. 'But it's like I told you, there really are no secrets.' He laughs again at people's unwillingness to believe him.

But I don't believe him either. Over an hour after we left the *cave*, I can still taste that 1999 white as vividly as when it first touched my tongue.

*

'Count on me,' Virgile had said.

I was in fact counting first on his friend Luc. Putting February's irritations behind me, I had commissioned him to procure me a Christmas truffle back in November, but last week he reluctantly admitted there was not so much as a whiff in the whole of the region. Everyone, it seemed – even Manu, presumably – was paying the price of a hot, dry August.

'Don't worry about Luc,' Virgile promised me. 'My family's full of truffle hunters. There's never a shortage in the Vaucluse.'

But now it is Christmas Eve, and for the first year that any of them can remember, the combined expertise of the Jolys has failed to unearth a single specimen even for their private consumption. His mother is making do with dried *cèpes*, he tells me.

I am wondering what alternative compromises may have occurred to Sarah and the other houseguests who have volunteered to cook my unfamiliar capon. (In the excitement of the Saturday morning market, it struck me as a more authentically 'local' choice than turkey for tonight's dinner.) But at Virgile's suggestion, I have delegated Christmas decoration duties as well so that I can join him for a final tasting of the new wines before we both drive up to sample this 'austerity-cookbook' *chapon sans truffe*.

We are working our way through the various *cuvées* that I have been privileged this year to follow from grape to glass – or rather from pruning cut to bud and thence to leaf and flower and grape . . . and only finally to glass.

The Cinsault is light and amiable; the Syrah (the two different *cuves* now blended) is dark and concentrated but relatively severe; the Carignan (similarly blended) is gutsy and spicy; and the Grenache – despite the recent traumas – perhaps the most fruitily engaging of all. The mixed *vin de presse*, on the other hand, is predictably bitter on the finish but it may yet be useful in the final blend. Then lastly there is the special Nébian Cinsault: the sweetly concentrated, utterly irresistible '*confiture*'. Virgile is now very excited about this. Two years in wood, he believes, will make it even more impressive, and although the style will only be achievable in exceptional years, he is resolved from this point on to target everything he does at Nébian towards the possibility.

'It's a bit early to say for certain,' says Virgile, 'but a lot of people think this is going to be the best vintage since the Languedoc got serious.'

'I was really lucky then . . . But you haven't yet started your pruning?' I ask, with a curious sense of reluctance to broach the subject. I suppose it was pruning time when we first met and to ask the question is to acknowledge that the year has nearly run its course.

'I prefer to leave it until after Christmas, when the sap will be rising,' he says. 'Apart from being too busy. The last of the *malos* have finished, you see – even the Grenache – so I've been doing the final rackings. And I've also been off to the Cognac region, choosing barrels for next year. I found this incredible guy. Really small scale. Even lets you choose the particular trees that you want him to use, if you can wait two years. Which sadly I can't . . .'

He will be barrel-ageing all of this year's Coteaux du Languedoc over a second winter, he explains. The early bottling of the first half of last year's production was driven purely by cash flow. With Puech behind him, only the Cartagène and the proportion of the wine that has to be declassified as *vin de pays* will be released in the spring.

'But that reminds me, I've forgotten to book the bottling lorry!' he announces to my surprise.

It is not that the thing itself is unfamiliar. Only the other day, when I visited Daumas Gassac, one of these giant bottling factories on juggernaut wheels was making short work of their 2001 white. I just hadn't expected Virgile to be filling Saint Saturnin's square with one of them next year. Times have changed more quickly than I would have thought possible in January.

'Don't I get a kiss, then?' asks Babette, as a lungful of cigarette smoke blows past my left cheek.

I owe this eleventh-hour marker of my social progress to a lack of commerciality on her part, which must, I think, be one of the core skills acquired at café-management school. New Year's Eve is a date in the calendar when much of the village might be expected to venture forth for festive refreshment. Yet perversely this is just when Babette can be relied upon to hang up her 'closed' sign.

She is not, however, the first to arrive at my party. Manu predictably claimed that prize but he is sadly unable to shower Babette with further cousinly kisses. This is because the hanging of the fairy lights was not an unqualified success. The lights themselves look well enough – or as well as can be expected, given his wife's refusal to pay for the replacement of the numerous defective bulbs. The trouble was that Mme Gros's preferred *emplacement* for the illuminations was higher than a man of Manu's stature should really have tried to reach, even from the top of his longest ladder. And although his fall, when it came, was partly broken by a pile of fallen branches, gathered from my little forest and waiting to be cut into Yuletide logs, they failed to prevent him from cracking his jaw.

He is thus heavily strapped and bandaged and not at all in kissing mode tonight. Indeed, the discomforts of merely eating appear to have lost him several kilos over the Christmas period. His only consolation is that the doctor's advice that he should drink everything, including wine, through a straw seems to have accelerated his already unrivalled imbibing rate.

'Good stuff, this,' he congratulates me between slurps and gurgles.

December

It is in fact some of the château's 'house champagne', sent up by Krystina. Presumably she did not want to be embarrassed in front of the handsome young man who seems to be her latest disciple.

'Greek God,' insisted Babette, when she tipped me off last week. 'But it'll never last. Only history he's interested in is the history of Krystina's alimony.'

'He makes even me feel old,' admitted Virgile, when the golden youth made his first public appearance on Krystina's arm this evening. 'But then, Versace jackets never did suit me,' he added as the boy dropped one of Krystina's Christmas presents casually in a corner.

I feel rather less casual about my own present from Krystina. Heaven knows how she managed it but she found me a bottle of Fine de Faugères dating from the nineteenth century. The exact date was unfortunately obscured by the thick black marker pen, with which she had written 'Thanx – It was Fun – Luv K' across the label. I have hidden it where Manu will never find it on any of his 'caretaker' visits next year.

'Are they planted?' Virgile whispers theatrically, already briefed by me that the same degree of secrecy is desirable for his own gift.

I know it will be several years before any of the three tiny truffle oaks in his Christmas Eve parcel yields its hoped-for riches – by which time, I hope to have found a way to live here full time. But I would still rather Manu remained ignorant of their location.

'I'm still dithering about where to put them,' I reply no less furtively, 'and I've only tomorrow to decide.'

Normally, I would have asked Manu's advice on these things, but in the circumstances I had to fall back on the nature book. Somewhere well drained, it said. But then again, not too dry. Shaded, but then again not dark. I ended up completely confused.

'I'd better come up to help before you go,' Virgile offers. 'But I brought you this . . .'

He is drowned by the courageous attempt of Mme Gros at his elbow to engage M. Mas in a polite discussion of the Christmas truffle crisis.

'Enormous!' she shouts above his ever-screeching hearing aid.

'*Enormous!*' she repeats at ear-splitting volume, having shrewdly assumed his toothless response to be the usual confession of failure to hear.

The extra decibels assure her the attention of most of the gathering, as she broadcasts her privileged enjoyment of what sounds like the largest example of truffle life reported in the whole of the Languedoc.

'My husband has his sources,' she informs us all smugly.

'I brought you this as well,' Virgile tries again.

He allows me a covert glimpse of a bottle in a carrier bag, which I am clearly meant to hide along with Krystina's brandy. It is unlabelled but he tells me it is a hand-bottled, advance sample of his superior, barrel-aged Coteaux du Languedoc from last year.

'We ran out of time on Christmas Eve and you'll not be here for the bottling.'

He looks at his feet.

'I'm going to miss you,' he says, embarrassed. 'I'll miss your feedback,' he adds. 'No really. Especially now that Olivier . . . Well, anyway, I'm really pleased with that,' he continues more chirpily, with a gesture towards the wine in the bag. 'I'm convinced it's one for long keeping. Ten years maybe to show its best.'

'Perhaps I should take it back to England – as a reminder,' I say and then I look at my own feet. 'I'll miss you too,' I mutter. 'I'll miss your *cave* almost as much as this house . . .'

'Are you two getting maudlin?' asks Sarah, from behind the

tray of *canapés* that took her most of the day to prepare. 'You've been monopolizing this boy for long enough,' she rebukes me, as her arm slides under Virgile's and she leads him away to a quieter corner, leaving me alone for a moment with the carrier bag. But only for a moment, because Manu's infallible antennae have already detected its bottle-shaped contents and he is limping over in the hope of investigating.

'Tried them yet, have you?' he mumbles, as ebulliently as the facial dressings allow. 'You've given them pride of place, I see.'

It is fortunate that my present from him was the one that needed no concealing. Its length rather precludes concealment. Indeed, as Manu has proudly noticed, it tends to dominate even this, my longest room. I have always thought these long-handled fruit-picking devices measured a couple of metres at the most. But with Manu's newfound fear of ladders, I suppose the outsized model was only to be expected – especially with even more of the picking burden falling on him next year.

'Been talking to that Virgile fellow,' Manu changes the subject. 'He's got some very interesting ideas, you know. Surprised you haven't picked up a bit more from him, given how much time you've been spending down there. I mean, he tells me for instance . . . Well, this is maybe a bit technical for you . . . But he says that, if I worked with lower yields, I'd get higher *alcohol*. Never thought of it like that but it certainly bears thinking about. Always willing to learn,' he chuckles, as he hobbles away in pursuit of more of Krystina's free-flowing champagne.

'Do they give you a lot of holiday?' Mme Gros accosts me animatedly, her steely grey hair tonight somehow radiant with optimism. 'It must be breaking your heart,' she adds cheerfully, her own cardiac condition remaining conspicuously sound, as she accepts an unaccustomed, celebratory second Noilly Prat. 'Leaving your lovely house. Leaving all of us to our own devices. Of course, we'll do all we can to keep an eye on things. Pop a bag of your fruit in your deep freeze, when you can't be there at picking time. Anything along those lines,' she assures me and she wafts herself exultantly away to monitor her husband's consumption levels.

'Such a shame,' agree the Vargases in reedy unison, as they struggle to juggle glasses, plates and walking sticks between two pairs of hands. 'Letting go of the land again, just when you were beginning to get on top of it. We'd offer to help, at least with the olive trees,' their frail duet assures me warmly. 'But the truth is, we're finding our own a bit of a struggle these days.'

'You can leave the vines to me,' says Virgile, joining us. 'It's the least I can do.'

'But they're right,' I acknowledge glumly, as the Vargases excuse themselves to totter away to a sofa. 'I can never make sense of this place in a few weeks a year.'

'Then stay for another fifty-two,' Virgile dares me. 'Stay for ever.'

'Be realistic!' I laugh, unsettled by the intensity of the challenge in his stare. 'I've got to go back to work. I need the money.'

'I am being realistic. Remember my Che Guevara postcard?'

' "Demand the impossible"?'

'Why not? I mean, how much money do you need to live here?' he presses. 'You can let your English house again. Or sell it. You can be practically self-sufficient here.'

'I can't.'

'Think of the new fruit trees. Think of your truffle oaks.'

'I just can't.'

'Think of all you've learned. Especially after what the Vargases have just been telling me. Apparently half your land here is *Appellation Contrôlée*. You didn't know that, did you? You should stay and make wine.'

'Don't be daft. I couldn't possibly.'

'You could,' says Virgile with another of his challenging stares. '*Si tu veux, tu peux.*'

Acknowledgements

There are many thanks now due and some that are overdue:

to Robin Baird-Smith, Emma Bradford, Jill Lloyd-Davis, Julian Mannering, Neil Philip and Philip Pullman, who all helped to counsel, encourage and steer me in finding my way into the unfamiliar territory of a second career;

to Mandy Little of Watson Little and Gail Pirkis of John Murray who finally gave me the best of welcomes to this strange new world of publishing;

to all my friends and family who suspended, or at least concealed, their disbelief along the way;

to Anne Boston for so many helpful suggestions on the manuscript;

to Adrienne Fryer who put pictures to my words and bore every pernickety change so cheerfully;

to Gareth Vaughan who first inspired my passion for wine;

to Liz and Mike Berry of La Vigneronne who first persuaded me that the Languedoc was the world's most exciting vineyard;

Acknowledgements

to Bridget and David Pugh of Le Mimosa, whose matchless restaurant has made many before and after me fall in love with the region and whose introductions to local wine-makers have been invaluable;

to all of the wine-makers featured in this book for making the wines that they make and for welcoming me with so much courtesy and patience – I hope that I have done something near justice to their achievements and philosophies;

to Virgile Joly, in particular, for sharing a year so generously and for being the real *'héro de l'Hérault'*;

to Jean-Marc at L'Horloge and Pius and Marie-Anne at Le Pressoir for both inspiration and sustenance, while I researched this book;

to Michèle Willemin who created the closest place in the Languedoc (or probably anywhere) to paradise;

and most especially to Andrew McKenzie, without whom this book would have been, in so many ways, impossible.

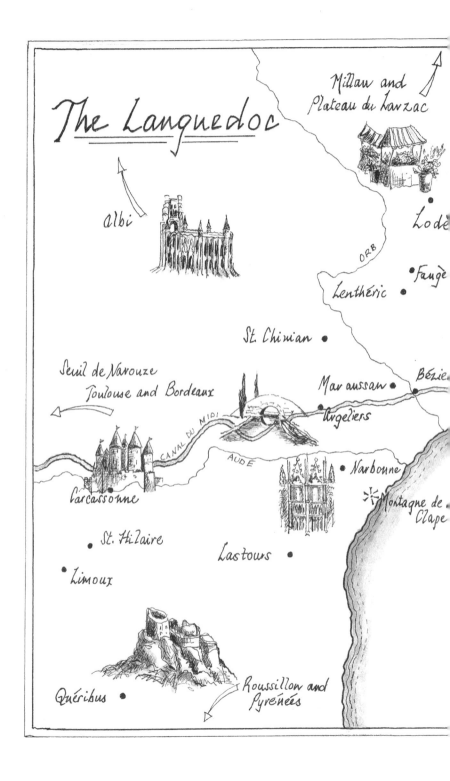

The Languedoc

Millau and
Plateau du Larzac

Albi

Lodè

ORB

Faugè

Lenthéric

St. Chinian

Seuil de Naurouze
Toulouse and Bordeaux

Maraussan

Bézie

CANAL DU MIDI

Argeliers

AUDE

Carcassonne

Narbonne

Montagne de
Clape

St. Hilaire

Lastours

Limoux

Quéribus

Roussillon and
Pyrénées